BEHIND *the* MORMON CURTAIN

BEHIND *the* MORMON CURTAIN

Selling Sex in America's Holy City

Steve Cuno

PITCHSTONE PUBLISHING
DURHAM, NORTH CAROLINA

Pitchstone Publishing
Durham, North Carolina
www.pitchstonebooks.com

10 9 8 7 6 5 4 3 2 1

Library of Congress Cataloging-in-Publication Data

Names: Cuno, Steve, 1954- author.
Title: Behind the Mormon curtain : selling sex in America's holy city /
    Steve Cuno.
Description: Durham, North Carolina : Pitchstone Publishing, [2021] |
    Includes bibliographical references. | Summary: "A behind-the-scenes
    investigation into Salt Lake City's prostitution industry and how it
    intersects with Mormonism"— Provided by publisher.
Identifiers: LCCN 2021028199 (print) | LCCN 2021028200 (ebook) | ISBN
    9781634312172 (hardback) | ISBN 9781634312189 (ebook)
Subjects: LCSH: Prostitution—Religious aspects—Church of Jesus Christ of
    Latter-day Saints. | Mormons—Sexual behavior—Utah. |
    Prostitutes—Utah—Interviews. | Prostitution—Utah.
Classification: LCC BX8643.P75 C86 2021 (print) | LCC BX8643.P75 (ebook)
    | DDC 289.3/32—dc23
LC record available at https://lccn.loc.gov/2021028199
LC ebook record available at https://lccn.loc.gov/2021028200

He that is without sin among you, let him first cast a stone at her.

—John 8:7

Contents

Author's Note 1

George Carlin's Infamous Septet

*If someone says "move the box," they'll never be able to match the
power of "move the damn box" or something stronger.*

—Jeff Wagg

One of the tracks on comedian George Carlin's fourth album, *Class
Clown*, was a version of his routine "Seven Words You Can Never Say on
Television."[1] It drew little attention until a New York City radio station
aired it, and a member of a conservative media watchdog group heard it
in the company of his 15-year-old son. The man complained to the Federal Communications Commission (FCC), claiming his son shouldn't-a
ought-a been exposed to such language. Never mind that it was 1973,
when 15-year-olds were exposed to all seven words in school hallways
every day.

A series of First Amendment battles ensued, inevitably finding their
way to the Supreme Court. The result was the Safe Harbor Doctrine,
which says it's okay to broadcast naughty words between 10 p.m. and
6 a.m. The court's reasoning was that most kids would be in bed during
those hours. If your kids complain when you send them to bed by 10, tell
them their argument is not with you but with the U.S. Supreme Court.

We owe the concerned father a debt of gratitude. Due to his tireless efforts, Carlin's septet of naughty words attained legendary status.

In connection with a stubbed toe or parking ticket, I may on occasion avail myself of one or two of the scandalous seven. But I avoid using them in my work, even when I'm writing between 10 p.m. and 6 a.m. Until now, the most colorful word I ever published was *shit*, and, at that, only twice in the course of three books and some 200 articles. The prior sentence marks only my third written *shit*. And *that* sentence marks my fourth. In this book, a few more are coming up.

You will also encounter a more infamous member of Carlin's septet that I had until now managed to avoid using in print altogether. It starts with *f*, ends with *k*, and, no, it isn't *flank*. I could have substituted another word, but my regard for Carlin, my interviewees, and your intelligence forbade. Take, for instance, a comment that one of my interviewees tossed out as cheerfully as you or I might toss out, "It's sunny outside." I think you'll agree that something valuable would be lost were I to attempt cleaning it up, say, like this: "I love to copulate. I just copulate and I get paid. What could be better?"

I am a recovering prude, so I empathize if your sensitivities recoil. But there is much to learn from the good people you'll meet in these pages, so please tell your sensitivities to flanking adjust.

Author's Note 2

The Tricky Business of Inventing Names

I would venture to guess that Anon, who wrote so many poems without signing them, was often a woman.

—Virginia Woolf

The sexual service providers quoted in these pages agreed to speak with me only on condition of their and their clients' anonymity. Erring on the side of caution, I changed key identifying details. If you think you recognize anyone in these pages, a word of caution before you risk embarrassing that person or yourself: you are probably mistaken. Of course, providers work under pseudonyms, and only in a few cases did providers share with me their real names. Still, to keep everyone doubly safe, I traded their real pseudonyms for fake ones, the irony in "real" versus "fake" pseudonyms not lost on me.

Coming up with pseudonyms for pseudonyms proved trickier than I'd anticipated. I'd no sooner pull a name from the air than I'd become aware of a provider working under that name. So if you happen to know a provider who goes by, say, Eva, Jewel, or Koko, be assured that she is not the Eva, Jewel, or Koko you'll meet here.

The only people who appear in this book under their real names are: Nikki, who courageously uses her real name as a public advocate for sex worker rights and asked me to call her Nikki in this book; Moab City Police Chief and former Salt Lake County Sheriff Jim Winder, who graciously agreed to be interviewed on the record; people whose actions and names are matter of public record; and, well, me. If I were going to invent a name for myself, trust me on this, I'd have come up with something way cooler.

Prelude

"Well, This Is Awkward."

It takes two bodies to make one seduction.

—Guy Wetmore Carryl

Eva preferred attending church without drawing attention to her looks. It was something of a losing battle. She was of Latin American descent, in her mid-twenties, fit, five-foot-two and buxom, with plump lips, dark lashes, and long, thick, black hair that struck a contrast against her pale complexion. The shapeless dark green dress she pulled from the closet could do only so much toward making her unremarkable.

Having grown up Mormon, Eva knew well the importance of not "becoming pornography"[1] through immodest dress. Form-fitting clothes were out. Skirts and shorts were to reach the knee. Sleeveless tops were a no-no. Heaven forbid Mormon females should inadvertently plant lust-ful thoughts in the defenseless soil of male Mormon minds. To expect men to take responsibility for their thoughts at the sight of an exposed shoulder or glimpse of thigh was to expect too much.

Dressing for clients, of course, was another matter.

Eva walked the short distance from her rusted, single-wide mobile home to the church building where her ward, that is, her local Mormon congregation, met. She lived in Rose Park, a lower-income neighborhood on the west side of Salt Lake City. Her walk took her past the county fairgrounds, a campground, the local power utility's main office, a vintage strip mall, one of Salt Lake's many corner 7-11 stores, and a laundromat whose exterior was covered in graffiti courtesy of a local gang. Bloods or Crips? She wasn't sure.

Mormon meetinghouses aren't hard to pick out. Most are of brown or gray brick, have a steep-pitched roof over the chapel area, and feature a crossless spire. Mormons believe in Jesus and the Bible, but crosses never found their way into the culture. "I do not wish to give offense to any of my Christian brethren who use the cross on the steeples of their cathedrals and at the altars of their chapels," said then-Mormon apostle Gordon B. Hinckley, most likely giving offense to his Christian brethren who use the cross on the steeples of their cathedrals and at the altars of their chapels, "but for us, the cross is the symbol of the dying Christ, while our message is a declaration of the living Christ."[2]

Arriving a few minutes before 9 a.m., Eva sat quietly near the back of the chapel and waited for the Sunday service to begin. At the chapel's front, a young woman played hymns on an organ custom-built for Mormon churches by Johannus Organs, headquartered in the Netherlands. Around her, fellow ward members greeted one another and chatted. Seated on a dais facing the congregation was the ward bishopric—the bishop, his first counselor, and his second counselor—unpaid ministers with duties akin to those of a pastor with a pair of assistants.

It was the second counselor's turn to conduct services. He was a picture of wholesome Mormon living: thirtyish, well-built, gray suit, white shirt, blue tie, and an off-the-ears haircut that would have passed a Marine sergeant's scrutiny. At precisely nine o'clock, he stepped to the pulpit, adjusted the height of the microphone, and said, "We'd like to welcome you to sacrament meeting on this lovely Sabbath day morning." He announced a congregational hymn and the name of the person who would offer the opening prayer. This would be followed by communion, or, as Mormons call it, the sacrament. Mormons partake of bread, but, since alcohol is forbidden, they substitute water for the wine. Following the sacrament, two ward members would deliver talks.

The service took just over an hour, after which adults and children filed off to their respective Sunday classes. Eva teaches four-year-olds. Her eyes glisten when she talks about the kids. You can tell she loves them.

That evening after church, Eva changed into her work clothes. She traded the modest dress for a tight black minidress with a plunging neckline. She applied heavy makeup, donned false eyelashes, and stepped into black, rhinestone-studded 4.8-inch stiletto heels. After a final mirror-check, she drove in her late-model luxury sedan to a four-star hotel in downtown Salt Lake City for a rendezvous with a new client. The Mormon Church discourages working on Sundays, but Eva figured the Lord wouldn't mind if she ever so slightly bent the rule. As a self-employed sexual services provider,[3] she understood the importance of making herself available at a client's behest. Surely the Lord understood that, too.

The new client happened upon Eva's advertisement while searching the Internet. It featured provocative photos of Eva, albeit with her face obscured. Smitten, the man sent her a text message requesting a rendezvous.

First meetings are a hazard of the trade on both sides. For all Eva knew, the man might be a thief, rapist, murderer, monument to poor hygiene, or undercover police officer. For all the client knew, Eva might look nothing like her photos, grab his money and run, set muggers upon him, murder him like Aileen Wuornos (who was famously portrayed by Charlize Theron in the movie *Monster*), or turn out to be a police decoy waiting for him with handcuffs—and not the fun kind.

Still, there were precautions each could take. Eva made it a practice to ask prospective clients for names and phone numbers of providers they'd already seen. Though not foolproof, checking references reduced her risk of running into an undercover cop or finding herself naked in a hotel room with a psychopath twice her weight. Eva called the man's references, and they assured her that this fellow was on the level. Nice guy, they told her, gentle, generous, and damn good looking. That's music to a provider's ears, so she agreed to meet him.

The client exercised caution at his end, too. He told Eva he'd found her on The Erotic Review (TER) website.[4] Operating from the Netherlands not far from Johannus Organs, TER is a place for johns[5] to rate providers on appearance and performance and, at their option, add detailed reviews. In a probably vain attempt to protect itself and users from soliciting and trafficking charges, TER's disclosure statement stipulates that all reviews are, wink, wink, "fictional." Checking TER wasn't foolproof, either—law enforcement agencies can post reviews for decoys, and scammers can post reviews for nonexistent providers—but it lowered the client's risk of disappointment, ripoff, and arrest.

Eva started in the profession at 19, so by this time she had racked up pages of positive reviews. Most affirmed that she was a great provider, and all affirmed that she really was the woman in the photos. The new client contacted her with confidence, assured that a delightful evening awaited him.

Eva parked her car in the hotel garage and texted a terse "I'm here" to the client. He immediately replied with his room number.

Having met more than a few clients at this hotel, Eva knew her way around the lobby. Pushing through the revolving door, she walked purposefully past the registration desk and across the lobby to the elevators. The purposeful walk mattered. Though there was no law against walking into a hotel lobby looking sexy, her outfit more than suggested why she was there, and any hesitation on her part might give hotel security justification to stop and question her. She didn't worry about the young man and woman working at the front desk. Eva sometimes slipped them crisp, folded portraits of Andrew Jackson, which helped them not to notice her comings and goings.

She rode the elevator to the third floor, found the room, and knocked lightly on the door. She took care to stand just outside the view of the peephole. She wasn't sure why she did that, but other providers did, so she did, too.[6]

Eva wasn't prepared for what she saw when the door opened.

The other providers hadn't exaggerated. The man standing in the now open doorway and facing her *was* damn good looking.

He was also familiar.

In fact, Eva had no difficulty placing him. She had seen him just that morning. Conducting services at church.

Her new client was the second counselor in her ward bishopric.

The usually talkative Eva stood speechless. The increasingly crimson-faced second counselor managed to open his mouth but not to speak.

Peering past him into the room, Eva spotted a pair of champagne flutes next to a bottle of bubbly on ice. So much for "alcohol is forbidden." She detected the smell of weed, also forbidden to Mormons. On the bed was an array of toys. It seemed that the second counselor, clearly no newcomer to the hobby,[7] had planned quite the party. What he hadn't planned was what to do in the event that the obscured face on the body he'd ogled online turned out to belong to a member of his ward who esteemed him a representative of the Lord Jesus Christ.

I'm busted, was Eva's first thought. Serious as the Mormon Church is about not working on Sundays, it's deadly serious about not having sex with anyone besides your lawfully wedded spouse. In Mormondom, sexual sin ranks as the third most heinous variety of sin you can commit.[8] It's grounds for disfellowshipment, in which church privileges are temporarily suspended, or for excommunication, in which membership is revoked.

Eva's follow-up thought was, *No, he'll keep his yap shut.* The second counselor had too much to lose. He'd be tossed out of the bishopric and excommunicated. There'd be ward gossip, lots of it. Odds are his wife would leave him and take the kids. His employer might fire him.

At last finding her voice, Eva said, "Well, this is awkward."

After a pause that surely felt longer to both of them than it really was, inspiration at last struck the second counselor. "I think," he stammered, "you have the wrong room."

"I think so," Eva quickly agreed before hurrying away as briskly as her stiletto heels permitted.

The second counselor melted back into the room and gently closed the door.

* * *

Eva shared stories from her life as a provider as we lingered over alleged Mexican food at Del Taco, a primarily western U.S. fast food chain with fare no better than you'd expect. Del Taco was her choice. I was willing to pop for someplace better. Honest.

No onlooker would have guessed Eva's profession that day—she wore sweats, her makeup modest, her hair pulled back into a ponytail—but an eavesdropper might have, for she spoke unabashedly and loudly. I thought I detected the occasional double take from customers seated nearby. Fortunately, no kids were around.

Continuing her story, Eva told me that on the following Sunday at church, it was as if the encounter never happened. She and the second counselor paid each other no heed.

Neither Eva nor the second counselor was in danger of disfellow-shipment or excommunication. Before church leaders can disfellowship or excommunicate someone for having nonmarital sex, they must first find out about it. In a church claiming that all leaders at every level are guided by revelation from God, you might think the Holy Spirit would tap the bishop on the shoulder and whisper in a still, small voice, "Guess what your second counselor and Eva did. Er, almost did." But God, who prefers working in mysterious ways, usually waits for the guilt-ridden to come forth and confess—or for busybodies to rat them out, which the church encourages. Eva did not feel guilt-ridden and so did not come forth and confess. Not surprisingly, neither did the second counselor, and no busybodies had been in the hotel to witness their brief exchange. Eva resumed her life and professional activities as if nothing had happened. So did the second counselor. The Holy Spirit, for reasons of its own, kept mum.

We can surmise a few things about the second counselor with a high degree of confidence. He was probably married and had kids, such being not quite but nearly a prerequisite for a call to the bishopric. He held down a day job outside of his church duties. He probably hid his hobbying from his wife, or thought he did.

This much about the second counselor is certain: as part of his bishopric duties, he was a member of the Ward Disciplinary Council. Once called "church courts" and unconvincingly referred to as "courts of love," Disciplinary Councils are convened for Mormons accused of having committed serious sins. Most sins aren't all that serious. Say you snuck a beer, flipped off some bozo for not letting you merge, or pleasured yourself thinking about a *Cosmo* cover you saw at the grocery store. Of such you may repent discreetly and on your own. But it's another matter when it comes to committing a felony, having gay sex, fraternizing with polygamists, preaching false doctrine, publicly criticizing church leaders—or engaging in nonmarital sex. Do one of those and you will find yourself before the Ward Disciplinary Council, your church membership in danger.[9]

The Ward Disciplinary Council consists of the bishop and his two counselors. In other words, it's the bishopric. It's just that when you appear before them to be tried for having been seriously naughty, the church prefers the other moniker. If the Ward Disciplinary Council finds you guilty after hearing the evidence, the bishop has the option of letting you off the hook with a stern warning, disfellowshipping you, or excommunicating you.[10]

All of which gives us one more piece of information about Eva's second counselor: on behalf of God, he sat in official judgment of people for doing exactly as he did in his secret life. There was, however, one major difference between him and them. He hadn't been found out.

Eva was well aware that her occupation might someday land her before the Ward Disciplinary Council. Should that happen, she assured me when I asked, she would not out the second counselor. Even if he voted to excommunicate her.

The irony clobbered me. Between the church leader whom society praises and the prostitute whom it reviles, in this instance the reviled prostitute would show the greater integrity.

It was neither the first nor last time the thought would cross my mind.

You may wonder how the second counselor lives with himself. But then, he is not unusual. You haven't heard the smallest part of what goes on behind the Mormon Curtain.

Chapter 1

Logo for a Call Girl

*"She will not speak!" murmured Mr. Dimmesdale, who had been
leaning over the balcony with his hand over his heart as he had
waited to see how Hester would respond. Now he drew back with
a deep breath. "The strength and generosity of a woman's heart!
She will not speak!"*

—From Nathaniel Hawthorne's *The Scarlet Letter*

1

"I make a lot of money as a call girl."

The seeds for this book were sown some 20 years ago when Linda paid
a visit to my small marketing firm. Settling into a chair across the desk
from me, she described the wholesale auto parts business she was starting. She had purchased delivery vans, leased a building, filled it with inventory, and hired two employees. She wanted my shop to create a dis-
tinctive logo and a compelling brochure.

I admire entrepreneurs. I'm interested in their stories, from how they
came up with their business idea to how they raised their startup capital. Some entrepreneurs find the latter question intrusive, but most are

proud of their success story and eager to share. I ask it because it helps me to know them and their business better. It also helps me to know if they'll be able to pay their invoice. Call me mercenary, but completing an assignment only to learn that my client is too broke to pay for it is not my preferred way of doing business.

When I asked Linda how she'd funded her business, she looked around to ensure no one else was in earshot before answering.

From there, our conversation took something of a detour. That can happen when the person seated across the desk from you says, "I make a lot of money as a call girl."

For the sake of comedy I would love to tell you that I did a double take and nearly fell out of my chair. I didn't, but I was powerless to prevent my eyebrows from moseying up and my eyes from widening just a bit. I was prepared for something more along the line of "I took out a second mortgage," "I borrowed from family," or "I have investors."

I was at once fascinated and curious. Linda lived in what was to me and, I suspect, to most people, an unseen world. In Salt Lake City, no less. Where all it takes to become the object of steamy gossip is to have a member of your ward catch you holding a cup of coffee.

2

America's bastion of family values

You have doubtless heard of Salt Lake City. Against the backdrop of the majestic Rocky Mountain Wasatch Range, the Salt Lake metropolitan area has about 1.25 million residents and boasts amenities you might expect to find only in larger cities. On a visit, be sure to take in a Utah Jazz home game and performances by world-class Utah Symphony, Utah Opera, and Ballet West. You'll find abundant shopping and endless outdoor recreation—hiking, rock climbing, mountain biking, river rafting, and, of course, skiing. It's no wonder that the International Olympic Committee chose Salt Lake to host the 2002 Winter Games.

You have doubtless also heard that Salt Lake City is home to the world headquarters of The Church of Jesus Christ of Latter-day Saints,[1] better known by its nickname, the Mormon Church. If you've seen or heard the church's advertising campaigns, or if Mormons have proselytized you, you probably know that the Mormon Church presents itself as the acme of wholesomeness, a bastion of family values, a monument to home life depicted in 1950s TV shows like *The Adventures of Ozzie and Harriet*, *Leave It to Beaver*, and *Father Knows Best*.

Like most religions, the Mormon Church has plenty to say about sex. Hardly a General Conference[2] of the church goes by without stern warnings about the evils of masturbation, the importance of modest attire for females, the dangers of impure thoughts, the terrifying consequences of watching porn, and, of course, the devastating ravages of illicit sex. In this case, "illicit" would refer to any sexual activity outside of heterosexual marriage, and to any activity within hetero marriage that gets, shall we say, too creative.

It's no wonder, then, that Utahns remain largely unaware that a thriving prostitution trade goes on under their noses. They would be shocked to learn that people they know, people they would never suspect, engage in it. Prostitution is the kind of thing you expect to hear about in, say, New York City. When a U.S. congressman from New York was busted for texting photos of his privates to a teenage girl,[3] and when a New York governor was busted for patronizing a prostitute,[4] no one said, "You're kidding. In New York?" But that a sanctified place like Salt Lake City would have quite the prostitution industry comes as a surprise to many a Mormon and non-Mormon alike.

It takes no more than a casual Internet search to come face-to-face with Salt Lake's considerable supply of sexual service providers. As I write,[5] 83 Salt Lake area providers are advertising right now on Eros.com. It's difficult to know how many of the 3,501 Salt Lake area providers listed on EroticMonkey.ch are active; a more reliable indicator is that 129 local reviews were posted in February 2020 alone. These numbers do not include providers taking a day off from advertising, providers advertising on other sites, streetwalkers, massage therapists who provide "extras," strippers, and providers who rely only on word-of-mouth. Nor do they include clients, who necessarily outnumber providers many times over.

It seems that even in Mormontown, the demand for sexual services is so strong that potential consequences such as shaming, censure, divorce, custody loss, arrest, fines, excommunication, and a criminal record are powerless to quell the hobby. They serve only to drive it underground.

3

"I bet you could get a lot of people in trouble."

I asked Linda if she'd mind setting aside discussing the logo and brochure long enough for me to ask a few questions about that largely unseen side of Salt Lake City. She didn't mind at all. "I don't get to talk about it that often," she said.

"You were able to save enough to start a business with vans, inventory, and warehouse space over and above living expenses," I said. "So I gather the money is good?"

Linda replied, "The going rate around here is around 150 or 200. I'm more high-end. I charge 500 for an hour. My regulars usually book me for two to four hours at a time. And they give me booze and cocaine. It's one of the perks." Recall that this conversation took place nearly 20 years ago. In today's dollars, the $500 per hour Linda that charged would be more like $750. Plus booze and cocaine.

I asked why she would trade such a lucrative business for the one she was starting.

"I'm not trading it," she said. "Not yet. I'll do both for a while. I want something to fall back on when I get tired of the game. Or when I'm not hot anymore. Whichever comes first."

Linda had not dressed for hotness. She wore business attire, her makeup was conservative, and she exhibited a professional demeanor. Dark roots betrayed the natural color of her blond, shoulder-length hair. I guessed that she stood about five foot six. She resembled businesspeople I encountered daily in my job. Yet it wasn't difficult to imagine that suggestive attire and severe makeup could bring about quite the transformation. Her face was pleasant, and to what I hoped was my surreptitious look she appeared fit.

"I bet you could get a lot of people in trouble," I mused aloud. I figured that men who could shell out one to two thousand dollars for a few hours of entertainment on a regular basis would be men of some standing. They would have much to lose should Linda, if you'll pardon the expression, chose to expose them.

"You have no idea," Linda replied, rolling her eyes. She entertained politicians, police officers, judges, defense lawyers, prosecutors, and doctors. All or nearly all of her clients were married.

And: nearly all of her clients were practicing Mormons. Some were rank-and-file church members, but not a few held leadership positions ranging from lower to higher in the church's hierarchy.

I'm a former Mormon. Having held lower-level leadership positions, I'd worked with church members, bishops, stake presidents, and other leaders. Even though I no longer believed in the church, I still respected and liked these men. It would not have occurred to me that some might hide secret lives in which they frequent sexual service providers.

"But I would never get them in trouble," Linda continued, "and for sure I wouldn't blackmail them."

I asked why she wouldn't. I suspected I knew what she would say, but I asked anyway.

"It would be wrong," she said. "Confidentiality is an unwritten rule in this business. Besides, I don't want to hurt anyone. I'm not cruel."

Yep. That was what I thought she would say.

I asked if she had ever been busted. She hadn't.

"But suppose someday you were busted," I said, "and suppose the judge or prosecutor was one of your clients. Then would you out him, or threaten to?"

"I'd keep quiet," Linda said. "I hope he'd go easy on me. If he didn't, I hope he'd feel like shit."

Linda's integrity struck me, much as would the integrity of Eva and others when I put the same question to them about two decades later. Here were powerful men sneaking off to pay Linda for sex, who in their professional lives and church duties joined in railing against the likes of her and, even more hypocritically, against the likes of her clients. Yet, even in the face of prosecution at their hands, Linda would guard their secrets.

Granted, one could argue that Linda had less to lose. She wasn't a bishop, judge, or CEO, and she didn't keep her profession a secret. For her, a conviction might entail a fine and a night in jail. For her clients, an arrest could prove life-ruining, even if no conviction followed.

The situation I posed to Linda was hypothetical. From my experience in research, I know better than to assume that what people hypothesize they would do is a reliable predictor of what they would actually do. Yet the situation wasn't hypothetical in the case of Koko,[6] a provider whom I would later interview. She had accompanied a busted friend to court. When the judge entered the courtroom and took his seat at the bench, both women recognized him as a regular client. Both kept their mouths shut.

Having already ventured well into the area plainly labeled None of My Damn Business, I ventured further by asking Linda if her family knew that she was a sex worker. "My ex-husband knew," she said. Linda, who loves to dance, sometimes worked as a stripper between one-on-one appointments. At a bachelor party where she was one of two hired strippers, a handsome graduate student offered her cash for a blowjob. They repaired to a private room, where, post-fellatio, Linda told him he seemed like a pretty cool guy. They exchanged phone numbers, began dating, and eventually married. Linda continued working as a provider. In time they had two daughters. When I met Linda, the girls were in elementary school.

About ten years in, the marriage ended. In the course of one particularly ugly argument, Linda's husband called her a common whore. Think about that: the man who'd introduced himself to her by paying her for a blowjob, the man who didn't mind living well for years on her considerable earnings as a provider, that man called her a common whore. "You can't imagine how it hurt," Linda said, her hazel eyes moist. He followed up with a threat to tell his family what she did for a living. That one made her laugh. She replied, "You're the one who wanted to keep it a secret from them, not me."

I could feel my perspective shifting. A few minutes of hearing Linda's experiences was fast humanizing a population that to me, I now realized, had always been little more than a concept, an object, a caricature, a TV and movie stereotype. Linda was a real person. An individual. She had depth, intelligence, manners, perseverance, moxie, business acumen, hopes, dreams, trials, concerns, boundaries, disappointments, achievements—and feelings. She was a mom who, like all moms, worried about and wanted the best for her kids. She had been deeply hurt by an ex-husband. She had a mortgage and a car payment. And now, she had an extra business to run and employees to manage.

Prostitution was what Linda did. It was not who she was.

Linda spoke with candor. She was neither defiant nor boastful, but neither was she abashed or apologetic. I found myself admiring this person, empathizing with her in her trials, and appreciating her willingness to trust someone she'd just met with a peek behind her personal curtain.

4

Curiosity reignited

Following Linda's visit, my shop went to work on her logo and brochure. We presented our finished work a few weeks later. Our business thus complete, we parted. I never saw her again.

Nearly two decades later, as I pondered possible topics for a new book, I recalled my conversation with Linda. My curiosity reignited. Just how many providers were there in Utah? How about gay providers? Noncisgender[7] providers? What was it like to be a sexual services provider in Utah? Did it differ from providing sexual services in other places? Were Mormon johns unusual? Were they married? Did they have children? What church positions did they hold? What did they do for a living? How did they handle the guilt? Did they even *feel* guilt?

There was no turning off my curiosity switch. I resolved to look into the sex trade in Utah. Over the next three years, I contacted and interviewed female and male providers, johns, massage therapists, attorneys, mental health professionals, and police officers. I researched the history of prostitution in the United States in general and in Utah in particular. I dug into legal issues.

What follows is an account of what I discovered and how I discovered it.

Chapter 2

Meeting Annie (While Avoiding Arrest)

*Well, there's a book that says we're all sinners and I at least chose
a sin that's made quite a few people happier than they were before
they met me, a sin that's left me with very little time to consider
other extremely popular moral misdemeanors, like usury,
intolerance, bearing false tales, extortion, racial bigotry,
and the casting of that first stone.*

—Sally Stanford

1

"Honest, Your Honor, it's for a book."

"Do not under any circumstance pay a call girl for an interview."

My attorney friend Max was emphatic. We were enjoying lunch at
Los Garcia, a Mexican restaurant in Sandy, Utah, one of my favorite
haunts. I count the owners among my good friends. I experience withdrawal symptoms when I go too long without their *camarones endiabla-
dos.*

"Why not?" I asked between mouthfuls of spicy shrimp and gua-
camole. "Sure, paying for sex is illegal, but interviews? Lots of people

charge for interviews. It's not illegal."

"Let me put it this way," Max replied. "Suppose she's under surveillance. The minute they see you hand her money, you're caught in the act of paying a prostitute. Now, imagine standing before a judge and saying, 'Honest, Your Honor, the money was for an interview. I'm writing a book.' It might be the most creative excuse the judge has heard all day, but if the judge doesn't buy it, which is likely, you'll look like you were trying to put one over, and you'll be worse off for it."

"But I'm not trying to put one over," I protested. "I'm writing a book. I can produce my notes and my in-progress manuscript as evidence. I can show articles and other books I've written."

"But you can't prove the money was for an interview *only*."

I saw his point. I recalled a hapless john who posted online that he carts along a video camera whenever he visits a provider. His plan in the event of a bust, he said, was to claim he was shooting a porno with himself in a starring role. Commenters made fast work of him. While the U.S. government has no law against producing pornographic videos, individual states and cities can and do outlaw it. Even where producing porn is legal, a host of regulations apply. Finally, they pointed out, it would take more than a camera to pull off that defense. Without a bona fide studio, production assistants, lighting equipment, and a foothold in the business, he'd have no credibility. In the end, he would only insult a judge's intelligence by thinking such a flimsy claim might fly. And, as Max pointed out, insulting a judge's intelligence is seldom the best strategy.

It wasn't difficult for me to see how a judge would put "it's for a book" in the same league as "I'm shooting a porno." So, in theory, Max's advice made sense. In practice, I soon found that only a few sexual service providers were willing to interview for free. Pleased or even flattered as they were at the prospect of being interviewed for a book, most insisted on their regular "donation," as they like to put it in their ads. To me, it seemed reasonable enough. "I charge for my time," explained one. "How you use that time is up to you. If you want to use it for talking, that's fine."

Which, it turns out, isn't unusual. "Some of my regulars only want to talk," she continued. "They don't even touch me. They pay me just to sit there and listen." Most succinct was the provider who texted, *No thanks unless you're paying for my time and information.*

I usually follow advice from attorneys. Not this time. If I wanted to conduct interviews, I was going to have to pony up. I'd just have to hope that no one carrying a badge and prone to jumping to conclusions would be watching.

I was well aware that researching this book was going to be expensive. The highest amount I forked over was for a joint interview with two providers. They often work together, so they wanted to interview together. As I was leaving, they handed me back $100 of their usual combined fee. "Because you're hella fun," said one, the other nodding her assent. I felt flattered.

More important, researching this book was going to be risky. The possibility of arrest was but one danger. I'd read first-hand accounts from johns who stepped into a provider's hotel room only to be clobbered on the head and wake up later without their wallet. One woke up missing his wallet and car keys, which he correctly took as a sign that his car would not be waiting where he left it.

Having a keen interest in staying out of jail and an equally keen interest in not being mugged, I resolved to choose and approach providers with the same caution a smart prospective john would use. Of course, that meant I'd need to learn how a smart prospective john would choose and approach providers. The information was readily available, because quite a few johns share tips online. The challenge was to sort johns who knew what they were talking about from johns who, like the "I'm shooting a porno" guy, only thought they knew.[1]

One point on which smarter johns agree is that once you're caught in the wrong place with the wrong person, there's no getting out of a ticket or arrest. They advise seeing only providers who have lots of positive online reviews. A provider who has no reviews, has only recent, too-good-to-be-true reviews, or has rave reviews from reviewers with no history of

reviewing other providers might be a scammer or part of a sting operation. It struck me as not unlike the process of choosing among products
on Amazon. Johns also suggest using a reverse-image search app like
TinEye to see if providers are using someone else's photos.

But even with precautions, they added, there are no guarantees.

Not terribly encouraging, I thought.

2

Googling for sex workers

Providers make their living providing, so they're as motivated to be found
as prospective clients are to find them. My first Google search produced
a number of websites where Salt Lake area providers advertise. The websites ranged in quality from professional to slapped together. Provider
ads featured photos, sometimes videos, a self-promotional paragraph or
two, a phone number, and an invitation to call or text. To avoid tempting arrest, all stopped short of explicitly offering sexual services. Many
included the line, "Payment is for my time and companionship only."

Threats of prosecution for aiding and abetting traffickers have pressured some websites to ban sexually oriented services advertising and
some to shut down completely. Still, a number persist, some taking more
risk than others. Many are headquartered outside of the United States.
Even so, responsible website operators toe the legal line and take a proac-
tive stand against trafficking. Eros.com, for instance, has a "report trafficking" link on every page. Clicking will take you to a "prevent trafficking" page with a list of warning signs to watch for and anti-trafficking
organizations to contact.[2]

Not eager to leave behind my IP address, I used the Tor[3] browser to
visit Eros and other sites. I didn't want merchants retargeting me with
ads, I didn't want anyone sending me viruses, and I didn't want hackers
poking around my bank accounts, even though they'd be bitterly disappointed. Nor was I terribly keen on being traceable if I unwittingly
happened onto a site under government surveillance. To the best of my

knowledge, I visited only legal websites, but I have always felt that waving a flag and saying, "Hey, Uncle Sam, look at me!" doesn't make for the best policy.

Browsing the Salt Lake area ads, I found providers' self-descriptions of little use. Most contained empty, interchangeable clichés. Here are some typical examples:

> I'm very educated, sophisticated, and passionate. I have a great personality, love to laugh, and have fun!

> I'm very loving, sensuous & generous with the right person.
> I am bubbly and very friendly. I can guarantee you will love me!

> I am a soft-spoken, passionate, very sensual, all-natural woman who has a rare mixture of incredible sensual appeal.

> My sparkling smile will without a doubt brighten your day.

> I'm your next muse. You deserve a relaxing, enjoyable, sexy unforgettable time with me!

> I am a girl who's always smiling and laughing.

The real difference among ads is to be found in the photos and, where available, the reviews. Perhaps that's why some providers dispense with the self-promotional spiel and post only photos. I wondered if they'd picked up the idea from Tinder. Or vice-versa.

Having compiled a list of providers I felt comfortable contacting, I turned my attention to persuading them to trust this total stranger. For all they knew I was an undercover cop, a serial killer, or a pervert getting off on asking intrusive questions under false pretenses. Until there were providers who would vouch for me, I figured the best way to earn sex workers' trust would be first to give them mine. I would share my real name, email, website, and phone number, and hope I'd have no reason to regret it. Here's the text I created and sent:

> I'm a published author at work on a book about the profession in Utah. The book will be supportive of providers. I believe your stories are important, and that the media, the justice system, and society in general treat you unfairly.
>
> May I interest you in being interviewed for the book? Identities of providers and clients will NOT be revealed. I'm not proposing to become a client or to engage in illegal activity of any sort.
>
> I invite you to check out my website so you can be assured I'm legit. Then, if you would consider talking with me, please shoot me a text or email. I hope to hear from you soon.

I wasn't prepared for what happened next.

Which was nothing.

Not even a "drop dead" or a "go away."

Weeks passed. I was all but ready to give up when a text message arrived from Annie. It said, *Just had a cancelation. Want to talk?*

I'm in my 60s and a widower. My kids are grown and on their own. I closed my office a few years ago and now work from home, where two neurotic German shepherd dogs keep me company. As a result, I'm often available for impromptu meetings. I told her I could leave right away and suggested meeting over coffee at Starbucks.

Just come to the apartment, she replied, and texted the address. I thought, *Let's hope a vice squad doesn't choose tonight to stage a bust. Note to self: don't tell Max.*

About 20 minutes later, I pulled into the parking lot of a 200-unit, middle-class apartment complex in Murray, a Salt Lake suburb. I texted Annie to let her know I was there, and she texted back her apartment number. It's not unusual for a provider to withhold her apartment number until you arrive. It ensures you won't knock on her door before she's ready for you. It also ensures that a departing client won't be heading out the door as you're heading in, which could be uncomfortable. Especially if you know each other.

3

Annie

Annie greeted me with a cheerful smile. She had showered while I was en route, so she came to the door wrapped in a white, terrycloth, knee-length robe, her damp, light-brown hair pulled back into a ponytail, her face scrubbed clean of makeup.

Our interview began with a brief tour of the one-bedroom apartment. It was well cared for, clean, not posh but by no means dowdy. No one actually lived there. Annie and a handful of providers used the place to entertain clients, sharing equally in the rent and scheduling around one another's appointments the way office workers schedule shared conference rooms. Months later I would interview Veronica in the same apartment.

The solitary bedroom was tastefully sensuous but not bawdy. A black comforter with a pattern of intertwining silver and white vines lay over a king-sized bed. Translucent maroon drapes hung over opaque blinds covering the only window. A black light rested on a dresser under a large, well-placed mirror.

The door to the adjoining master bathroom had been removed. A bead curtain hung in its place. I asked if removing the door was a security measure of some sort. "No," Annie said with a good-natured laugh, "the bathroom is so small that when you're sitting on the commode it's hard to close the door."

We repaired to the front room for our interview. Its appearance gave no hint of the transactions that took place down the hall. In one corner sat a wing chair on the diagonal, facing a couch against the back wall. Before the couch stood a coffee table. In short, it was like any front room in any middle-class apartment.

Annie had settled onto the couch, drawing her legs under her, and directed me to the wing chair. Hers was a natural, unpretentious de-meanor. Conversation with Annie was like conversation with any spe-cialist in any field.

A good fifteen minutes had passed, and no one had burst through the door and yelled, "Police!" I began to relax.

4

"I think she killed my father."

Some of the providers I interviewed had happy, functional childhoods. Not Annie. She was four years old when her uncle began repeatedly rap-ing her and her three siblings. The scene she described could have come straight out of a horror movie. "He put on a werewolf mask, dragged us one at a time into a closet, and raped us. It was fucking terrible."

He was never arrested. All four kids were adopted out that year, split between two families. Annie and a younger sister went to one family. Her older sister and younger brother went to another, where, soon after, the adoptive father began raping the older sister. When that sister reached her teenage years, one of the rapes resulted in conception. "He gave her a coat hanger abortion at home," Annie said. "My sister is now a basket case, strung out on every drug you can name. She has three kids, all tak-en from her due to her drug abuse. My brother is in his late twenties and has a heart condition from meth use. His heart functions at 12 percent."

Annie's adoptive mother, Marion, was a bright spot in her life. "I loved her," Annie said. "She died a few years ago. She was my best friend."

Annie became sexually active at 14. "I started playing on Livelinks just to fuck around," she continued. Livelinks, which is still in operation, was something of a precursor to online chat rooms. Late-night commer-cials depicted good-looking women and men enjoying telephone con-versations, while a voiceover urged lonely viewers to call and make new friends for free. Of course, to access the more advanced features—that is, to have the kind of fun the beautiful people in the commercials seemed to be having—you had to let the service add by-the-minute charges to your phone bill. The charges can add up, as Annie learned a few weeks later when Marion confronted her with a huge phone bill. That was the end of Annie's time on Livelinks. For the time being.

Annie became pregnant at 15 but lost the baby. When Marion discovered that the father was 19, she pressed charges against him. "I was livid with her," Annie said.

Annie dropped out of high school at 16 and, a year later, married. It wasn't a dream marriage. They separated 16 times over the next six years. Shortly before the marriage's legal end, Annie moved in with a "dreamy, gorgeous" boyfriend. It was that dreamy, gorgeous boyfriend who one day told Annie that it was time she started paying her fair share of household expenses. He suggested prostitution. "I was infatuated with him," she said, "and I loved sex. My reaction was, 'Okay, I'll do it for you.'"

She returned to Livelinks, this time to set up liaisons. "I made seven hundred dollars on the first day," she said. "My first year, I made over a hundred thousand dollars. Not bad for a 24-year-old high school dropout. I was amazed and hooked."

Not long after, Marion began having financial troubles, so Annie helped her out with the bills. It was inevitable that Marion would sooner or later ask. "I know you don't have a job," Marion said, "so where is the money coming from?"

Annie chose not to lie. Drawing a deep breath, she answered, "Mother, I spend time with men for money." Then she waited a seeming eternity for her mother, an actively participating Mormon, to explode.

But Marion didn't explode. Leveling her gaze on her daughter, she said, "As much free pussy as I gave away in my day, I wish I would have made some money."

I burst out laughing. "I love your mother," I told Annie.

"Yeah," Annie replied, "me too. My mother was what I call a Mormon gangster. She drank and popped pills, but she was a believing, active Mormon, and she attended church and was kind and nonjudgmental."

After a pause, she added, "I think she killed my father."

Killed your father? How? Why? Why do you think so? I was crazy curious, but Annie's only further comment on the subject was, "Sometimes I think her kindness and acceptance of others were, for her, like a kind of penance."

Annie broke up with the dreamy, gorgeous boyfriend but remained in the business. "I started for him. Now I was doing it for me."

Not that all was well. "I was smoking crack and popping ecstasy like candy. So at 26, I moved out of state, cleaned up, got a regular job, and got off hardcore drugs." As of two months prior to our interview, Annie had been drug-free for six years. There was no hint of pride, just relief and gratitude at being one of the lucky ones.

5

He pressed a gun to her temple

Some providers tour the country and allow clients the privilege of covering travel, lodging, and dining expenses. A client may buy a provider a plane ticket to his home state. Transporting a person over state lines for purposes of compensated sex is a felony under the federal, ironically named Mann Act, but willing providers tend not to file complaints. Short of that, many providers travel on their own dime, having found that most cities have no shortage of hobbyists eager to hand over cash to meet them. It doesn't take very many encounters to pay for plane tickets and hotels.

During a stay in Fair Oaks, Virginia, Annie ran into trouble. "I rented a nice room in the Hyatt," she said. "The real Hyatt. Not Hyatt Place or anything like that. I was 27, about, and these were the days before I started checking references. If someone passed the LE test, that was good enough."

"LE" is short for "Law Enforcement." The so-called "LE test" usually consists of asking a client outright if he works in law enforcement, asking him to show his genitals, and inviting him to touch the provider in the genital or breast area. The idea is that cops must say they're cops when asked, that cops are not allowed to expose themselves, and that cops are banned from touching providers.[4] Most of my interviewees had been around enough blocks to know that the LE test is bunk, some having learned the hard way. The few who still bought into it were loath to give it up. The only argument that seemed to give them pause was to ask them to substitute *narc* for *undercover cop*. "Do you think narcs are required to say 'yes' when a dealer asks, 'Are you a narc?' Do you think they're not allowed to touch the drugs?"

The man at Annie's door that night was not a cop, the LE test's futility notwithstanding. But he was by no means safe.

He rapped on her hotel room door at the appointed time. Through the peephole, the five-foot-three Annie saw a tall, bulky man. "He was wrapped up and in a hat so his face was hidden," she said, "so he looked a little scary. But I was tipsy, so I let him in." Once he was inside, the hat and wrap came off, and Annie was pleased to see that her guest was muscled and handsome. The positive impression was short-lived. She greeted him with a hug—and he responded by heaving her to the bed, where he brutally raped her. At last breaking free, Annie ran to the bathroom and desperately searched for her douche kit. Thinking she was looking for a weapon, the man pulled out a handgun and followed her into the bathroom, where he grabbed her and threw her against the vanity. The man's pants were around his ankles and Annie was naked. Pressing the gun to Annie's temple, he said, "What the fuck are you doing?"

"I wasn't scared," Annie told me. "I know what a real gun looks like. This was a realistic looking pellet gun. Still, what if I'd been wrong?"

Drilling the gun harder into her temple, the man said, "I know you've been working all day. Where's the money?"

"My pimp has it," said Annie, who had no pimp. Earlier she had noted a room across the hall with a "Do Not Disturb" tag hanging from the knob. Now she gave that room's number to her assailant. "That's his room. Go ask him with that gun. He doesn't have a gun." Annie explained to me, "I knew if I could get him out of the room I'd be okay."

The man didn't go for it. He ordered her to stay in the bathroom while he ransacked her room, looking for her money. He pulled up mattresses, opened drawers, and "thoroughly tossed the place." Annie had $1,500 stashed behind a painting. He didn't find it.

Annie remained in the bathroom with the door closed. Her cell phone rang. A friend was calling. Annie grabbed her phone and yelled into it, "I'm being robbed! I'm being robbed and he has a gun!" Her assailant dropped the search and tried to reenter the bathroom. Annie fought to keep the door closed while continuing to yell into the phone. "Finally," she said, "he booked it."

The brute was through with Annie, but she wasn't through with him. He had called to set up the appointment, which meant that Annie had his phone number. A quick Google search revealed that he was a male escort[5] working in the Washington, DC area. She easily found his escort name and, with a little more digging, his real name. She called and kept calling his phone. He didn't answer, of course, but she left threatening voice mail messages. Next she began incessantly texting him. "I have friends who are cops and they know where you are," she told him, a claim she backed up by texting him his full name and address, "and I'm sending them after you."

To me she said, with a satisfied smile, "I terrorized him."

You don't mess with Annie.

These days Annie agrees to see new clients only if they have references from other providers she knows and trusts. But it's rare that she'll see a new client at all. "I stick with clients I know and like," she said. "It's fun again. When it was nothing but dicks, back-to-back, day in and day out, the money was great, but it was exhausting. Now I'll schedule a client a week out and let the anticipation build. There's a thrill to the waiting game."

6

What if cops are waiting outside to grab me?

Annie answered my questions with candor and directness. She made no attempt to justify, defy, or apologize. She put on no airs. She could have played the femme fatale but chose not to. As she shared horror stories of rape and other abuse, there was not so much as a hint of "poor me." She came across as real, simply herself. Clearly, she felt no need to impress. Which impressed.

Annie said she had more to tell, but our conversation had already gone on for nearly two hours. She suggested adjourning and reconvening a few weeks later. We agreed on a follow-up appointment, but she canceled without explanation the day before it was to take place. After that, my text messages went unanswered. When I later returned to the apartment to interview Veronica, I asked her about Annie. She would say only that Annie was safe and "taking a break."

Heading for the door after my chat with Annie, I recalled reading that sometimes cops will watch a known provider's apartment and stop presumed clients on their way out. Or they might follow a presumed client's car at a distance, hoping a minor traffic violation will provide a legal reason to pull him over. Visiting a provider's apartment is not a crime, but unnerved johns often needlessly and foolishly blurt confessions. It seems there's something about being pulled over by a cop and having a flashlight aimed in your face that makes you forget you're allowed not to answer questions and not to volunteer self-incriminating information.

No cop stopped me. I walked safely and uninterrupted to my car. I was a compulsive mirror-checker during the first few miles of the drive home. If police officers were following me, they did a great job of remaining inconspicuous, and I did a great job of not committing even the tiniest moving violation.

My first interview had been productive and *enjoyable*. I was eager to continue. Annie offered to vouch for me to other providers, which vastly improved my odds of securing more interviews. Having been in the profession for some time, Annie was known and liked. With her endorsement, once-silent providers began replying to my texted inquiries and agreeing to meet.

Arriving home, I killed the engine and remained in my car, reflecting for a moment. "What a nice person!" I said aloud to the empty passenger seat.

As we were wrapping up our interview, Annie had said, "This was like therapy. Better, in a way. I see a therapist, but I haven't told her what I do. So, thank you."

Annie had opened up to me at no small risk. She had set aside the contrived, sexy persona to reveal the real, vulnerable person. She had trusted me to protect her anonymity and to write about her with fairness.

And then, of all things, she thanked me.

"I hope you remembered to thank *her*," the empty passenger seat replied.

I assured it that I had.

Chapter 3

A Brief History of Mormon Sex

*The union of the sexes, husband and wife (and only
husband and wife), was for the principal purpose of bringing
children into the world. Sexual experiences were never intended
by the Lord to be a mere plaything or merely
to satisfy passions and lusts.*

—Mormon prophet Spencer W. Kimball

1

The Mormon psychosexual pickle

If you're new to the Mormon Church, now might be a good time for a
bit of context. It may provide a better understanding of the psychosexual
pickle in which Mormons find themselves the moment they so much as
entertain a sexual thought.

While nearly every religion more or less agrees with "thou shalt not
commit adultery," most leave adherents to mind themselves from there.
But some religions set forth stricter, more explicit sex rules, take them
way the heck more seriously, keep tabs, and impose penalties. The Mormon Church is of the latter sort. It dictates to members the purpose of

sex, when sex is permitted, what sexual activities are not allowed, and what sexual thoughts not to think, which is most sexual thoughts. As for keeping tabs, the church instructs local leaders to ask members in one-on-one "worthiness interviews" about their obedience and encourages members to inform on one another. Breaking the rules can result in a summons to a disciplinary council, which may in turn result in disfellowshipment or excommunication, not to mention gossip and shaming.

An executive summary of the Mormon Church's history and policy with regards to sex might read something like this:

- The Mormon Church, properly called The Church of Jesus Christ of Latter-day Saints, claims to be the only true church, guided by a prophet who receives revelation from above. From the prophet down to the local level, all church leaders are entitled to receive revelation pertaining to their individual assignments. You defy their council at the peril of your church membership and eternal well-being.

- For the first 80 years of the Mormon Church's existence, Mormons vehemently defended polygamy as a commandment from God. It was not a two-way street, however, for only men were allowed multiple spouses. Today the Mormon Church would just as soon everyone forget its polygamy days and excommunicates anyone who practices or advocates it.

- Today the Mormon Church presents itself as a defender of one-man, one-woman marriage and "family values."

- Mormon bishops are instructed to hold regular, private "worthiness interviews" with church members age 12 and up. One of the questions they're required to ask is whether the church member obeys the "Law of Chastity," which pretty much boils down to this: *Procreation is the primary purpose of sex. Do not have sex with anyone besides your lawful, of-the-opposite-sex spouse. Even with your spouse, don't engage in anything that might shock your nonagenarian prophet. This includes oral sex. From time to time, expect your bishop to check up to ensure you're not giving your genitals too much leeway. Never masturbate. Dress modestly. Push all inappropriate sexual thoughts from your mind. Violating the Law of Chastity is the third most serious sin you can commit, right after denying a sure witness of the Holy Ghost and murder.*

Not surprisingly, Mormon policy regarding the authorized use of genitalia has been known to foster a good deal of sexual repression.

The remainder of this chapter is for those who would like to delve a little deeper. I'll meet back up with the rest of you a few pages from now.

2

A prophet caught with his pants down

Mormons believe that Christianity abandoned its roots long before the Roman emperor Constantine got ahold of it in the fourth century CE. It wasn't until 1820 that Jesus gave it another go. On a spring day in the woods of upstate New York, he appeared to 14-year-old Joseph Smith Jr. and told him that the churches of his day were "an abomination in his sight."[1] Ten years later, Smith, now a prophet, seer, and revelator,[2] restored the one true church, that is, "the only true and living church upon the face of the whole earth, with which I, the Lord, am well pleased."[23]

Jesus told Smith to call the restored church The Church of Jesus Christ of Latter-day Saints,[4] "Saints" meaning "followers of Christ,"[5] but outsiders lost no time in dubbing it the Mormon Church. The nickname stuck. "Mormon" comes from the Book of Mormon, which a fellow named Mormon engraved on plates of gold around 400 CE. Mormon was a white, Christian Native American prophet descended from Jews who had left Jerusalem 800 years earlier for a promised land known today as the Americas. The book is a sacred history of God's dealings with Mormon's people. In 1823, an angel led Smith to a spot in the woods near his home where the golden book lay buried. Retrieving the book, Smith translated it "by the gift and power of God." His translation method consisted of placing a "seer stone" in an upturned hat, burying his face in the hat to block out ambient light, and gazing at the stone, which displayed translated phrases for Smith to read aloud while his scribe wrote them down.[6] Mormons accept the Book of Mormon as scripture equal in authority to the Bible.

The Mormons revered their young prophet, figuring that anyone holding regular conversations with Jesus must be nigh unto perfect. So you can imagine their surprise when, within about a year of having founded the church, Smith was caught *in flagrante delicto* with his wife's 14-year-old housekeeper.[7]

Smith fessed up, but not to adultery. He explained that God had ordered him to take multiple wives, just as the Old Testament patriarchs had done.[8] The distraught Smith had begged God to spare him the burden of having to bed lots of women, but God was not to be dissuaded. In the end, Smith had no choice but to do as he was told. Thus, he and Fanny—no kidding, that was the housekeeper's name—weren't committing adultery. In the eyes of God they were husband and supplemental wife. Smith explained to his closest associates that they, too, were commanded to take multiple wives. This seemed to go a long way toward quelling their initial outrage and opening their minds to the possibility that maybe there was something to this new polygamy commandment after all. They were, however, to keep the practice secret from the church at large.

The divine edict for Smith to accrue extra wives came as a surprise to a lot of people, none more so than Smith's lawful wife, Emma. Smith hadn't told her about the new commandment because, well, God told him not to tell her. God, it seems, was no less afraid than Smith of Emma's temper.

The prophet continued hustling women until his death at age 38. *Hustling* is not an unfair word choice. Smith pressured at least two young women into bed with claims that a sword-bearing, invisible angel stood at the ready to hack him to bits unless they complied. Not wanting to witness much less cause the prophet's dismemberment, the frightened young women capitulated.[9] Nor did Smith's eye fall only on single women. When he fancied a married woman, he would send her husband on an extended errand and hustle her while the man was away.[10]

Smith's appetite for young, single women led to his being tarred and feathered in 1832, but it was his appetite for married women that led to his death in 1844. In the nearly all-Mormon town of Nauvoo, Illinois, Smith made the mistake of hitting on the wife of one his closest associates. Enraged, the husband decided to blow the lid off of Mormon polygamy. This the husband accomplished by publishing the aptly named *Nauvoo Expositor.* Among its compendium of insider accounts was this harrowing description of Smith's entrapping women into what many were calling "spiritual wifery":

> It is a notorious fact, that many females . . . have been induced, by the sound of the gospel, to forsake friends, and embark upon a voyage across waters that lie stretched over the greater portion of the globe, as they supposed, to glorify God. . . . When in the stead thereof, they are told, after having been sworn in one of the most solemn manners, to never divulge what is revealed to them, with a penalty of death attached that God Almighty has revealed it to him, that she should be his (Joseph's) Spiritual wife. . . . She is thunder-struck, faints, recovers, and refuses. The Prophet damns her if she rejects. . . . She thinks of the great sacrifice, and of the many thousand miles she has traveled over sea and land, that she might save her soul from pending ruin, and replies, God's will be done, and not mine. The Prophet and his devotees in this way are gratified. The next step to avoid public exposition from the common course of things, they are sent away for a time, until all is well; after which they return, as from a long visit.[11]

Smith, whom not surprisingly the Mormons had elected mayor, persuaded the city council to declare the *Expositor* a public nuisance. He then ordered the newspaper and its printing press destroyed, an order that the Nauvoo marshal carried out.[12]

The action didn't go over well with the state of Illinois. Smith and three associates were arrested and jailed. They occupied an upstairs room with an unbarred window to the outside. A visitor smuggled a six-shooter to Smith, which came in handy when an armed mob stormed the building two days later. Smith and the mob exchanged shots. With three bullets spent and three misfires, Smith ran to the window. Four shots spun him around, two hitting his chest and two hitting his back. Crying out "Oh lord my god," Smith fell from the window to his death, leaving behind some thirty to fifty grieving widows.[13]

For about six months following Smith's death, a number of aspiring prophet-successors arose. In terms of numbers, the winner was Brigham Young. Young led the greater part of the Mormons out of the United States into the valley of the Great Salt Lake in Mexican territory. There he brought Mormon polygamy into the open. Seven months later, Mexico ceded the territory to the United States, which lost no time enacting never before needed anti-bigamy laws. The Mormons defied the law, knuckling under in the early twentieth century only when the government began seizing church property and jailing church leaders.

Today the Mormon Church excommunicates anyone practicing or advocating polygamy. "I condemn it, yes, as a practice," Mormon prophet Gordon B. Hinckley told CNN talk show host Larry King during an on-air interview, "because it is not doctrinal.[14] It is not legal and this church takes the position that we will abide by the law."[15] King was at the time married to a Mormon woman and living in Provo, Utah.[16]

Taking the church's capitulation to the U.S. government as a sign of apostasy, polygamy-practicing splinter groups immediately began popping up. They are still to be found in Utah, Idaho, Colorado, Texas, other U.S. states, Mexico, and Canada. Lilly, a Chinese-American who owns an Asian massage parlor in downtown Salt Lake City,[17] told me of a customer who had four wives and 24 children. At the conclusion of his massage, the man proposed to her. He was in the market for Wife Number Five and, having met Lilly, suddenly felt that God wanted him to take a Chinese wife.

Lilly declined, if you can imagine.

3

A madam partners with the Salt Lake City Council

While polygamy was making Mormons infamous, prostitution thrived in late nineteenth- and early twentieth-century Mormon towns as much as it did in all other cities with the population to support it. The sex trade in America was an open secret, tolerated as a necessary evil. Most states and municipalities had no laws against it.

Commercial Street[18] emerged as Salt Lake's red light district in the 1870s.[19] By the turn of the century, concern about its proximity to the city's business center led to proposals not to shutter but to relocate it. In partnership with Belle London,[20] the town's leading madam, the Salt Lake City Council set aside Block 64 for the profession's new home. Block 64 sat about a mile west of Commercial Street, bounded by the streets 500 West, 600 West, 100 South, and 200 South. The locale seemed ideal because:

> there were railroads on three sides of it, it divided two school districts (so children wouldn't have to walk past it), and because, "the 'foreign element,' (Greek and Italian workers) had so destroyed the area that establishing prostitution there would not harm it any further and could even be rationalized as catering to the immoral foreigners."[21]

No less than the Mormon Church–owned *Deseret News* praised the proposed relocation as "commendable," questioning only whether the move would prove "practicable."[22] Perhaps the editor knew better than to rail against prostitution while defending polygamy.

The new brothel was by no means modest in size. A downtown Salt Lake City block takes in 435,600 square feet, about ten times the area of a city block in, say, downtown Portland, Oregon.[23] Nor was it inconspicuous, less because of its numerous parlors, cribs, bars, and gambling establishments, and more because of the largely taxpayer-funded stockade surrounding the block:

The stockade consisted of nearly 100 small brick "cribs" which were ten feet square with a door and window, and built in rows. . . . Within the stockade there were also larger parlor houses and storehouses for liquor—an essential component of the stockade operation. The stockade had three entrances, each guarded to both keep children and "undesirable" guests from entering as well as to warn of the periodic police raids.[24]

The stockade opened for business on December 18, 1908, and for three years served as the proud home of Mormontown's red light district. Each month, London visited police headquarters and paid fines on behalf of the stockade's inhabitants. The fines were more akin to a tax, representing a considerable and dependable source of municipal revenue. In return, police tipped off London before conducting the occasional, perfunctory raid.[25]

It's unknown why London shut down the stockade a mere three years after opening it. Some sex workers returned to Commercial Street, while a good many took apartments across the street on 200 South, colloquially called Second South. Today, locals make humorous references to Second South as a red light district, but most have no knowledge of the street's history, much less that a stockade-enclosed brothel once stood there.

4

Brothels in other nearby Mormontowns

Belle London wasn't northern Utah's only well-known madam, nor was the stockade its only in-your-face establishment. At about the same time London was building her reputation in Salt Lake, another madam was building her own in nearby Park City. Perched on the Wastach Range of the Rocky Mountains about 43 miles southeast of Salt Lake City, Park City today sports world-famous ski resorts. Visitors spend a fortune on lodging, food, ski equipment, skiwear, and, of course, lift tickets. If you stroll Park City's historic Main Street, you'll pass expensive art galleries, numerous restaurants, and no shortage of gift shops. Visit Park City in January and you may run into celebrities attending the Sundance Film Festival, founded by the Sundance Kid himself, Utah resident Robert Redford. Had you visited in February of 2002, you would have found yourself amid crowds attending the Winter Olympic Games.

But when Rachel Beulah stepped off the train in Park City in 1878, Park City was a mining town. Six years earlier, a newly completed arm of the Transcontinental Railroad had begun bringing record numbers to the area. In those days, where there were railroads and mining there was prostitution, and Park City was no exception.

Likely having worked as a prostitute in her native Ohio, Beulah resumed her profession in Park City, unaware that she would soon become one of the town's most prominent citizens and, eventually, one of its most colorful historical figures. Her star began rising shortly after her marriage to George Urban in 1898. About that time, locals had decided they didn't care for having a red light district close to their homes. Seeing this as an opportunity, George and Beulah built "the Row," sixteen cribs in an adjacent area now known as Deer Valley. As the Row's madam, Rachel Beulah Urban picked up her endearing nickname, "Mother Urban." Park City Museum volunteer Chris McLaws wrote:

> Rachel had a big heart, giving generously to the poor and needy. She was a large woman, weighing about 200 pounds, with a peg leg and a pet parrot that swore at passersby from the front porch. As a madam, Rachel took good care of her girls, which is likely how she got her nickname "Mother Urban." She wanted them to be cultured and educated. They weren't allowed to walk the streets and if they broke the rules, she bought them a one-way ticket on a train out of town.[26]

In her book *Red Light Women of the Rocky Mountains*, Jan MacKnell wrote, "One old-timer recalled that if there was a death in the family, Mother Urban would discreetly visit in the night and give money to the family."[27]

Urban died from stomach cancer in 1933 and was interred in the Park City Cemetery. There is some disagreement regarding her send-off. Citing Gary Kimball's book *Death and Dying in Old Park City*,[28] McLaws states that the city threw Urban a lavish and expensive funeral.[29] By contrast, MacKnell writes that "by then there was nobody left to pay for her headstone."[30]

Utahns have an easier time reconciling prostitution as an open secret in Park City as opposed to Salt Lake. With its millionaire-owned vacation homes in the surrounding mountains and year-round tourism, Park City tends to be more liberal than the typical Utah town. Though that's an admittedly low bar, locals facetiously characterize Park City as "in Utah but not of it," a play on a common admonition among Christians to be "in the world but not of it."[31]

No less colorful and no less known than London and Urban was madam Rossette Duccinni Davie, whose Rose Room brothel flourished during the 1940s in Ogden, Utah. Like Park City, Ogden was a railroad town. It sits about 40 miles north of Salt Lake and about 50 miles southeast of Promontory Point, where the Golden Spike marks the celebrated completion of the transcontinental railroad. Author Tyler Hoffman wrote that Davie "was an affluent member of the community and would regularly be seen walking the streets with her pet ocelot—a dwarf leopard."[32]

According to Associated Press, "Rose Davie, as she was known, pulled down $30,000 a month in her prime and withstood several prostitution charges before she was ultimately done in by a federal tax evasion charge."[33] Davie and her husband were thought by some, including historian Val Holley, to be police informants, or at least to have bribed sheriffs not to mind the goings-on at the Rose Room.[34]

Rose Room clients entered the building from Ogden's 25th Street, exiting onto perpendicular Lincoln Avenue. During Prohibition the brothel was also part of an underground system of tunnels used to run bootlegged alcohol. Today, the building houses a nightclub.[35]

Like Salt Lake's Second South Street, Ogden's 25th Street has a persistent reputation and provides fodder for innuendo. And like their neighbors to the south, few Ogden residents who joke about the street know its real history.

5

Turnaround

By the 1970s, the image of the Mormon Church had undergone a remarkable turnaround. With the specter of polygamy fading, Americans had begun associating Mormons with wholesome values and strong families.

The church may have uptight parents to thank for its transformation. Teenagers and young adults in the 1960s and '70s were challenging social norms. Many parents were beside themselves at the sexual revolution, long hair on boys, bralessness, environmentalism, equal rights, career women, unisex fashions, and other affronts to once-accepted norms. In Mormons, these parents saw an encouraging contrast. Mormon boys had short haircuts. Mormon girls dressed modestly. A Mormon woman's place was in the home. Mormons didn't sleep around, swear, use tobacco, drink alcohol, abuse drugs, or even consume coffee or tea. They were law-abiding and respected authority. They were all about family. They were consummate patriots. They preached against premarital sex and stood for the sanctity of—this time around—monogamous marriage.

The church lost no time in capitalizing on the turnabout. It produced and ran heartrending, pro-family commercials tagged with, "A message from The Church of Jesus Christ of Latter-day Saints. The Mormons."[36] At the same time, church leaders drilled into members that, as representatives of the true church, they were to present a good example of righteous living. Sermons told tales of Mormons who sinned and regretted it because a non-Mormon had witnessed it and now would never join the church.[37]

The combination of post-hippie parental angst, clean-cut Mormon kids, pressure to show a good example, and a strong public relations campaign worked. More and more, non-Mormons were praising the exemplary Mormon family that lived on their street.

6

Count the shakes after you pee

Of the Mormon Church's many sexual don'ts, masturbation enjoys frequent mention. Possibly the most infamous example is found in the late Mormon apostle Boyd K. Packer's 1976 sermon, "To Young Men Only." Likening testicles to "a little factory" and nocturnal emissions to a "release valve," Packer cautioned against tampering with said valve. "For if you do that," he warned, "the little factory will speed up. You will then be tempted again and again to release it. You can quickly be subjected to a habit, one that is not worthy, one that will leave you feeling depressed and feeling guilty. Resist that temptation. Do not be guilty of tampering or playing with this sacred power of creation."[38]

More recently, the church produced and released a video teaching that if you know of someone who masturbates, failing to inform that person's bishop is like leaving a wounded soldier on the battlefield.[39]

So constant and so emphatic is the church's anti-masturbation rhetoric that some Mormon boys grew up terrified that exceeding three posturination shakes counted as masturbation. When I first heard that, I thought it was a joke. I later heard from a number of Mormon men who grew up with precisely that fear.

Besides masturbation, Mormon kids are taught the evils of fornication and anything remotely approaching it. For Mormons, "anything remotely approaching it" covers a wide range of behaviors. "Immodesty, necking, and petting," wrote Mormon apostle Bruce R. McConkie, are "a form of sex immorality."[40] Letting a romantic interest touch "any part of your body covered by your bathing suit" is "a form of fornication" requiring repentance and confession to a bishop.[41] "Immorality does not begin in adultery or perversion," taught Mormon prophet Spencer W. Kimball. "It begins with little indiscretions like sex thoughts, sex discussions, passionate kissing, petting and such, growing with every exercise."[42]

In a well-known Sunday school lesson for teenage Mormon girls, a teacher arranges sticks of gum on a plate and invites each of the girls to take one. One stick, however, has been opened and chewed. When no one selects the chewed piece, the teacher explains, *If you're naughty with boys, you'll be like that chewed piece of gum. No one wants to marry a chewed piece of gum.* There is no corresponding lesson for Mormon boys.

Some Mormons take not fornicating so seriously that they perform marriages for their pets before letting them breed. At first I thought that was a joke, too. Nope.

Modest dress is another frequent Mormon topic. At Mormon youth dances, chaperones will turn away any girl who shows up in a dress that's sleeveless, doesn't reach the knee, or is "too form-fitting." Other chaperones hover about the dance floor, guarding against too-sexy and too-close dancing. I spoke with a Mormon bishop who boasted of patrolling youth dances, armed with a teddy bear. If he couldn't fit the teddy bear between a boy and girl, they were dancing too close.

Church-owned Brigham Young University's dress code states that women's attire "is inappropriate when it is sleeveless, strapless, backless, or revealing; has slits above the knee; or is form fitting. Dresses, skirts, and shorts must be knee-length or longer. Hairstyles should be clean and neat, avoiding extremes in styles or colors. Excessive ear piercing (more than one per ear) and all other body piercing are not acceptable."[43] Female students living in BYU dormitories have been made to line up and kneel on the floor, and young women whose hems didn't touch the floor were sent back to their rooms to change.

For men, the code states, "Clothing is inappropriate when it is sleeveless, revealing, or form fitting. Shorts must be knee-length or longer. Hairstyles should be clean and neat, avoiding extreme styles or colors, and trimmed above the collar, leaving the ear uncovered. Sideburns should not extend below the earlobe or onto the cheek. If worn, moustaches should be neatly trimmed and may not extend beyond or below the corners of the mouth. Men are expected to be clean-shaven; beards are not acceptable. Earrings and other body piercing are not acceptable."

All of which may explain why, in 2014, the Mormon blogosphere exploded when attorney Kate Kelly, excommunicated for challenging the church's refusal to ordain women to its priesthood, was *photographed in a sleeveless dress!*

Kelly dubbed it "dressgate."[44]

7

What's that you're doing in your bedroom?

The Mormon Church has sex rules for married couples, too. Though leaders talk more often about the don'ts, they will on occasion concede a do or two. In those rare instances, they manage to make sex sound not quite as appealing as paying a parking ticket.

On the *not-to-do* side, Mormon couples are counseled to avoid anything that's "unnatural" and, in a feat of circular reasoning, anything that's "inappropriate." Mormon prophet Spencer W. Kimball wrote, "If it is unnatural, you just don't do it. There are some people who have said that behind the bedroom doors anything goes. That is not true and the Lord would not condone it."[45] He also said, "Married persons should understand that if in their marital relations they are guilty of unnatural, impure, or unholy practices, they should not enter the temple unless and until they repent and discontinue any such practices. . . . The First Presidency has interpreted oral sex as constituting an unnatural, impure, or unholy practice."[46]

Birth control is both on and, more recently, not on the *not-to-do* side. In April 1969, Mormon prophet David O. McKay said, "We believe that those who practice birth control will reap disappointment by and by."[47] Six years later, Kimball declared, "Sterilization and tying of the tubes and such are sins, and except under special circumstances it cannot be approved."[48] Married Latter-day Saints took statements like McKay's and Kimball's as orders from God not to use birth control. As a consequence, many Mormon couples felt it their duty to crank out as many kids as they could, as fast as they could. A mother's physical health was some-times a consideration, but until recently her mental health was less of one. Others, loath to risk adding to however many mouths they were already struggling to feed—Mormons take the whole "multiply and re-plenish the earth" thing literally and seriously[49]—rationalized abstinence as not birth control and kissed their sex life goodbye.

Some Mormon men sought another solution. "When I first moved to Utah I worked at Planned Parenthood," a now retired social worker told me. "Many Mormon men who didn't want more kids would come in for a vasectomy and didn't want to tell their wives."

Today the church allows that "decisions about birth control and the consequences of those decisions rest solely with each married couple." There is, however, a proviso: "Those who are physically able have the blessing, joy, and obligation to bear children and to raise a family. This blessing should not be postponed for selfish reasons."[50]

On the *to-do* side, you won't hear anything approaching encourage-ment to *enjoy* sex. This is about as close as it gets: "Sexual relations within marriage are not only for the purpose of procreation, but also a means of expressing love and strengthening emotional and spiritual ties between husband and wife."[51] Hot stuff.

So it is that many Mormons arrive at their wedding night not just sexually inept but sexually confused if not afraid. The transition from *don't use your genitals* to *now that you're married you can use them* is not an easy one. In order not to do anything "unnatural, impure, or unholy," many Mormons err on the side of caution, avoiding anything more ad-venturous than a quick execution in missionary position. Many Mormon women experience difficulty transitioning from *only sluts do it* to *you're married so now it's okay*. Some raised on *only bad girls like it* feel guilty if they happen to *enjoy* marital sex at all.[52]

To be fair, the church has come a long way since the late Mormon apostle J. Reuben Clark taught, "Remember the prime purpose of sex desire is to beget children. Sex gratification must be had at that hazard."[53]

Mormon sex, it appears, is not for the faint.

8

Abuse, cover-ups, victim blaming, and bishops who teach lasciviousness

Mormon bishops and other leaders conduct regular, one-on-one worthiness interviews with adults and with youth age 12 and older. The church's *General Handbook* lists interview questions bishops are required to ask. One of them is, "Do you obey the law of chastity?" While that's intrusive in its own right, some bishops have been known to wax more explicit, creeping out some kids and sending others home with new ideas they can't wait to try. A Mormon apostle once admitted over the pulpit, "One of the General Authorities once interviewed a young man who . . . made confession of a transgression. . . . The General Authority was amazed at the sordid nature of what the young man had done and asked, 'Where on earth did you get the idea to do things like this?' He was shocked when the young man answered, 'From my bishop.'"[54]

While the majority of Mormon leaders act within the bounds of propriety, there are some who do not. As I write, a Mormon who had presided over thousands of missionaries stands accused of having sexually assaulted young women in his charge[55]; multiple bishops stand accused of fondling children in private interviews[56]; as many or more bishops stand accused of putting sexually explicit questions to children during private interviews[57]; a number of bishops stand accused of counseling battered wives to "stay with their abusers for the sake of the marriage"[58]; a Mormon general authority stands accused of fondling his grandchild, offering to pay her father—his son-in-law—for silence, instigating and facilitating the father's divorce, and, working with fellow general authorities and local leaders, orchestrating a cover-up that included witness tampering[59]; accusations have arisen of abuse of Native American children under the church's now shuttered Indian Placement Program[60]; a prominent Mormon filmmaker has admitted to fondling a 13-year-old in his home during a son's sleepover[61]; and more. Each case has come with the usual complement of cover-ups, clandestine legal settlements, and bullied silence. Abuse and cover-ups are not the exclusive domain of the Roman Catholic Church.

By 2018, after victims had surfaced in sufficient numbers to raise sufficiently loud protests, the church made a concession: parents were now permitted to sit in on bishops' interviews with their children.[62] The same year, carefully worded and sandwiched in the middle of a General Conference talk, Mormon apostle Quentin L. Cook tiptoed to within several hundred miles of publicly acknowledging the incidence of sexual abuse within church ranks:

> During my lifetime, worldly issues and concerns have moved from one extreme to another—from frivolous and trivial pursuits to serious immorality. It is commendable that nonconsensual immorality has been exposed and denounced. Such nonconsensual immorality is against the laws of God and of society.[63]

Critics were quick to point out that Cook had understated if not trivialized the problem, that the passive-voice "has been exposed and denounced" failed to note that it wasn't church leaders but outraged members who did the exposing and denouncing, and that "nonconsensual immorality" was a downright wimpy choice of words leaving room for victim blaming. Their fears were not without precedent. Like many organizations and society in general, the church was no stranger to victim blaming. Mormon apostle Richard G. Scott said in April of 1992:

> The victim must do all in his or her power to stop the abuse. Most often, the victim is innocent because of being disabled by fear or the power or authority of the offender. At some point in time, however, *the Lord may prompt a victim to recognize a degree of responsibility for abuse.*[64]

Like many religions, the Mormon Church seems to place greater priority on protecting the organization than on justice and healing for victims. A 2019 *Vice News* article revealed that the church's hotline for reporting sex abuse didn't ring at church headquarters but at a church-retained law firm, whose priority was not victim support but containment.[65] And the church's 2006 *General Handbook* stated, "To avoid implicating the church in legal matters to which it is not a party, church leaders should avoid testifying in civil or criminal cases or other proceedings involving abuse. . . . Church leaders should not try to persuade alleged victims or other witnesses either to testify or not to testify in criminal or civil court proceedings."[66] A more recent edition says, "Church leaders should not involve themselves in civil or criminal cases for members in their units, quorums, or organizations without first consulting with Church legal counsel."[67]

9

Meddling in gay sex

In 2004, about two-thirds of Utah voters approved an amendment to their state constitution banning anything that looked, walked, or quacked like gay marriage, civil unions included. The amendment's passage was not surprising. The church publicly urged members to vote for it, and Utah is about two-thirds Mormon.

In 2008, the church launched a massive, would-be incognito effort to ensure the passage of California's proposed anti-gay marriage amendment, Proposition 8. The extent of the church's involvement remained under the radar until Wikileaks revealed just how much the church had meddled.[68] "Mormons tipped scale in the ban on gay marriage," trumpeted the *New York Times* and other media.[69] Revelations soon followed as to the extent of the church's prior meddling in Hawaii, Alaska, Nevada, and Nebraska, sparking outrage across the nation. For the church to tell its members how to vote on marriage laws *may* have been defensible as a moral stand, but its meddling with non-Mormon voters was seen as an overstep. Some saw it as a possible violation of the Johnson Amendment, which bars tax-exempt organizations from endorsing or opposing candidates and attempting to influence legislation.[70]

To some, the Mormon Church was once again rebranding itself, this time as an anti-equality, anti–human rights organization. Mormon apostle Dallin H. Oaks likened the Proposition 8 backlash against the church to intimidation inflicted upon African Americans in the American South during the Civil Rights era. His remark was not well received.[71]

Beyond offensive, the Mormon Church's public condemnation of homosexuality may well be deadly. Author Gregory A. Prince dedicates a chapter to suicide in his book *Gay Rights and the Mormon Church*. Here is its sobering opening paragraph:

> The tragic connection between homosexuality and suicide is well-known, as is the dramatic (eightfold) reduction in risk of suicide if LGBT youth are accepted within their families. Yet the incidence of teenage suicide in Utah, the most Mormon state and country, is rising at the highest rate in the country.[72]

According to the Public Health Indicator Based Information System,

> The Utah suicide rate has been consistently higher than the national rate. In 2018 (the most recent national-level data year available, data from the National Center for Health Statistics), the age-adjusted suicide rate for the U.S. was 14.78 per 100,000 population, while the Utah suicide rate was 22.13 per 100,000 population during the same year. Utah had the 6th-highest age-adjusted suicide rate in the U.S. during 2018.[73]

It seems likely, even obvious, that Mormon Church policy contributes to Utah's unusually high LGBTQ suicide rate, but the data are insufficient to assert as much with certainty. Death certificates tend to list the means of suicide, not suicide itself, as the cause of death. Death from a self-inflicted gunshot wound, for instance, might be listed as "death by accidental shooting," and a self-hanging might be listed as "death by asphyxiation."[74] Moreover, Utah medical examiners are not required to note or ask about a deceased person's sexual orientation or gender identity. Privacy-minded, bereft families often prefer that official reports omit such details.

Fuzzy data are one reason that many organizations concerned with the wellness and safety of the LGBTQ community avoid accusing the Mormon Church outright. Another is that bluntness can backfire from a public relations standpoint. Church sympathizers and defenders raised an outcry when comedian and talk show host Ellen DeGeneres read this statement on air in 2018: "The leading cause of death for Utah kids, ages 11–17, is suicide. Suicide in Utah has increased 141 percent because of the shame they feel from the Mormon Church."[75] One response, a guest opinion in the *Idaho Statesman* headlined "No Correlation between Youth Suicide and Church of Jesus Christ of Latter-day Saints," claimed:

> Michael Staley, who works for Utah's medical examiner and ranks among the most respected researchers on this topic, said in an interview with *Q Salt Lake*, a Utah LGBT magazine, his initial findings do not support the narrative that Utah youth suicides are rising as a result of the Church's traditional teachings on sexuality or LGBT issues. "There's no data to show that, period," Staley said. "The people who are driving that narrative are going to be disappointed."[76]

To claim "no correlation" and "no data" is an exercise in intellectual dishonesty. The Mormon Church has been unabashed in its anti-LGBTQ messaging, especially targeted to youth; the relationship between the LGBTQ community and suicide is established[77]; and suicide is the leading cause of death of Utah children between 10 and 17 years of age.[78] Moreover, only in the majority-Mormon state of Utah has the incidence of LGBTQ-related suicides increased, even as church leaders have doubled down on their anti-gay rhetoric and policies. To be sure, correlations do not establish causation, but they *are* data and can *suggest* causation—as the above most certainly do.

Another reason that some organizations avoid hitting the Mormon Church head-on is that doing so tends to make church leaders dig in their heels. If the goal is to effect change, patience and tact may prove better tactics. The gentler approach has yielded some positive results, for the church's policies regarding the LGBTQ community have evolved.[79] Past church leaders refused to acknowledge homosexuality as an orientation, whereas most today have either come around or learned to avoid the subject. The church no longer holds that identifying as gay is de facto sinful.[80] In 2012, the church pulled quite the surprise by publishing an official church website, mormonandgay.org,[81] which among other messages states, "LGBT people who live God's laws can fully participate in the church."[82] In 2010, the Mormon Church expressed support for a Salt Lake City ordinance banning housing and employment discrimination on the basis of sexual orientation or gender identity,[83] ending the city council's internal debate and allowing the measure to sail through.[84] In 2019, the church reversed its four-year-old policy against baptizing children of married gay parents.[85]

Yet for all steps forward, there are inevitable steps backward. In 2021, the Mormon Church excommunicated a mental health professional for her "conduct contrary to the law and order of the church," which consisted of "repeated, clear and public opposition to and condemnation of the church, its doctrines, its policies, and its leaders." Her alleged contrary conduct was that "she supports same-sex marriage, counsels that masturbation is not a sin and insists pornography should not be treated as an addiction."[86]

In other words, she chose the standards of her profession over dogma. How dare she!

10

Naughtiness, Mormon-style

You have to feel for Mormons. They're told not to obsess about sex by a church that obsesses about sex. They're told not to indulge in sex that's unnatural or inappropriate by a church that defends a founding prophet who married and bedded some thirty to fifty women, not all of age, not all single, and some under threat. They're told what they can and cannot do in the bedroom, and what they should and should not think about pertaining to sex.

If there are Mormons who hunger for a bit of naughtiness, the church must bear some responsibility. Its continual harping on sexual don'ts cannot but place sex front and center in more than a few Mormon minds. Oppression and shaming may bolster the effect. So may the pressure to be good when non-Mormons are watching, pressure that becomes conspicuously absent when no one is watching.

Perhaps that's why Harvard economics professor Benjamin Edelman's research published in 2009 showed that Utah led the nation in per capita paid porn subscriptions[87] and why in 2015 Utah ranked seventh in the nation for paid memberships on the extramarital dating site AshleyMadison.com.[88] And perhaps that's why in 2016, critical thinking–oriented website ProCon.org ranked Utah 28th in the nation for "unlawful promotion of or participation in sexual activities for profit."[89]

And perhaps that's why more Mormons than you might think, including Mormons you'd least expect, pay for sex.

Chapter 4

Secret Sexual Activities of Mormon Men

"Promiscuous" is the label that we use as a pejorative for people we think are having more sex than we are.

—Matt Dillahunty

1

"What *don't* they want to do?"

Most of us accept and follow all kinds of unwritten rules. There's no disputing that you must immediately touch the plate that a server warns you is too hot to touch, that it is unwise to reveal what you honestly think to anyone who says "tell me what you honestly think," and that contorting your body helps make the bowling ball go where you want.

When it comes to sex, an unwritten rule that's been around for centuries states: *The more creative your sexual fantasies, the more you damn well better keep them to yourself.*

If you happen to belong to a religion that presumes to intrude into your bedroom, you can add this unwritten corollary: *Disclosing your fantasies risks horrifying your spouse and may diminish your chances for continued sex at home.*

And this one: *Your spouse might lament to church leaders, who may take you aside to tell you how deeply concerned they are about your spiritual well-being, and who may repeat your fantasies in confidence to their respective spouses, who may in turn repeat them in confidence to their friends, and so forth, until you wonder why everyone at church is looking at you funny.*

On the other hand, with few exceptions, admitting your fantasies to a provider is relatively safe. Fantasy fulfillment is their business. And so is confidentiality.

With that in mind, I looked forward to asking providers, "What are some of the weird requests your clients have made?"

Tina, a lingerie model as well as a provider, is a five-foot-five American-born Latina with large brown eyes and an aquiline nose. A registered nurse, she keeps her license current even though she doesn't practice. Despite having been enviably endowed by Nature, she has twice undergone breast augmentation. She is soft-spoken and eminently kind. To my question about weird requests, she chuckled, "What *don't* they want to do? There. There's your chapter in one sentence."

I don't like admitting this, but my original intent for this chapter was to uncover activities that struck me as funny so you and I could laugh at the expense of johns who engage in them. You may have gathered as much by my use of the word "weird." My attitude began changing when I spoke with Veronica, a 34-year-old fair-skinned brunette whose eyes barely hinted—at that, only after she told me—that one of her parents was Polynesian. She had an honest, irrepressible cheerfulness about her. "After 14 years in the business," she said, "what's weird? Nothing blows me away. All of my clients are total gentlemen, respectful, wonderful. Some I've known for over 10 years. *Love* isn't the right word, but I *care* for them, about them. I like making them happy. They know they can ask me anything and they don't have to be embarrassed."

Nikki self-identifies as a sugar baby.[1] She doesn't advertise; all of her clients are regulars paying a fixed monthly retainer. A mutual friend had arranged for us to speak over lunch at the Asian Star restaurant in Midvale, a Salt Lake suburb.[2] You could tell she worked out, and you wouldn't have guessed that she had just turned 40. Brushing back her shoulder-length brown hair, she said, "Ours is a shame culture. I am about healing. I'm about cool and powerful experiences that society denies itself."

Later I would meet Rose, petite and in her late 20s, when she accompanied a male provider to his luncheon interview.[3] "I *want* to help them work out their fantasies," she said.

Betty and Boop expressed a similar sentiment. "I've seen so many men for so long," Boop said, "we're like, I don't know, is this weird?"

You read the last two aliases right. They often work together, so they asked to be interviewed together. I had barely pulled out my pen and yellow pad when the more animated of the two asked, "What names are you going to give us in your book?" I replied that I hadn't thought about that yet, that I would cook up aliases later. The other, who was more reserved, put a finger to her chin and said, "I think I'd like to be Betty." Betty it would be, I told her, whereupon the first burst into a wide-eyed smile and said, "Ooh! Then I want to be Boop!" They played off of each other well. Betty, a second-generation U.S.-born Latina, is slender with dark hair and lashes. "I'm the quiet, seductive type with the look of a teacher who dresses a shade too sexy," she said. "Clients fantasize falling in love with me." Boop calls herself a "Blaxican." Rubenesque, curvaceous, and mahogany complected, she told me her birth father is African American and her birth mother Mexican. "I'm more like the sorority party girl everyone wants to fuck," she said. I could see why clients would enjoy seeing them together. *This will hands down be my most entertaining interview*, I thought. Correctly, as it turned out.

"The thing is, we try to be nonjudgmental," Betty said.

"Exactly," Boop said. "I may not understand a behavior or request, but if it's within my boundaries and it'll make someone happy, then I'm glad to fulfill the fantasy. Being nonjudgmental is important, because more than sex, clients crave security and acceptance." She talked about the importance of assuring clients they're not freaks or bad, of letting them express their secret desires and feel validated instead of shamed.

"But my favorite," Boop added with a mischievous smile, "is the guy who lays back and lets me do what I want."

The more I saw of providers' nonjudgmental, caring perspective, the more it dawned on me that I'd been approaching the subject with the very shaming attitude I'd thought myself above. Fantasies and activities were still topics of interest, but now I began putting the question in terms of *unusual* and *creative* requests instead of *weird*. Whatever harmless activities consenting adults choose to enjoy, I finally came to understand, more power to them.

To be sure, some of what I heard made me chuckle, and some of it made me wince. You may chuckle or wince, too. That's okay: wincing and chuckling needn't be condemning. And who knows? Maybe you'll pick up an idea or two you'll want to try on your own. By all means, go for it. I promise not to scorn you or make fun of you.

2

Dress-up and anal

"These," Veronica said, pulling out a dresser drawer, "belong to a client." In the drawer was a stash of lingerie. "He doesn't dare keep these at home," she said. "He's a regular client and he's very Mormon. He books three hours and always has me invite another girl." She and the other provider each charge $300 for an hour—*a gentleman doesn't negotiate*, her online ad firmly states—which means this regular client regularly pays $1,800 per session. "We spend the first two hours doing his makeup, hair, and nails. Then he dresses up in the lingerie, puts on spiked heels, and struts around the apartment while we tell him what a hot, beautiful girl he is."

I asked, "That's it? Then he goes home?"

"No, then we fuck him."

"Meaning he fucks you, I assume."

"No," she said. "We fuck him. With a strap-on."

Veronica likes him and enjoys his sessions. She and her fellow provider have a blast doing his makeup, hair, and nails, telling him he's "such a hot girl," and, yes, penetrating him. They like knowing they're letting him enjoy a behavior he could never request, much less try, at home. They like providing a safe, confidential venue where he feels accepted, fantasies and all. "One of my clients who loves anal is very thoughtful," she said. "He comes in from the East Coast. He always cleans himself out the night before. He comes prepared. I do him with a strap-on, too."

Boop, too, has male clients who keep lingerie and outerwear at her apartment. Others simply borrow hers, and some bring lingerie they purchased for their wives that their wives refuse to wear. One fellow pilfered a good quantity of his wife's lingerie and brought it to a session for Boop to wear. "I wondered if he'd killed her," she said. "I watched the papers for a while."

Once the men have dressed up, Boop said, "I beat them off or spank them. Most of the lingerie guys don't fuck. It's more about them being the female. They want me to dominate them." Usually, that means anal penetration. "Every guy wants to be fucked up the ass," Boop said. "Dildos, toys, you name it."

It was with Boop's encouragement that Betty, who worked in the Los Angeles area, decided to give working in Salt Lake a try. Boop had asked her, "You don't mind anal, do you?" Actually, Betty replied, she did mind. Boop clarified, "Not your ass. Theirs." That, Betty said, was fine with her.

"I never did anal on guys in LA," Betty said, "but I do lots of it here. It's like the ultimate fantasy for the sexually repressed Mormon." Yet afterward, she said, the men are often apologetic, even ashamed. "I'll get 'I never do this but,' 'I'm married but,' 'I've been working a lot but.'" One of her regular Mormon clients, "a really well-groomed guy who wears garments"—sacred white underwear that temple-attending Mormons are required to wear at all times[4]—always arrives visibly eager for her to "put stuff in his ass." During the act he is ecstatic and vocal but after climaxing becomes quiet, detached, businesslike, and eager to get away.

Often men worry aloud to their providers that enjoying anal penetration and cross-dressing means they're gay. Unlike Jerry Seinfeld, they don't quickly add, ". . . not that there's anything wrong with that,"[5] because in Mormondom there is everything "wrong with that." Providers find themselves having to reassure clients that it is as possible for straight men to dress in lingerie and enjoy penetration as it is for nonmurderous cosplayers to enjoy dressing up as Darth Vader.

"Mormon bishops are the most messed up," Boop said. "I tell them, 'Listen, that's how you reach the prostate. It's not your fault that's how you're made. It's okay. It doesn't make you gay.'"[6]

That "maybe I'm gay" is more terrifying to a Mormon bishop than "I just stepped out on my wife" and "I just paid for sex" speaks worlds about the church's anti-gay obsession. Yet if Mormon men would allow themselves consolation, they might find it in the fact that cross-dressing for play is not as unusual among their peers as they might think. Koko is one of Salt Lake City's longest-standing and busiest providers. In her late 40s and barely five feet tall, she has pages of positive online reviews. Of Asian extraction, she was adopted as an infant by a Mormon family and raised in Salt Lake City. The scarcity of Salt Lake area Asian providers outside of massage parlors gives her a marketing edge, even though her speech is pure metropolitan American and her knowledge of her birth country, its culture, and language is nil. "One of my clients, a married Mormon dude, went home wearing my clothes and lipstick," she told me, "and I went home with his whole paycheck. I wondered what happened when he got home." Another of Koko's clients, a "total Mormon businessman," never requests sex or even touches her. He pays her to "watch him put on lingerie and makeup and then sit next to him while we smoke together."[7]

3

A child molester approaches the wrong provider

There is one version of the dress-up game that makes some providers uncomfortable. "I don't like it when guys ask me to dress up like a little girl or like their daughter," Boop said, her usual buoyant expression dissolving into consternation. "I won't do that shit."

Koko has a different take. "Some guys ask me to act like I'm six or seven. You know, like this," she said and, switching to a childlike voice, squealed, "Hi Daddy." Resuming her normal voice, she continued, "They want to fantasize molesting me. I go along with it. It doesn't mean they're pedophiles. It could just be a fantasy. But if he is a pedophile, I like to think maybe I'm sparing a little girl somewhere."

Boop made an exception—or a seeming one—in the case of one man who wanted to act out a pedophile fantasy. Merely discussing it on the phone seemed to arouse him. Creeped out, Boop drew a breath to tell him to take a hike when he let slip, "And my daughter is getting too old." With that, Boop agreed to the role-play. She suggested meeting in a public park and heading to her apartment together from there. To keep things looking legit, she told him, she'd be wearing sweats and running laps when he arrived. "I'm looking forward to meeting you," she said, signing off. What she didn't tell him was that the police, whom she contacted next, would look forward to meeting him even more.

Meeting Boop at the park ahead of time, police officers agreed to keep out of sight while Boop ran laps. When the client arrived and approached her, police came out of hiding, cuffed him, and hauled him away. Now needing to calm her nerves, Boop decided to run more laps. She passed out on the second lap, perhaps due to hypoglycemia with an assist from stress. She awoke in a hospital bed to the glad news that the pedophile was in jail and that his daughter was safe.

And, she wasn't under arrest. Contacting police was a greater act of courage for Boop than one might at first realize. Besides the potential for retaliation from the man after he served his time, Boop put herself in danger by admitting to police that she had agreed over the phone to sell sexual services. For all she knew, the police might have arrested her for owning up to being a provider and not bothered going after the pedophile.[8] Or they might have arrested them both.

Someday I may be able tell that story without choking up.

4

Skip this part if you're squeamish.

* * *

I'm not kidding. The further you read in this section, the more you may find it stomach-turning. I won't be offended if you skip to the next section, "A quick side-trip to California."

* * *

"One guy," Jewel told me after the salads arrived, "paid me to kick him in the balls and step on them while he came." She is 29. Her father is African American and her mother Native American. She told me she identified more as Native than African.

Wincing, I asked, "He didn't want you to kick him hard, did he?"

"He did."

Still wincing and now experiencing a bit of sphincter tightening, I said, "Were you able to make yourself do it?"

Nonchalantly stabbing a helpless crouton with her fork, she replied, "Not the first time."

Nikki, too, had a client who wanted her to slap, squeeze, and bite his balls while he climaxed. She couldn't bring herself to do it. Less severe but no less wince-inducing for me was the client who asked Lilly to bite his nipples—hard. Like Nikki, she declined. "He doesn't know how hard I can bite," she said.

"Nut-punching is a common request," Rose assured me. "Especially when they're trying to come. Punch them in the nuts while you're sucking them off. I'm right there, their nuts are in easy reach, so okay."

Betty recalled, "There was this guy who wanted me to fist him in the ass. When I pulled out my fist there was blood. It sickened me for weeks." As she spoke, I could see that the memory still grossed her out. I understood, for just hearing about it grossed me out. "That's why now we always wear gloves for anal," Boop said.

Every provider I spoke with routinely receives golden shower requests, that is, the client wants the provider to pee on him. A bit of online research revealed that golden showers aren't an uncommon type of foreplay. Some providers are willing, some aren't. "A client asked me for a golden shower," Jewel said. "I was fine with it. He got undressed and lay down in the tub, and I squatted over him and urinated on him. Then I gave him head. He was happy."

Having defined golden showers, I probably don't have to tell you what brown showers are. Its clinical name is *coprophilia*, though it is sometimes referred to as *scatophilia*. The American Psychiatric Association briefly mentions it as a fetish in its *Diagnostic and Statistical Manual of Mental Disorders*, more or less stating that it needn't be considered a problem as long as, well, as long as it's not a problem. Some of the providers I spoke with receive the occasional brown shower request. All have declined. I spoke with only one provider who tried it once, not with a client but with a boyfriend. I didn't ask for details.

One brown shower hopeful has texted every woman in Tina's escort agency with a request to "shit in each other's mouth and then vomit on each other." To date he has had no takers. Boop has received brown shower requests, too, which she always declines. "Why do people want to be pooped on? What is this? No judgment, but hard to wrap your mind around."

Annie entertained a fellow who found flatulence arousing. The word for that is *eproctophilia*. I admit it struck me as gross, but it was a welcome change of subject from brown showers. The man lay on his back and begged Annie to fart in his mouth. She was happy to oblige, however, the ability to fart at will is not to be found among her talents.[9] The client suggested using a douchebag—a literal one, not a boor hanging out in a singles bar—to pump air up her butt. I'm not recommending that—check with a physician first—but Annie said it worked. Squatting with her butt hovering just over the client's open mouth, she managed a respectable fart. Inhaling deeply, the client moaned his contentment.

5

A quick side-trip to California

Betty splits her time between Los Angeles and Salt Lake. "Aside from men who like anal, I haven't had many requests in Utah you'd call unusual. I could share some from working in California if you want." What she shared was interesting, so I decided to include it. I promise to return to Utah and Mormons shortly.

"There's a man there who hires lots of women at once. He tells them to wear high-heeled, open-toed sandals. Open-toed is a must. He has boxes of cordial cherries. He places the cordial cherries all over the floor and has the women walk slowly around the room, crushing them under their high-heeled sandals."

I asked how he found gratification in that activity. "He gets off on pretending the cordial cherries are bugs," she said. That certainly cleared *that* up.

The cordial cherries reminded Betty of other food fetishes. "One man hires ten women at a time to sit down, naked. Then he brings out ten flats of eggs. He has the first women crack an entire flat, one egg at a time, against her forehead. Then he has the next woman do the same thing, and so forth, until all the eggs are broken and all the women are dripping with raw egg. It's not cheap. These women charge $500 apiece." I'm no mathematician, but by my calculation, this fellow's fetish costs him $5,000 per hour. Plus eggs.

She considered for a moment and added, "Another guy bought 50 pies and paid a girl to let him throw them at her."

In Los Angeles, she said, "a man hired thirty of us girls to come to his home at the same time. He had a female coordinator take us into a large room. She had us strip, gave us each a blindfold to put on, and told us to stand at attention. Then the man came into the room. He chose us at random, one at a time, taking us gently by the shoulders and moving us around the room like chess pieces. He kept this going for three hours. Thirty girls for three hours is a lot of money." I turned to my calculator app for that one: $45,000. "His house was something else," Betty added. "You know he wasn't hurting financially."

I asked, "That was it? He just moved you around?"

"That was it. He left the room when the three hours were up. The female coordinator thanked us and told us we could take off our blindfolds and go home."

"How did he get off?" I asked.

"I don't know," Betty said, shrugging. "I was blindfolded."

Betty told me of meeting a new, sight-unseen client in a park. He asked her to arrive fully dressed and be sure to wear socks and hiking boots. She was to sit on a bench, wait for him to show up, and identify herself not by speaking but by locking eyes with him. When he arrived, he removed her hiking boots and socks, opened a package of new white socks, put them on her feet, and spent the next hour smelling her feet.

"I could tell you about BDSM if you want," Betty offered. BDSM stands for *Bondage, Discipline, Sadism, and Masochism.* The American Psychiatric Association once classified BDSM as a form of mental illness but declassified it in 2010, so you may now enjoy BDSM without calling your sanity into question. We'd already ventured well into California, so I figured we might as well venture into BDSM while we were at it. "Go for it," I said.

At a licensed BDSM club in Los Angeles, Betty said, she allowed a client to hogtie her, hoist her up using some sort of crane, and insert thin, acupuncture-like needles into the sides of her breasts. "I enjoyed it," she said. She assured me that the needles were fresh from the package and sterile, an assurance that did little to quell my visceral response. I have to look away when I get an injection.

Betty explained that BDSM is legal in California provided that it hurts. Only if it feels good, she said, is it prostitution and therefore illegal.[10] Rejoining the conversation, Boop said, "Obviously that's flawed reasoning, since the whole point of BDSM is that pain feels good."

"There was no vaginal, anal, or oral insertion," Betty said. "That's illegal. Usually the guys just come in their pants." After a pause, she added,

"I like BDSM. I like the art of it."

"It's pretty," Boop said.

6

What passes for wild for Mormons

Highly religious U.S. states tend to be repressive when it comes to sex. Alabama banned the sale and possession of sex toys, a law that a federal judge eventually struck down.[11] Texas law doesn't ban sex toys but limits the number you can own to six.[12] And in Springfield, Missouri, you damn well better not show so much as a hint of "underboob, sideboob, and all areas of the butt."[13]

Utah's taboos are not so much legislated as ordained by the Mormon Church. The result is that for a lot of Mormon clients, the slightest deviation from missionary position is enough to fulfill their wildest fantasies. "A lot of repressed men are amazed with delight that a blow job is on the menu," Nikki told me, "because they've never had one." Oral sex, other providers confirmed, is the ultimate fantasy for many a Mormon man.

Nikki said, "I've known men, grown men, married men, who don't know female anatomy. Some have never seen it and just want to look. They'll ask, 'Can I just see it?' 'Can I touch it?' 'How do I lick it?' I give them a safe place with no mockery. I'm not going to shame them. I will coach them."

A social worker who reviewed an early version of this manuscript said, "This reminds me of a fellow classmate when I was getting my MSW. We had a lecture on sex, as we would be counseling couples after we left school and went on to professional lives. This young Mormon man who'd married a divorcée with a couple of kids raised his hand and asked what a clitoris was. Most of the women muttered 'His poor wife.'"

"Lots of guys are into stockings and heels," Veronica told me. One of Lilly's regulars brings a fresh pair of pantyhose for her to put on at the outset of his sessions at her massage business. Then he proceeds to lick her toes, moving slowly up from there. A one-time customer asked Lilly to sell him her panties. "I will tell you where I buy them," she replied, "and you go buy a pair." Not surprisingly, he wasn't satisfied. "They're part of a set," Lilly said. "They match the bra. You want to buy the set?" The man offered $50 for the set, but Lilly had paid $85 for it. The conversation ended with Lilly exercising her right to keep her panties and bra and the customer exercising his right to storm away angry. "I'll never come back," he glowered. Lilly said to me, "Some threat, huh."

When Lilly declined one fellow's request for a hand job, he brightened and asked for a foot job instead. Foot jobs, evidently, are not an unusual request. "I didn't want to work his dick with my feet, either," she said. "I told him I don't do that." What she didn't tell him was that her objection wasn't to hand or foot jobs but to him personally. "He was too forward," she said. "Creepy."

Jewel recalled a client who craved humiliation. That, too, is not unusual, although this fellow's approach to it may have been. "He paid for a full hour. He didn't have me undress. He had me sit facing him, with all my clothes on, while he stood in front of me with his pants down around his ankles. Then he jerked off while I watched him and—don't ask me why he wanted me to do this—he told me to puff my cheeks."

I had to ask. "You sat there with puffed cheeks the whole time?"

She did.

"Without cracking up?"

"I held it together."

"How on earth did you manage not to crack up?"

"The five hundred bucks he was paying me," she said.

I wasn't quite sure how puffing her cheeks constituted humiliating him. "That wasn't the humiliation part," she said. "He wanted me to call his friends on speaker and tell them what he was doing while he did it so he could hear them laugh at him. I passed on that one."

A male massage therapist whose female clients sometimes pay him for more than a massage told me, "It's often the woman's husband who sets up the appointment. He wants to watch or listen in. This one woman had left her bedroom window open. I thought that was strange. Later, I found out her husband was outside, listening."

Koko told me of a client who liked her to "tie him up, hang him from a hook in the ceiling, punch and kick him, and leave him there." I later offered that as an example when Betty and Boop asked what I might consider an unusual request. Boop exclaimed, "I saw that guy too!"

Tina has a regular client who likes her to strip to her lingerie and lie down next to him while he masturbates to SpongeBob SquarePants cartoons. "He came seven times in one hour," she marveled. (I marveled, too.) If watching SpongeBob cartoons in her company pleased him, she was happy to oblige. I imagine it took no small amount of courage for the man to confess this desire to another person, paid or not. He must have been relieved when Tina accommodated rather than mocked him.

Another client pays Tina to sit on his chest while he masturbates. "I think I crush him," she said. "He likes it, because that's what his babysitter used to do with him." The babysitter's actions would have constituted felony child abuse. I hope a harmless fetish was the only long-term effect.

A man who admitted to having difficulty erecting at home was pleasantly surprised to see his member stand at full attention in no time as he lay on Lilly's massage table. Delighted, he forwent the hand job, ended the session, and raced home to engage in sex with his wife "while it still worked." Lilly said, "I hope it lasted for him."

A surprising number of men who hire providers do not want sex. A man in his 70s pays Tina to sit and talk, fully clothed. "Another guy pays me twenty-five hundred dollars to listen to him bitch about his ex-wife," she said. "There's no touching, no stripping down to my lingerie. He pretends I'm his live-in therapist. Once he made me spaghetti and meatballs." Another client pays her $1,500 to sit and talk with him. "The only physical contact he asks for is a good-bye hug before I leave."

Veronica spoke of two regular clients who never touch her. One, a "garment-wearing Mormon businessman," simply looks her in the eyes and masturbates while rhapsodizing about her beauty. "He loved showing up when I was pregnant," she said. "It was a real turn-on for him." The other client also looks her in the eyes and, likewise, waxes eloquent about her looks while he masturbates. After climaxing, he becomes withdrawn and businesslike. No longer able to look her in the eye, he hurries awkwardly away. He pays for the full hour even though his visits never last longer than fifteen minutes.

When Michelle invited her favorite client to name his ultimate fantasy, she braced herself for a kinky request. Slender with a generous bust, she stands five feet, three inches tall, has a light olive complexion and dark brown hair, and speaks with the faintest touch of a Mexican accent. "He was so sweet," she said. "His fantasy was for me to spend the night so he could wake up with me in the morning and make me breakfast. I warned him that I snore." The next time she went to see him, after sex she surprised him by asking, "Are you going to make me breakfast in the morning?" He was visibly pleased. "He makes a good cup of coffee," she added.

Rose told me of a client who likes to say, "I love you," and hear her say it back to him. "Thing is," she said, "some guys really do fall for us. Or think they do. It can get really uncomfortable and sometimes you have to drop them. This guy, it's just part of the fantasy for him, so I go along with it."

Every provider hears from young men who want to lose their virginity. For Mormons that's easier said than done, for the Mormon Church forbids nonmarital sex. Some simply feel it's about time they had sex while others feel a need for practice before making the attempt with a real lover. My interviewees were ambivalent about virgin clients. Tina declines them. She feels the first experience should be with a special, truly intimate partner. Koko is of like mind. "I won't take guys younger than me, and I don't take guys who want to lose their virginity. 'I don't want to be your first,' I tell them, 'go find a nice girl and have a relationship.'"

Providers who told me they agree to see virgins also told me they weren't terribly thrilled about doing so. Ineptitude aside, some virgins are dealing with other deeper issues. Jewel has found that men who hire her for their first experience show ambivalence, being at once eager and reluctant to proceed. "It's annoying," she said. "And some men lie about being virgins, hoping I'll give them extra care and time. It doesn't work on me."

7

Lesson from a doorknob

A marriage counselor told me of a Mormon client who could climax only while gripping a doorknob. Lucky for the client, the doorknob didn't have to be affixed to an actual door, so he kept an uninstalled one on his nightstand within easy reach. Less lucky for him, his wife had grown understandably weary of sharing her husband with a piece of hardware. "Wait, I'll get the doorknob" could be something of a mood-killer, she explained. Any amorous mood that struck with no nearby doorknob was doomed to failure. Besides, now and then, she said, the client's wife could do with a bit of attention from both of his hands.

A few sessions into counseling, it emerged that two influences from the husband's teenage years had combined to create the doorknob fetish. The first was the Mormon Church. No religion takes masturbation more seriously. Hardly a General Conference of the church goes by without a stern lecture from a church leader in his 80s or 90s about the evils of masturbation. The badgering does little to stop kids from masturbating, but it's quite effective at making them feel terrible about being normal.

As a Mormon teen, the doorknob man didn't let the church's admonishments stop him from slipping into the bathroom to pleasure himself. This brings us to the second influence, namely, the bathroom door. It had no lock. To ensure no one blundered in on him as he stood pleasuring himself with one hand, he desperately gripped the doorknob with the other. In time, gripping a doorknob became essential to his ability to climax.

The story ends well. With time, counseling, and a patient wife, the man was able to let go, figuratively and literally, of the doorknob.

Knowing the man's backstory made it easier for his wife to understand his doorknob fetish. It makes it easier for you and me to understand it, too. Yet even without the backstory, we could agree that there's nothing morally wrong about a doorknob fetish. Unusual and inconvenient, sure, but last I checked, *unusual* and *inconvenient* weren't in any dictionary under *immoral* or *perverted*.

What may first strike you or me as odd may in fact be perfectly understandable with a bit of backstory. But when no one's rights are infringed and no one gets hurt, we neither need nor deserve explanations as to why consenting adults enjoy what they enjoy. Humanity demands only that we let them enjoy it free from shaming and other forms of harassment.

Chapter 5

The Life of a Mormontown Sex Worker

I was with a woman. Somebody's mother. Her husband didn't care about her anymore. This woman hadn't had an orgasm in maybe 10 years. Took me three hours to get her off. For a while there, I didn't think I was going to be able to do it. When it was over, I felt like I'd done something, something worthwhile. Who else would have taken the time, or cared enough, to do it right?

—Julian Kay (Richard Gere) in *American Gigolo*

1

Real people

When I met Jewel, she was a picture of elegance. Twenty-nine years old, five-foot-eight and trim, she had almond-shaped eyes, a latte-brown face with reddish undertones, and waist-length micro braids. Her fuchsia lipstick matched a form-fitting, calf-length dress. So perhaps you can understand my experiencing something of a paradigm shift when, during a text exchange a few days later, she said she was at home doing her family's laundry. *Having only seen you dressed to the nines*, I texted, *it's strange to picture you doing plain old everyday housework.*

She replied, *Would it help if I said I was naked?*

The exchange served as a reminder that providers do not live in the illusory experience they create for their clients. They sell fantasy, but in real life they fix meals, drive kids to school, help with homework, handle household chores, pay bills, get colds, fill up at gas stations, make friends, have significant others, go to movies, lock horns with teenagers, watch Netflix, visit restaurants, clubs, and other venues, date, and shop for groceries.

Most providers I met were of northern European descent. Women of Latin American descent were a close second. I also met women with African, Native American, Asian, Polynesian, and Mediterranean roots. Some heritages seemed evident, while others I would not have guessed had not the providers volunteered them. All but one were U.S. citizens. Curious as to how closely my sample reflected the mix of providers advertising that day, a Wednesday at 11:30 a.m., I visited Eros.com and counted local ads, taking care to omit visiting providers. Forty-seven listed themselves as "Caucasian," 16 as "Exotic" (usually a Latin or other mix, though sometimes "Exotic" is code for "I'm not telling"), ten as "Latin or Hispanic," and one each of "Asian," "Ebony" (African American), and "Native American." Three had left the ethnicity field blank.

Many held a day job apart from sex work. Annie, for instance, makes $12 per hour as a housekeeper in a two-star hotel. I asked why she kept a low-paying day job when she makes $200 to $300 an hour as a sex worker. "No one has ever asked me that before," she said, mulling. "It gives me a bank account and taxable income, which I need when I apply for rent or credit. But that's not the real reason. I think I do it for my sanity. I guess it keeps me grounded."

Marci, Alison, and Debbie, who didn't sit for an interview but answered sundry questions via text, are a dock loader, banker, and dental hygienist, respectively. Jewel is a cosmetologist. Rose, who holds a baccalaureate in health sciences, worked at a neurofeedback[1] facility for teen offenders. Nikki, the first in her family to graduate from college, holds a Bachelor of Science in business, an Associate of Applied Science in audio engineering, and a Master of Science in technology. Prior to becoming a provider, she'd had a successful, years-long career as a stockbroker.

In addition to being a registered nurse, Tina is a licensed, legal escort. If she likes you and feels assured of her safety, she may provide services the law does not allow. "I make three times as much escorting than I did as a nurse," she said, "and I don't have to pull triple shifts."

Betty has worked as a mental health professional. She holds a Bachelor of Science in social work and Associate of Arts degrees in human services and chemical dependency treatment. She has also worked as an executive assistant, a film industry production assistant, and a pastry chef.

Boop holds a Bachelor of Arts in speech and communication. When we spoke, she was one year from adding a second bachelor's degree to her resume. She interned as a photographer and videographer with a major telecommunications and publishing company. She has tended bar and worked as a server in a comedy club. Like all of the providers I interviewed, Boop is a sex worker by choice. Unlike the others, however, she comes from money. If she wanted to quit, her parents would support her in comfort. "I'm a child of privilege," she said.

Work and education aside, Boop is fiercely committed to her high-functioning autistic son. "He takes music lessons," she said, showing no lack of maternal pride, "and he's good at it." Twice during our interview, we paused so that she could call him. "School just got out," she explained. "I need to see how his day went, make sure he's where he needs to be, and make sure he turned in his homework."

I spoke with some providers who are bilingual. Betty studied and mastered American Sign Language in college. She also took and understands Spanish. Toni, who answered only a few questions via text, said she is in her 50s and, raised in the United States by Thai parents, is fluent in Thai. Tina speaks fluent Spanish, her parents having emigrated from Mexico. Lilly speaks fluent English with a slight Chinese accent. Michelle was 14 when her family left Mexico and came to Utah via a brief stay in California. Her accent is barely detectable, while her English vocabulary and usage could put many a person born and raised in the United States to shame.

Boop speaks no Spanish even though her birth mother is Mexican, but she studied and understands French. And, she added, she speaks fluent Hebrew. A Hebrew-speaking provider might not be remarkable in cities that boast significant Jewish populations, but Jews account only for about a half-percent of Utah's population.

I asked Boop if she spoke Yiddish. She said, "Only enough to swear."

2

The money

If there's a common denominator among providers, it's that the money attracted them to the trade and keeps them in it. New providers are often pleasantly shocked at how much they can make. Rose could hardly believe it when her first client handed over six $100 dollar bills without a fuss. "If I'd known it would be this easy," she said, "I'd have started years ago."

Taking in $100,000 or more in the first year is not unusual for the subset of providers I met. Moreover, these are cash transactions with no paper trail. I'll go out on a limb and assume that most providers don't declare their earnings on a Form 1040 and most clients don't issue them a Form 1099. That would make $100,000 the rough equivalent of a $140,000 taxable income.

Tina charges $300 for seminude and nude body rubs,[2] including touching, fondling, and, sometimes, kissing. "A hundred of that goes to the agency," she said, referring to the escort agency that represents her, "and the rest goes to me. But then there's tipping. It's up to me to make it worth it to the client to spend more. I keep 80 percent of tips and give 20 percent to the booker who takes calls and makes appointments for me. I think that's only fair. Some customers keep bookers on the phone a long time. They really work for the money." She reserves sex for only preferred clients. "At first I wouldn't, but now I will for the right price. I found my price when I was broke and had three kids to care for." And what was the right price that she found? "I charge a minimum of an extra thousand dollars for sex."

She takes in anywhere from $300 to $8,000 in a day. "The most I ever made in one year was $150,000," Tina said. That's the rough equivalent of a $207,000 taxable salary. "During Sundance [Film Festival], I made $28,000 in one month."

Jewel started in the business at 19. "At first I'd get fifteen hundred to three thousand for a few hours stay. I was 19 and loved making that much. But now you have to lower your price to compete. There are just too many girls out there who charge less. I charge three hundred for an hour. That's still more than some girls. Sometimes a guy will say, 'Well, so-and-so will do it for eighty dollars.' Fine, I tell him, then go see so-and-so. It's my body, and I set my own price. Nobody can tell me what to sell it for. But if a girl is willing to work for eighty dollars, you should run away."

Overwhelmed by their initial earnings, not a few providers begin spending out of control. *No problem*, they reason, *I can make it back to-morrow.* That often leaves them dealing with the same budget crunches that lower wage earners face. Early in her career, Jewel spent her money as fast as it came in, mostly on clothes, nightclubs, cars, and travel. It's something she now regrets. "Now I see young girls doing the same thing, and I want to tell them, no, don't do it, save up."

Veronica began providing sexual services at 20. She had been scrap-ing by since the age of 16. By then she had two children by a deadbeat boyfriend who had recently abandoned them. Then the deadbeat's *ex* dropped his *other* two children at Veronica's door and disappeared. Ve-ronica did not for a moment consider not assuming responsibility for the children. For four years, she worked minimum wage jobs and made ends meet by shoplifting. She was 18 when a friend suggested escorting, tim-idly broaching the subject with, "It's not for everyone." Two years later, Veronica was ready to give it a try. She started with an escort agency and eventually went on her own. She no longer needs to shoplift. To busybody accusers who might ask what her children would say if they some-day found out what their mom did for a living, I couldn't help feeling the answer might be, "Thank you."

Koko stays in the profession not for enjoyment but for the money. She charges a flat $200 for a session. The fee includes sex and, on request, accompanying the client on a dinner date at no extra charge. Most pro-viders tack on an additional fee for a dinner date. "It's no different from going to bed with a guy after he spoils you on a date," she said, shrugging. "Except, we're smarter. Why not take the money? I might as well make money at it."

Due to medical and other expenses, Koko is not in the best financial shape. She waxes philosophical when it comes to money. "Do not value material things," she advises. "I grew up with plenty of money. I've made good money. It doesn't make a difference in happiness."

As with any business, being a provider entails overhead. Betty ex-plained, "It takes a lot of time and money. There's apartment rent, which isn't cheap. We spend a lot to be presentable. There's hair, makeup, wax-ing, threading, weaves, facial upkeep, pedicures, washes, lotions, douch-es, soaps, and wigs. We have gym memberships and personal trainers. We get massages, all to keep up our stamina. The food we eat so we don't look bloated isn't cheap. We have to pay for lube, toys, batteries, drinks, outfits—clients don't want to see you wearing the same thing twice—condoms, and candles. Keeping the apartment is like running an office. We have to buy housecleaning supplies, laundry, towels, linens, a washer and dryer, and laundry detergent. We need computers and Internet. We have to keep bottled water, booze, wine, beer, and weed on hand for cli-ents. You have to be able to relate to your clients, so we keep up on the news so we can be interesting and stay topical. Sometimes there are fines. And attorney fees."

I asked Betty to estimate her and Boop's monthly overhead. After pausing to tally, she said, "Three to five thousand a month." That sur-prised me. It also surprised Tina, who likewise maintains an apartment for work and is every whit as professional. She did a double take when

I repeated to her Betty's estimate. "I use a little makeup palette I bought two years ago," Tina said. "She must be buying the most expensive lingerie and caking on top-of-the-line makeup. Guys don't mind seeing the same outfit. They're more focused on what's underneath."

Betty and Boop didn't disclose their annual earnings. If the fact that they can afford three to five thousand dollars per month in overhead is an indicator, I think it's reasonable to assume that they do quite well.

3

"How I became a sex worker"

Question six on my list of interview questions was, *What made you decide to become a sex worker?*[3]

Much like Annie,[4] Jewel entered the trade under pressure from a boyfriend. "My boyfriend and I were dealing drugs," Jewel said, "and this was another way to make money. He pushed me into it and was my pimp." In time she dumped the boyfriend and continued providing sexual services on her own.

Boop, who has been in the trade for twelve years, said, "In my high school in the Midwest you were a slut if you held hands with a boy. I transferred to a different high school where no one knew me and I could fuck whoever I wanted. In high school I figured out I could make money at it."

It was Boop who introduced Betty to the trade. They were roommates, living in Los Angeles at the time. Knowing she could trust Betty not to judge and not to blab, Boop disclosed her occupation to her. Not one to pull punches, Boop unapologetically said, "Guys pay me to fuck," and awaited Betty's reaction. Betty's reaction was immediate. "I was like, oh, I like her even more now," Betty said. "Everyone knew I was into BDSM. I worked as a stripper and an actor, which is not a whole lot different, and I did erotic massage. So I wasn't judgmental."

Two years passed. Saddled with school debt, Betty told Boop she was considering entering the trade. "You can make money," Boop encouraged her. "Don't you like to fuck?"

Michelle fled her family's dysfunctional home at 16 and barely supported herself by working at a fast-food restaurant. At 19 she began working as an escort, which was legal, and provided protected sex for a minimum $200 tip, which wasn't. Within five years she bought a house. She took business classes. At 26 she gave up sex work, married, and became a restaurant manager. She is now in her early thirties, and her confidence and determination are evident. I left our interview thinking, *She will achieve whatever she sets out to achieve.*

Tina began her career in sex work as a stripper in Las Vegas. "I love the perks of self employment," she said, referring to her work as a provider. "I make my own schedule. I've never been busted. I'm licensed and careful. I've never had an STI, never had a pregnancy scare. It's not as dirty as it sounds. It's more honest than picking up a girl in a bar and pretending to be into her. All cards are on the table."

Koko was 16 when she noticed classified ads for escorts and private dancers. She asked her mother what they were. Her mother dodged the question, but Koko remained intrigued. A few years later, finding herself pregnant by a boyfriend who'd assured her he was sterile—"He may have thought he was," she said—she turned to providing to cover the cost of an abortion. "By the time I reached 20 or 21, doing sex for money was a regular thing."

For Sally, who spoke with me on the phone but did not want to meet in person, providing was something of a godsend. "After my divorce I was a junkie living on the street," she said. "I have a friend who was escorting. I gave it a try. Now I'm clean and I have my own apartment and food in the fridge. I'm thinking about going to college. I can afford it now."

A case can be made for including women who work in legal, northeastern Nevada brothels among Salt Lake area providers.[5] Wells and Elko are about a two-and-a-half and three-hour drive west of Salt Lake City, respectively, and home, respectively, to two and four legal brothels.[6] Like most Nevada brothels, they have websites displaying photos of women "currently appearing" and listing available services in forthright terms. They are statutorily forbidden from posting prices. Visitors relax, have a drink, and visit with sex workers in a bar and lounge area. The sex worker's job, of course, is to entice a visitor to accompany her to her private room in the back. That is where the conversation about pricing takes place.

On a visit to Elko, I stepped inside one of the brothels and took a seat at the bar. After the discretion I'd taken pains to exercise when visiting Salt Lake area providers, there was something surreal about brazenly walking into a Nevada brothel in broad daylight, knowing that it was perfectly legal for me to be there. The lounge was quiet, empty but for a frail, older woman tending bar. Soon a bead curtain separating the lounge from the back rooms parted, and through it stepped Ling, a Chinese woman in her late twenties wearing a red and black embroidered bustier, fishnet stockings, and an opened, flower-patterned robe. She took a seat next to me. Business was slow, so she chatted for a few minutes.

An immigrant, Ling was working as a server in New York City's Chinatown when she noticed an advertisement from Sue's Fantasy Club, a legal, all-Asian brothel in Elko, Nevada. She liked the prospect of leaving behind the brisk New York pace. She lives and works in the brothel. "All my customer nice," she said, "and money good. I take vacation in China every year. Sometimes take two."

She has many regular customers from Utah, she told me, struggling with her English. She guessed that half to 75 percent of her clients come from Salt Lake City. Others, she said, come from California and from Nevada towns that don't allow prostitution. I asked if any of her regulars were Mormon. She asked how she could possibly know. I pulled out my iPhone, googled Mormon underwear, and showed her a photo. "That Mormon?" she said, showing surprise. "Many customer wear."

4

Sex workers talk about their work

I met Utah providers who had been in the trade from six months to more than 20 years. Though some began under pressure from a boyfriend, not one was forced and not one remained in the trade against her will. None were longing to get out, though some talked about someday retiring. The word "escape" didn't apply and never came up.

All enjoyed the money, most enjoyed the sex, and quite a few but not all enjoyed the human connection. As for the "not all," sex work is to them a job like any other. Tessa, who was willing to speak on the phone only briefly, said, "I get tired of fucking all the time."

Koko, too, has little enthusiasm for the job. "I don't like sex," she said. "I never have. It's like I'm dead down there, like Novocain when you see the dentist. I'm trying to learn to like it. I can enjoy spending time with a client if he's likable, nice, or charming. But the sex, no. I don't mind if a friend touches me if it's not sexually." I asked if she liked being touched affectionately. "I don't know," she replied. "I've never experienced that."

She has tried, unsuccessfully, to break into other careers. She has taken numerous healthcare, business, and accounting courses. "Trouble is, I've been busted. It's right there on my record. Busted for prostitution. No one wants to hire a hooker." She reflected a moment and added, "Actually, lots of people want to hire a hooker. Just not for accounting."

Jewel has no compunctions about being a provider but would prefer her children not know what she does for a living. Lately, she has cut back on her activity. "My daughter was getting old enough to start asking where are you going and why are you dressed like that," she said. "I'm old enough to choose what I do with my body, but my daughter isn't. I don't want her thinking about it at her age."

I asked how she would feel if her daughter someday entered the trade. "It's her body," Jewel said. "She can make the choice if she wants when she's old enough. She's too young now to know what she'd be getting into. I mean, the secrecy, STI risk, crazy clients, jealous girlfriends, and law enforcement."

Jewel showed me a photo of herself and her daughter standing side by side. "Isn't she pretty?" Jewel asked, slipping into proud-mom mode. Jewel has been blessed with youthful looks, and her teenage daughter is mature for her age. I was hard-pressed to tell them apart and said so. "I know, right?" she said.

Jewel enjoys interacting with some of her clients and endures others. "It's not all bad," she said. "I've met some great people. But I don't think anyone gets into it for enjoyment."

She hadn't, apparently, met Boop. "Oh my god," Boop effused when I asked how she felt about her job, "I love it. I love to fuck. I just fuck and I get paid. What could be better?" And unlike Koko, who finds the white American male's Asian woman fixation profitable but tiresome, Boop appreciates it when race plays to her advantage. "I get a lot of athletes who have a black girl fantasy. Some are really well built. I'm like, 'Seriously, you're paying? You could get paid.'"

Annie expressed a similar sentiment. "I love dick," she said. "Always have. I was a hoochie mama since I was 14."

Betty grew up in "a strict Christian family" but, like Boop, has no moral quandary when it comes to receiving money for sex. "I think every female charges," she said. "There's emotional currency, money, contact currency. I believe sex work is work. You release endorphins. People need contact. I understand it's a service, but, still, it's contact. Skin-on-skin contact that people need."

Nikki finds fulfillment in the human connection aspect. "Most of this is just people wanting to connect. Sure, there's a sexual element. Sex is a part of it but it's not what people are looking for. When people feel lonely or alienated, we're told it's sex they want, but what they really want is to connect. Some of them just want to be touched. Some have never seen a naked woman before."

Tina is caring by nature, which is what motivated her to enroll in nursing school. It is a side of her personality that is not lost on clients. Many unload their woes on her, sometimes making her feel more like a mental health professional than an escort. "Many times we're like social workers," she said. "We do a lot of listening and empathizing. The ones who bother, that is. Some girls are like, 'Well, here I am, do what you want while I just lie here.'"

She has had to learn not to let thoughtless remarks from clients bother her. "It took me a while to stop taking things home with me," Tina said, "like some of the comments guys make when they think they're being clever or sexy. One guy asked, 'Did your boyfriend teach you this?' It was over the line. It bothered me. I had to learn to let stuff like that go."

Koko, too, is protective of her feelings. "I'm insecure about my looks. I don't think I'm pretty. I need to feel secure with a client in terms of not wanting to be judged by my appearance." I was a little surprised. I would not have described Koko or any of the providers I met as unattractive. Still, I'm well aware that self-esteem doesn't necessarily follow from looks. "Doesn't matter," she added, shrugging. "Sexy and pretty are different things. Some of these guys, you put lingerie on a fire hydrant and turn down the lights, they'll get horny."

Enjoy the work or not, appearing to enjoy it is part of the job. "We have to be good actresses," Jewel said. "We have to be on, upbeat, cheerful, and affectionate. We have to convince you you're the only one, that we're really into what's going on, even though you might be one appointment in a day filled with appointments. You have to look and act upbeat even when you have a broken heart or what have you. You always have to smile. Even if your car was just repossessed, you had a fight with your boyfriend, whatever, you have to smile. It's hard to keep it up."

5

A psychologist begs to differ

A smarter person might think twice about being on Match.com while working on a project like this one. On the heels of the mandatory first-date question "What kind of work do you do?" usually comes "What books have you written?" After we discuss the former Mormon polygamist wife's memoir that I co-authored,[7] the follow-up question is nearly always, "What are you working on now?" This has made for unusual first-date conversations.

So it was that I found myself discussing prostitution over brunch with a psychologist about my age. We'd arranged to meet at Eggs In the City, one of my favorite breakfast spots.[8] I told her that while some of the women I'd spoken with were certainly dealing with serious issues, most had struck my admittedly not credentialed eye as genuine and adjusted.

She didn't buy it. Having treated prostitutes trying to break free of the trade, her view was that prostitution was a tragedy, an inescapable trap. Women entered prostitution only under coercion, she maintained, or as a result of sexual or emotional abuse. Her experience was that providers had low or no self-worth, and that many were supporting expensive drug habits—all reasons, she said, that made breaking away difficult if not impossible.

Her assessment applied to some, but not all, of the women I interviewed. Indeed, I might have agreed with her had I spoken only to Koko. "I think almost everyone in the profession has been molested or raped, and does or did drugs," Koko had told me a few weeks earlier. "Many are broken after a rape. It's like, I'm tainted now, so why not just go ahead with it and get paid for it? A lot of it goes back to the crap I went through when I was younger. I guess being molested as a child can really mess you up. I'm not sure but I have a lot of the signs. The signs that make it so that I am disabled mentally."

Yet Koko is not a representative sample, and neither are the handful of providers my new psychologist friend treated. Well-adjusted providers would hardly be the ones showing up in her office to discuss a longed-for exit. Providers like Annie see therapists to discuss non-work-related issues and don't disclose their profession. My interviewees aren't a representative sample, either, but they do attest to the existence of providers who enter into and remain in the trade of their own free will.

Asserting that all sex workers are de facto mentally unhealthy ignores the fact that mentally healthy and mentally unhealthy are not an either/or but ends of a continuum. Asserting that all providers who think they're mentally healthy are mistaken is patronizing, and offering "no healthy person enters into prostitution" as evidence is blatantly circular. To be sure, I heard harrowing tales of rape, beatings, dysfunctional homes, bad husbands or boyfriends, and drug problems. But I also heard tales of safe, happy childhoods and well-adjusted lives—no rapes, no beatings, no dysfunctional homes, no bad husbands or boyfriends, and no drug problems.

Society and the media seem more inclined to paint providers than clients as broken. While our culture does its share of characterizing johns as sex addicts,[9] it is more willing to allow for a healthy man who pays for sex than for a healthy woman who sells it. It's "boys will be boys but there's something wrong with promiscuous girls" in a new suit of clothes.

If bad life circumstances create prostitutes, there should be a good deal more prostitutes. In one study, one in five women reported having been a victim of child sexual abuse.[10] One in five women do not become sex workers. Bad life circumstances might sometimes be a contributor to, but not a sole much less a necessary cause of, the choice to become a sex worker.

I spoke with providers who have not shed their self-esteem or surrendered their boundaries. On the contrary, many set their own rules and brook no breaking or even bending of them. Some, for instance, draw the line at penetration, and those who don't insist on protection. Some do not permit kissing. Some permit kissing but not kissing with tongue. All reserve the right to reject any client for any reason, and often do.

Lexie is a provider who discovered one of her boundaries after submitting photos to *Playboy*. The striking, naturally endowed blonde soon received back a generous offer for a pictorial. In the end, she declined it. Appearing in the magazine had seemed like a good idea at the time, but with the offer in front of her she had second thoughts. Undressing for clients in private was one thing, she explained, but putting her body on display before the world now seemed like quite another. "I don't want everyone seeing me naked," she said with a shudder.

The psychologist and I moved on to other topics, spending a pleasant hour or so. I didn't go on at length there as I have here. We were on a date and at Eggs In the City, after all. Besides, I'm no psychologist, and I don't take lightly the folly one risks in disagreeing with an expert. I have high regard for Isaac Asimov's warning about a "strain of anti-intellectualism . . . nurtured by the false notion that democracy means that 'my ignorance is just as good as your knowledge.'"[11] Even so, one psychologist's anecdotal experience, albeit informed, remains anecdotal; and no one, neither she nor I, is immune to confirmation bias.[12]

We split the check. Neither of us suggested a second date.

6

Close encounters of the off-duty kind

Inevitably in the course of being out and about in daily life, providers now and then spot or are spotted by a client. It's rarely a problem. An unwritten rule states that when providers and clients cross paths in the real world, they are not to acknowledge one another. No nod, no smile, no wave, and certainly no shouted greeting. It's not unlike the discretion mental health professionals and their clients exercise—which is not inapt, given how often johns open up to and make surrogate therapists of their sexual service providers.

"I see clients out with their wife or family all the time when I'm at the mall," Crissie said in our brief, text-only exchange. "We look right past either other. At most there might be a brief meeting of the eyes. That's kind of hard to avoid."

Chances are you wouldn't recognize Betty or Boop in public. At the end of their workday, they shed the wigs, switch their contacts to change eye color, don baseball caps, tone down the makeup, and dress modestly. "We have our standards, we have our pride," Boop said, "and we like our privacy like anyone else."

Koko was dining out when she saw one of her regulars, a judge, enter the restaurant with his wife and kids. His eyes paused only for a moment upon meeting hers, a subtle reaction no one else noticed. Composing himself, the judge ignored Koko and turned his attention to enjoying the evening out with his family.[13] "That's how it should be," Koko said.

Coincidence is no respecter of miles. After a weekend excursion to Las Vegas, Michelle and a trio of traveling companions stopped at a North Las Vegas gas station for fuel and snacks. A few days later, she received a text from one of her regular clients. "I saw you in Las Vegas," it said. He was driving home to Salt Lake from San Diego and had stopped at the same station at the same time. "That's amazing," she texted back. There was no worry that he would have approached her. He knew better, and she knew that he did. "Besides," she said, "he told me he was traveling with his wife and stepdaughters. No way was he going to say, 'Hey, I know you.'"

Unwritten rules are only as good as the parties' willingness to observe them. "Some guys are real dopes," Koko said. "Guys who've seen my ads have walked up to me in public and said, 'I recognize you. You're Koko.' Once a client walked up and started talking to me when I was out with my boyfriend. My boyfriend knew what I do, but the asshole who walked up to me didn't know he knew. He didn't think. He could have ruined my relationship."

On a visit to the pharmacy to fill a prescription, Koko had the misfortune of encountering a pharmacist who, evidently, spent a good deal of time surfing online provider ads. Recognizing her, he made suggestive remarks. When she tried to move her prescriptions to another pharmacy, he called her repeatedly at home, pleading with her not to transfer her prescriptions, asking what it would take to make her return to his store. Koko insisted on the transfer, an effort the pharmacist frustrated by omitting information on the necessary forms. Finally, Koko asked her physician to write new prescriptions that she could fill elsewhere.

Another man who had seen Koko's online ads began stalking her. He would phone and tell her where he had seen her on a given day. "You were home today, I saw you through your window." "Buying a new car?

You went to a dealership today." "I saw you leave at seven last night. Going to an appointment?" There wasn't much Koko could do about him. Having a record, she didn't feel that complaining to the police was an option.

Koko flatly declined a would-be client whom she knew from her personal life. He was her adoptive cousin, and he had molested her from the time she was five years old until she reached 11. Now that Koko was a provider, he pleaded for a rendezvous. She refused. One time he brazenly showed up at her door. Certain that at the sight of him Koko would fall into his embrace, he hadn't even bothered bringing cash. She turned him away, not kindly. "Trust me on this," she said, "it wasn't that he didn't bring cash. I would have turned him away if he'd shown up dripping hundred dollar bills."

There are other ways in which real and fantasy worlds collide. Over several days, a would-be new client had been trying to arrange a first meeting with Jewel. She never connected with the man, but she did with his wife, who happened to be holding his phone when Jewel replied to one of his text messages. The wife immediately called Jewel and demanded to know who she was. Jewel did her best to evade, but it soon became obvious that the man was busted and that continuing the charade was futile. "Look," the wife said, "it's okay to tell me. He's done this lots of times before." Relenting, Jewel admitted that the woman's husband had been trying to arrange a rendezvous. "She was really nice to me," Jewel told me. "We had a nice conversation."

Besides the challenges that come with being recognized in public, providers deal with the same sorts of #MeToo issues that women from all walks of life face. One evening Tina drove with her children to Walmart. The four of them had walked halfway across the parking lot when Tina heard a loud, sharp whistle, the kind used to summon a dog. Looking in the direction the sound had come from, she saw a group of young men driving slowly by, car windows down. One of them called out, "I want to suck your tits!" Recounting the experience, Tina rolled her eyes. "I have implants," she said, cupped hands hovering over her breasts. "I like the extreme look. But come on. My kids were with me. They know I'm an RN. They think I'm a homecare nurse."

Eva had a similar experience. She had taken her daughter to Burger King. Though not dressed for work, she hadn't tried to hide her curvaceous body either. A Boy Scout troop seated nearby began heckling her with suggestive remarks. The scout adviser made no attempt to rein them in. But then, the Scout Law and Oath don't explicitly rule out sexual harassment. Indeed, Boy Scouts of America only recently decided that the Law and Oath don't support cover-ups for scout leaders who molest their young charges.

7

The lingerie model

The city of Provo sits 45 miles south of Salt Lake City. It is home to Mormon Church–owned Brigham Young University, a fully accredited, four-year school boasting some 34,000 students. As you may have surmised, the school is named after Mormon pioneer and prophet Brigham Young. Of several contenders, it was Young who persuaded the greater part of the Mormons that he was the rightful successor to church founder Joseph Smith upon the latter's death in 1844. Young is something of a Mormon folk hero, viewed as a plain-speaking, no-nonsense pioneer leader.[14]

Provo is proud of its university. You can tell by many of the town's place names. There's University Parkway, University Avenue, University Car Wash—and University Mall, where Natalie happened to be shopping when a local modeling agency representative approached her about becoming a model. Only 15, Natalie, a natural blonde whose body had matured early, was flattered. "It was exciting. I did ads, clothing, runways, and more."

We met for lunch in Salt Lake at Brio Tuscan Grille, an upscale chain with, as the alert reader may have surmised from its name, Italian fare. To avoid drawing undue attention when meeting in public, I'd often ask providers to "show up dressed to clean the garage." Not all took me at my word, but Natalie, now 39, did. She wore a loose gray sweatshirt and ripped jeans. She had not done her hair or bothered with makeup. There remained a disheveled attractiveness about her, but no one would have recognized her as the lingerie model from sundry magazines.

Natalie was 18 when she noted an online friend doing bikini modeling in California. She flew to California on her own dime, where the friend introduced her to a California modeling agency. The agency signed her immediately. "They gave me lodging and board in a 14-bedroom mansion," she told me. "I loved the life. I had someone to do my hair and makeup. I was chauffeured around in limos. I had visits to the Playboy mansion. I auditioned for *Playboy* but wasn't accepted. Once I had lunch with Eddie Murphy. For an 18-year-old girl from Utah County, this was nirvana. And, of course, there was the dream of fame."

The agency taught Natalie how to model. There's more to it than looking pretty in front of a camera. Besides endless attention to hair and makeup, it involves contorting while trying not to look like you're contorting, and flashing a seductive smile while your body begs you to release it from unnatural, torturous poses. "You have to stand with your boobs thrust out, your back arched, and your ass pushed out behind you. Try doing that while you smile and try to look inviting. Plus, I have to work out a bunch of times a week to maintain my figure. Beauty is pain."

Natalie's dreams of fame didn't materialize. At 19, she returned to Utah, where an ad in the Help Wanted section headlined "Work in your bikini" caught her attention. She inquired, which was how she discovered body rubs. The advertiser had rented office space and divided it into a handful of small rooms, each furnished with a massage table. Customers, most of them Mormon men, showed up and paid $60 plus tip for a beautiful woman wearing only a bikini to run her hands or fingertips over his body. For many customers, that much was plenty arousing, and it had the advantage of being legal as well as something Mormon men could rationalize as landing within church standards. Whether a hand job, which of course isn't legal, was on the menu depended on the therapist and on how much the client was willing to tip.

Natalie didn't do hand jobs at first. There was no need; plenty of men were happy to pay to see her in a bikini and enjoy her touch. She gave $24 of the $60 fee to the boss, keeping $36 for herself. She kept 100 percent of tips, which usually started at $40 and went up. Tips of $100 or more weren't unusual.

But she disliked her boss. The other women working there disliked him, too. They encouraged her to open her own spa and promised to work for her if she did. When the boss was out of town, Natalie took advantage of being out from under his watch and opened her own place. True to their word, the others went with her. "Everything was strictly legit," she said. "I didn't do extras and I didn't permit the girls to do them either."

Her new business did well. Natalie hired a manager, freeing her to attend aesthetics school. It was during this time that the business plummeted from an average of eight appointments per day to an average of two, forcing Natalie to close the shop. She later learned that, contrary to reports from her manager and workers, appointments hadn't dropped. They were seeing as many clients as ever, not telling her, and keeping the money.

Natalie bounced from one spa to another. She left one after an ill-fated affair with the owner. She was forced to leave another because she refused to do hand jobs. Finally, she took work as an operator in a call center while continuing modeling and doing webcam work. At 24, she learned she was pregnant. She made plans to move in with the father, but ten weeks into her pregnancy he left her. Desperately in need of income, she returned to the body rub business.

This time she was hired to manage a spa where the women wore lingerie instead of bikinis. To ensure no one was doing hand jobs, she was to do room checks by "accidentally" walking in on sessions at random. That wasn't for her. She left her workers and their clients to their privacy and falsified her reports.

Natalie provided body rubs in addition to her duties as manager. Pregnant and needing money, she started doing happy endings. That satisfied many, but some clients pressured her for "full service," which is to say, sex. "Some of them had a pregnancy thing," she said. "One day a guy offered me $400. *What the heck*, I thought, *okay*. Afterward, I thought, *that was an easy four hundred bucks.* And I enjoyed it. I was single and had always been sensual. From then on, if someone asked for full service, instead of saying no, I asked how much he was willing to tip."

Natalie began advertising on a local website for hobbyists ". . . because, you know, the money." She enjoyed the sex, but money took over as her prime motivator. "I started getting loads of calls. My income jumped to $10,000 to $15,000 per month. I started living a rich life. Bought a car, a nice house, traveled." Soon her business doubled. "I bet it was because I made a shower available, so guys wouldn't take home smells. Plus it was a residential place instead of an office building." The humility underlying her comment struck me. Having seen her portfolio, I would suspect that Natalie's looks played a much bigger role in attracting clients than the availability of a shower.

When Natalie and I spoke she had over 200 regulars. She still models lingerie and has gathered a respectable following. At the time of our interview, she was a week away from trying the California modeling scene again.

8

"Give me sex or I'll tell my mom."

Not every man arrives at a provider's door ready to do business. Sometimes a fellow lingers only a few seconds, long enough to drink in the sight of the provider, and then bolts. It's rarely because the provider isn't what he'd hoped. More often, it's that the thrill of a brief face-to-face with a hot woman who isn't his wife is all the naughtiness he desires. And, of course, there's no cost.

Well, usually there's no cost. Boop recalled a fellow who, arriving at her apartment for his appointment, stepped inside, slipped off his shoes per her request, and looked her up and down for an extended, uncomfortable amount of time. Then he said he didn't have any money and turned to leave. Boop wasn't about to let him get away with it. "I said, 'Dude, you're a lookie-loo. There's a cancelation fee.' I pushed him out the door and kept his shoes. He phoned me from outside and said he needed his shoes. I said I'd sell them back to him for $50. He said no. 'Dude,' I said, 'what are you going to tell your wife when you come home with no shoes?' He paid and I gave him his shoes and told him never to call me again."

Likewise, a bartender in an Elko brothel told me that it's not unusual for men to visit the lounge long enough to stare at all of the women in the line-up or seated at the bar, and then leave without so much as buying a drink. Some may not have seen a provider who appealed, but repeated nonbuyers are probably, to use Boop's term, lookie-loos.

All providers have horror stories of clients with poor personal hygiene. "I was massaging a guy and when I got to his junk there was this horrible smell," Jewel said. "I stopped right there and made him go take a shower. Sometimes big overweight guys have problems with rashes and so forth. Guys with rough hands are a problem. It hurts when they touch you. I've turned away guys who showed up dirty or had black teeth. One guy dropped his tightie whities and there was a shit streak inside. I sent him away."

The providers I spoke with insist on condoms when sex is on the menu. Nikki said, "There's always the guy who tries to 'accidentally' sneak it in." A couple of Salt Lake area providers in the same price range have an apparently deserved reputation for skipping protection when things get hot. A reviewer on TER warned readers that one Utah provider sent him home "with a little extra" which, luckily, happened to be of a variety that antibiotics could wipe out. To the women I interviewed, that's not just unprofessional, but also disgusting, dangerous, and irresponsible. They make protection an absolute, nonnegotiable requirement.

Sex isn't always on the menu. Like many providers, Jewel advertises body rubs only. She'll include but not advertise a hand job but reserves full service only for a few, established clients. "Some guys demand full service and want their money back when they find out it's not available, even after they climax," she said. "One guy, when I wouldn't give him sex, threatened to tell his mom on me. He said she was a cop. When that didn't work he tried to grab his money back from me, and when that didn't work he tried to steal my car keys. He wrestled me into the hall. I was in my bra and panties. I was lucky that time. The desk clerk heard, came running, and made him leave."

Jewel lost her nerve the time a would-be new client led her into the basement of his home. He had decked it out like a dungeon. "The red light didn't freak me. The cameras didn't either, but I wouldn't have let him use them. But the walls, that freaked me. They were draped with plastic, like on the TV show *Dexter*. You know, the serial killer. So I left. Some things aren't worth five hundred bucks."

Tina has twice turned away men for appearing "too grabby, too eager. It was obvious they wanted cheap sex." Veronica has twice caught and evicted clients for trying to video their session without her knowledge or permission.

One client played upon Veronica's compassion. "He sent me a text message saying he just found out he had cancer," she said. "I felt terrible. I sent a sympathetic and sincere response." A few months went by before she heard from him again. "This time he said he was in the hospital, it was terminal, and he had only a few days or weeks left." Again, Veronica sent heartfelt sympathies. Not long after, a new text arrived from the same number from someone identifying herself as a nurse. She said she was following up on the man's request that she let Veronica know that he had died. "I sent sympathies and condolences to her," Veronica said. "A little while later, I got another text from the 'nurse.' She wanted to get together for a session." At that point, Veronica knew that the man hadn't died, hadn't been ill, and was posing as his own nurse. "I told him he was a sick puppy and not to contact me again."

9

Close encounters of the law enforcement kind

Providers are ever at risk that a new client will turn out to be an undercover cop. That's why experienced providers screen. A provider who doesn't screen may be inexperienced, low-end, reckless, or a police decoy, or she may naïvely believe she has some sort of a sixth-sense cop-detector.

For screening purposes, most providers are satisfied with references from two or more other providers. That doesn't necessarily leave a reference-less newbie out of luck. Many providers will accept a picture of photo ID like a driver's license or passport and a workplace phone number they can call to verify that the would-be client doesn't work in a police station. Higher-end providers who charge in the thousands may ask for all three—references, photo ID, and a workplace phone number. Johns willing to pay over $1,000 for a provider seem not to mind the extra hoops.

But police have a few tricks up their sleeves that can take the most cautious provider unawares. They can create fake references, IDs, and office phone numbers. They may offer to go easy on a just-busted john—who will pass all three forms of screening—in exchange for his wearing a wire to his next appointment with a provider. But that's rare. Even more rare is attempting to "turn" a busted provider. Her personal integrity and economics come into play. Fines and jail time aren't nearly as costly as not being able to work due to being known as a police informant. Most of the time, police go looking for prostitutes and johns the old-fashioned way, that is, with surveillance and undercover work.

Jewel learned by experience not to buy into the myth that police officers aren't allowed to let providers touch their genitals. "This guy came to my hotel room and undressed. After I touched his junk, he said he needed to use the bathroom. That was when I knew I'd been set up." Sure enough, less than a minute later, backup officers knocked on the hotel room door. "They booked me overnight and fined me. I had to be tested for AIDS and STIs."

Once Jewel made the mistake of agreeing to too much via text, which was used as evidence against her. It's one thing to claim never to have said anything incriminating, but text messages are impossible to deny. Experienced providers are careful not to text specifics or discuss them on the phone when setting up appointments. If a prospective client gets too specific, he is either a fool or a cop. Either way, the experienced provider knows she is better off terminating the conversation.

The precautions aren't foolproof, but they help. Most of the providers I interviewed had not been busted. Koko was one of the more unlucky ones. She has been busted five times, including once while on probation for a prior bust. She has been fined, jailed and fined, and jailed and fined with her car impounded. She wasn't sure whether she was careless or simply a frequent target. Perhaps it was neither, I suggested. She was the longest-standing provider I interviewed, having worked in the Salt Lake area for over 20 years. Over that length of time, she would have had more opportunities to encounter law enforcement than providers newer to the trade.

Busts are not an effective means of persuading providers not to provide. They are, however, remarkably effective for teaching providers how to avoid future arrests. Jewel learned not to text anything incriminating and not to suggest illegal activities once a new client arrived. "I let him do the talking and let him make the moves," she said, "and I keep quiet in case he's wearing a wire." Her new caution served her well the next time an undercover cop targeted her. When the gotcha moment arrived, the cop revealed his identity and told her she would receive a summons in the mail. "When he left without having me sign anything, I knew he didn't have anything on me." She was right. No summons arrived.

It would not be surprising if nonwhite providers were at greater risk for arrest and more severe sentencing. It would reflect the experience of nonwhites in America overall when it comes to law enforcement.[15] Jewel was standing on a sidewalk waiting for a friend when police pulled up and searched her. As far as she could tell, their "probable cause" consisted of her having committed an SAWB—Standing Around While Black. "They found weed in my purse and busted me. I didn't consent to a search, so it was a Fourth Amendment violation. You think that mattered?"

You could make a strong case for Traci's having been pulled over for the related crime of DWB, that is, Driving While Black. "I was driving my mother-in-law's new Cadillac," she said, "you know, the kind of car that if a black person is driving must be stolen. Especially late at night." The officer who pulled her over peppered her with questions. *Where are you going? Whose car is this? Where are you coming from? Where are you headed?* At length, finding nothing amiss, he let her go.

Traci's next DWB experience was nothing short of harrowing. Police had pulled her over for a legitimate reason: her car's registration had expired. In Utah, that's a common violation for which police usually hand the driver a ticket and leave. Not this time. The officer hauled Traci to Salt Lake City police headquarters, where she was made to strip and wait for her name to be called. She stood shivering in the cold of the station, doing her best to cover her breasts with one hand and her crotch with the other. She felt all eyes were upon her, which certainly was not just in her imagination. After an agonizing wait, a female officer called her into a side room and subjected her to a cavity search. Finding nothing incriminating, the female officer allowed Traci to dress. It was not until then that the female officer troubled to read the citation. "You're here for expired registration?" she asked. "I thought they picked you up for soliciting."

Traci felt she had no choice but to contain her outrage. An African American in a mostly white police station in Utah is wise not to raise a ruckus, even after being humiliated, dehumanized, and violated for an "offense" typically handled with a ticket and "Have a nice day and remember to take care of that registration."

"But here's the thing," Traci said. "They didn't know I was a sex worker. I don't have a record. They assumed I was a hooker because I'm black and I have big boobs. But there's no excuse for treating anyone that way, no matter what they think she is."

She reflected a moment. "I'm so glad police are getting vehicle and body cameras," she added. "I get pulled over less often now."

"Less often?" I asked.

"Less often," she repeated. "DWBs aren't going away anytime soon."

10

Rape, other forms of violence, and heartbreak

In the United States, neither society nor the justice system is known for showing a good deal of sympathy to rape victims. What little sympathy people and courts are willing to muster often drops to zero if the victim is a prostitute or even a legal escort. In many minds, a sexual services provider is the personification of "asking for it." Moreover, until recently in Utah, the provider who reported a rape risked landing in jail with a prostitution charge while her attacker went free. We have a system that treats a suggestively raised eyebrow in a bar as provocation for rape, and that treats selling sexual services as permission to rape.

About 15 percent of American women have been victims of rape. Roughly another 3 percent have been victims of attempted rape.[16] It would not be unreasonable to assume higher numbers within the sexual services industry. Half of the providers I interviewed were victims of rape or attempted rape, whether at work, outside of work, or both.

Tina's *earliest memory* is of being raped. She was three years old, and the assailant was her uncle. As a provider, she has been raped three times by clients. "My only defense was to try to relax as best I could," Tina said. "That way it was over faster and I'd have fewer injuries. It was all I could do. I couldn't go to the police. I'm a licensed escort. I make my living undressing in private for men. Do you think they'd believe I was raped? Do you think the charge would stick?" She reflected a moment and added, "You become numb to it."

Tina continued, "When I go see a client, I tell someone exactly where I'll be. If I don't check in when I say I will, they'll know I'm in trouble." What she said next was chilling: "I took a crime scene investigation class in high school. It fascinated me. For a while, I wanted to do forensics for a career. That's what ultimately led me to nursing school. Wherever I go, I intentionally leave behind DNA where police will know to look but a client won't find it and get rid of it. That way, if he murders me, he won't get away with it. I'll be dead, but he'll be caught."

Despite never having been raped by a client, Koko has had her share of scary client encounters, including an attempted rape. The assailant was an officer from Hill Air Force Base, about 30 miles north of Salt Lake City. "I said no to something he wanted to do and he got violent. I guess he wasn't accustomed to being told no. Instant personality change. He tried to rape me." A friend hovering nearby "just in case" intervened.

Another scary encounter involved guard dogs and a gun. "I went to a man's home," Koko said. "He had Dobermans. After letting me inside, he turned them loose outside. Then he pulled out a gun. I was afraid to walk out and afraid to stay." I asked what happened next. "I talked my way out of it," she said.

Jewel kept a .22 pistol in her purse in the early years. "I took it out only once, when a guy looked like he was going to attack and maybe try to rape me after I told him no full service. Sometimes I had my girl-friends and homeboys nearby for protection."

Not to be overlooked are Annie's earlier-described horrifying experiences of repeated child rapes at the hands of an uncle—while he wore a werewolf mask—and of the client who after raping her pressed a hand-gun to her temple and tried to rob her. Lilly, too, has fought off would-be rapists within the walls of her legal massage business.[17]

Nikki was a victim of acquaintance rape in her high school years and has been assaulted as a provider, too. "Once a medical doctor who wanted to become a client asked if I'd come to his office to get acquainted," she said. She usually screens prospective clients by getting to know them over lunch. "But," she said, "I thought, what could go wrong?" She soon found out. "He locked me in and tried to rape me right there." That time, she was lucky. She managed to fight him off.

In a Facebook post, Nikki wrote,

In my 35 years, I've seen a lot: I've been raped. I've been beaten. I've been lied to and cheated on. I've been divorced (twice), filed bankruptcy (twice), had cars repossessed, and a home foreclosed on. I've been discriminated against, bullied, and manipulated. I've had surgery to rebuild half of my face, and been within an inch of my life more than once. I've had broken bones, and spent a year in rehab. I lost a brother to heroin and have watched my sister battle it for over a decade. I've watched my weeks-old baby get test after test at the hospital, including three spinal taps. I've been fired, laid off, and transferred. I've used tips at the end of a shift to buy my kid food for the next day.

Nikki works hard to keep up her spirits. She continued,

But I've also picked myself up after every single one of those challenges and brought my life back. I've found my purpose and I live passionately and meaningfully every day. I'm raising two amazing and intelligent kids, and I'm starting a business by myself. I was the first in my family to graduate college, and now I have three degrees. I've received numerous certifications and awards, and an elite scholarship. I have an incredible partner who works hard every day to build our family and to keep learning and evolving together. I've rebuilt and retried. I've learned to keep loving and to keep smiling and to keep trusting. I see the world, and the people in it, as beautiful every single day and try to always smile at strangers.

A year before our interview, Boop experienced heartache when she traveled to another state to meet her birth parents. You may recall that her birth father is African American and her birth mother is Mexican, and that she cheerfully calls herself a "Blaxican." Her father was welcoming. So was her mother—at least, when they communicated by phone, email, and text. When Boop arrived at her birth mother's home to meet in person, she went for a hug—and her mother recoiled. "She pulled back and said 'you're so dark.' That broke my heart. My mother pulled away from hugging me because I'm dark? I'd even sent photos. We're okay now, but that broke my heart."

Natalie has known her share of heartbreak and trials. "When I was 13," she said, "my parents told me they were divorcing. It was traumatizing for me. It still hurts. I blamed my mother for the divorce and started running away from home. Years later I found out that my mom had given my dad an ultimatum. It was her or pot. He chose pot. I have to deal with the fact that for over a decade of grieving I have been blaming and resenting the wrong person." At 15, she moved in with a boyfriend who continually beat her. "Still," she said, "we were inseparable." She stayed with him for eight years.

Her boyfriend chose a New Year's Eve party at a friend's house to tell her they were through. The following day, he posted on Facebook that he was in a new relationship with another woman. "I was obsessed," Natalie said. "I texted him, 'I'm going to drive down to your work and I'm going to shoot myself right in front of you.'" Shooting herself was an idle threat—Natalie didn't own a gun—but driving to his work wasn't. When she arrived, "five or six police cars surrounded me. The police had their guns drawn and ordered me to show my hands out the window. Then they ordered me to get out of the car, put my hands on my head, and walk backwards." She did, and they handcuffed her. "I asked what I'd done, and the cop said I had a gun in my car. No, I didn't, and when they searched it they didn't find one." I couldn't help observing, and Natalie agreed, that surrounding her with drawn guns seemed like an odd approach to stopping someone from putting a bullet in her own head. *Don't try to shoot yourself or we'll shoot you.*

The boyfriend changed his phone number and had her served with a restraining order. The order stands to this day, and Natalie has honored it.

Somehow, I wasn't surprised when Natalie next told me she deals with post-traumatic stress disorder (PTSD). Koko, too, has been diagnosed with PTSD, as well as bipolar disorder, attention deficit hyperactivity disorder (ADHD), schizophrenia, depression, suicidal tendencies, and an autoimmune disease that she didn't specify. On the other hand, Annie's story reads every bit as much like a tragedy, yet she has emerged upbeat, composed, and positive.

Veronica's experience as a provider has been largely positive, something she doesn't take for granted. "I know some girls with horrible stories," she said. "I've never been beat up and never had an STI. I check regularly." Boop, too, has never been raped or molested. She is well past the traumatic incident of meeting her birth mother. "My adoptive parents were loving and protective," she said. "My dad owns a company so I had plenty of money as a kid. They paid my tuition and rent for years."

11

From stockbroker to porn actress to sugar baby

Nikki, born and raised in Utah, has been a sex worker since the age of 20. Her parents were "not particularly Catholic" but nonetheless prudish. They never talked about sex at home. When her parents were away from Utah, Nikki went to work serving cocktails at Southern Exposure, a strip club with two Salt Lake area locations and one Wendover, Nevada location.[18] It was her first experience with a sexually oriented business.

Then her truck broke down. A dealer hoodwinked her into signing a contract for a vehicle she could "use overnight while he worked on paperwork." The next day, the dealer informed her that what she had signed was an agreement to purchase the vehicle she thought was a loaner, and that she was now on the hook for a $2,000 down payment. "It was clearly his plan all along," she said. She needed to come up with two grand, and fast. That was when she saw an ad for a local agency that was looking to hire escorts.

"I argued with myself about calling, but curiosity won out," Nikki told me. "When I called, a woman answered the phone. That helped. She said, 'Just come in and talk with me,' so I did. They offered to let me give it a try. They lined me up with a client they knew well, someone they assured me was a gentleman. I went to see him, and I liked it. Most of this is just people wanting to connect. Sure, there's a sexual element. Sex is a part of it but it's not what people are looking for."

The agency charged 150 dollars per hour. Half of this plus 100 percent of tips went to the provider. Nikki performed lap dances and private, erotic dancing, and allowed touching outside the breast and genital area, all of which were legal. She also did hand jobs, which were not, but drew the line at full service. "They were super nice people and I made a whole bunch of money." She remained with the agency for 18 months.

In time, Nikki's mother found out about her daughter's new occupation. "She flipped out. She took the money they'd set aside for my college, used it to pay off my bills, and told me never to do it or speak of it again if I wanted to remain a member of the family. I felt emotionally devastated." Nikki withheld the information from both her stepfather and her biological father. The latter, a former police officer, she said, "had some cognitive troubles" due to an accident, and she worried about his reaction.

"I wanted my freedom of choice, but I chose my mom over the business," Nikki said. Later, putting her business degree to work, she took a job as a broker with a national investment firm. She was successful at her work and remained with the firm for 14 years. During that time, she had a child, married and divorced, and came to expect another child by a new man she was dating, whom she eventually married. "At first, he was reluctant to date. He made no bones about being polyamorous. He didn't want to date me because I was monogamous. I said, 'Hold on, this is important to you, so tell me about it.' I heard him out and realized that I aligned with him on nonmonogamy and liberty. I believe that sex can be healing. Open marriage wasn't right just for him. It was right for us."

After so many years in the investment business, Nikki was ready for a change. "I didn't like investments. By then I knew that, whatever I would do, it would have to do with sexuality. Toward the end of my investments career, I worked as a model for a man who taught sensual massage. He demonstrated on me to show the class what to do. As a demo model, I saw couples losing their uptightness. I saw that it was good for them, healing. Trouble is, the teacher couldn't keep the class going. So I taught my husband how to do sensual massage. This eventually led to going into the sensual massage business on our own. That was when I quit the brokerage business."

By the time Nikki left the brokerage, she had appeared in an adult film on her own and, with her husband, in two productions for Playboy's *Adult Film School* series. To my knowledge, Nikki was the only adult film performer I interviewed, so I asked her to tell me about the adult film world.

"It's not as hot as you'd think," she said. She and her husband auditioned by making a home video and submitting it to Playboy TV. Liking what they saw, the folks at Playboy flew Nikki and her husband to Texas to star in a professional production. They arrived at the studio at eight o'clock on the morning of the shoot. Shooting didn't begin until an agonizing 12 hours later. Makeup and hair accounted for only some of the setup time. Lighting, sound checks, set dressing, last-minute script changes, camera setups, getting the production crew in sync, and Murphy's Law accounted for the rest. There's no telling how long any of those steps might take, so actors remain on set to be available the moment setup is complete. Even if it means making them sit around, naked, for hours, which it usually does.

Once shooting begins, it's still "not as hot as you'd think." Nikki explained that sitting around naked for hours while a director, videographer, lighting director, sound director, and gaffers fuss over their jobs can take the hotness out of a sex shoot pretty fast.

Nor does the director simply roll tape, turn the actors loose, and, once they're spent, call out "that's a wrap." Lower-quality productions are made that way, and you can tell from the poor lighting, pacing, and sound, as well as from the lackluster action and, often, solitary camera setup. Playboy, however, had a brand to maintain. They used professional directors, camera operators, and other technicians who took pride in their work.

Like any quality production, a quality porno film requires shooting and reshooting scene after scene from different angles for an editor to cut together later. Every new angle requires taking down and moving the camera and lights, and setting up the sound anew. For the actors, it means reperforming the same scene over and over for each new camera angle. That alone can quickly dampen any feelings of hotness with which the actors may have started out.

There are myriad interruptions and retakes. Perhaps the woman's hair covered part of her face. Perhaps the man didn't look sufficiently turned on. Perhaps a crewmember sneezed, ruining the sound. Perhaps the lighting was off. Perhaps the boom mic intruded into the frame. Perhaps the actors needed to contort just a little more to place body parts in full view of the camera. Perhaps one actor farted and the other burst out laughing. "Shooting a porno isn't sexy," Nikki said. "It's tedious."

As the feeling of excitement gives way to the realization that you're not so much having hot sex in front of a camera as working to look like you're having hot sex, a new problem arises. Or rather, fails to arise. Waning excitement shows less on a woman than on a man. If you're old enough to be reading this book, chances are I needn't elaborate.

Consider the talent it takes to look like you're horny, spontaneous, and fully enjoying yourself under those conditions. I can't speak for you, but I will never again roll my eyes when I hear someone refer to porn stars as actors.

Likewise, do not envy the production crew for "all of the beautiful bodies and hot action they get to see." Any titillation that camera operators or gaffers may experience at the outset of their first porn production inevitably gives way to focusing on the demands of the job. By their second production, they might as well be shooting a tire commercial.

Returning home, Nikki resumed her work in the sensual massage business, but it was turning into something of a hassle. Clients often scheduled at the last minute. Her husband traveled for work, so each appointment request meant frantically searching for last-minute babysitters. It also meant having to lug a heavy massage table to the client's home or office several times in a week, sometimes several times in a day. Nikki began looking for a way to provide sensual services on a schedule she could control, and without having to wrestle the massage table in and out of her car.

She found the solution in the sugar baby business. A handful of clients paying to see her on a regular, prescheduled basis would make her life manageable. She found clients by advertising on websites and through the swingers community—people who get together for group sex and to swap partners. Salt Lake City, it turns out, has a thriving one.

For the first time, Nikki offered full service. "I have worked in the brokerage business and I have worked in the sex business," she said. "I had no idea there were so many predators out there. That's why I'm glad I left the brokerage business."

Nikki has consistent, regular clients. They schedule appointments in advance. She sees some weekly, some biweekly, and some monthly. This lets her plan her time and budget. It also all but eliminates the risk of arrest, since she seldom advertises, and getting together with clients looks as legal as any other get-together. She sells three hours for $600. The hours are the client's to use as he chooses. Sex is on the menu, but not all opt for it. Sometimes a client will take her on a public date, say, to dinner and the opera. Some just want to sit and talk with a pretty woman.

"Three hours can be a lot to fill," Nikki said, so she screens for clients with whom she can connect. "I'll meet a prospective client for lunch to get a feel for conversation and so forth."

Nikki is serious about selling sex as a service, and about its healing power. "My clients by and large are not datable," she said. "They can't communicate with women, have a handicap of some sort, their busy schedule forbids a real relationship, or they're in a loveless marriage. I give them a safe place. There's no mockery. I don't shame them. I validate them."

Nikki feels strongly about sex work as a service. So strongly, she said, that in a few weeks she would be delivering a talk about sex work at TEDx Salt Lake City.

Shortly after our lunch, I went online and bought tickets.

12

Nikki, sex worker rights advocate

On September 8, 2018, Nikki walked to the center of the stage in the main theater of Kingsbury Hall. The 2,000-seat hall was filled to capacity. Located on the University of Utah campus, Kingsbury is a venue of no small reputation. David Copperfield, Wynton Marsalis, and other big names perform there.

Nikki was the morning's seventh speaker. Suspended behind her in huge letters was the TEDx Salt Lake City logotype. She wore distressed jeans, a modest navy top, and a white jacket. There was not a hint of nervousness about her, despite 2,000 people seated before her and the fact that speaking at TEDx meant that people throughout the world would later see and hear her presentation. Yet in a follow-up interview, Nikki told me she had been terribly nervous. During one of many rehearsals, she broke into tears, uncertain that she could pull it off. As of this writing there have been more than 2.7 million views of her presentation on YouTube.

The polite applause that welcomes any noncelebrity to the stage swelled and ebbed. Then, Nikki addressed the crowd:

Some people think you can live without intimacy, without connection. I think that's total crap.

A few years ago, a client emailed me. He said, "Today a miracle happened. Since my wife passed, I've been very lonely. I haven't so much as been hugged in over two years. I'm not handsome, I'm not rich, I don't know how to talk to women. But you held me, you rubbed my back, you listened to me vent about my grief. This might just be a job for you, but today you saved my life."

Now, I'm not a psychiatrist. I'm not a doctor. I don't work for a crisis hotline.

I'm a sex worker.

Silence fell across the hall. After four seconds of it, I thought *What the hell* and started clapping. As if they'd been awaiting permission, the rest of the audience joined me with thunderous applause and cheers. These were not catcalls, mind you, but honest, supportive applause and cheers.

> And as a sex worker I see a side of people most of you don't.
>
> Just so we're on the same page, the term "sex work" refers to sexual encounters by consenting adults for some sort of payment. Now, before your imagination goes crazy, hold on, think about this. On average, studies have shown that sex lasts only 5.4 minutes. So if they're paying for an hour—or three—what are they actually paying for? They're paying for a place to be their true selves, a place to talk about challenges without being criticized, judged, a place to try new things without losing everything they've built. And, frankly, sex is a really strong need for them. It often consumes them. Because sex is how men feel loved and worthy.

I recommend viewing all 12 minutes of Nikki's excellent presentation on YouTube.[19] Skipping to her summation:

> My job includes consoling a man who misses his children on the other side of the country, to teaching someone about female anatomy, to reminding someone of what it feels like to be touched, who has been deprived for so long, to helping someone who is disabled feel "normal" just for a minute.
>
> Now don't get me wrong. This job's not glamorous, and it is certainly not easy. There's always a guy that wants to call all the time—you all know somebody like that, right?—or somebody that wants to do something really funky.
>
> But there's a greater good here. These people deserve to feel important, and connected, too, and if they could find that somewhere else they would have.

We're all people that need help, we pay for help all the time. We pay for tax attorneys, we pay for car repairs, we pay for childcare, housekeeping. There's just this huge stigma around sex.

Just as much as we seek healing for our minds and our bodies, we ought to be free to seek healing for our hearts and, well, our parts, too. Just as you'd hire a mental health professional, I'm a sexual health professional. But it's not about the sex. It's about intimacy, and connection.

Nikki is unique—and heroic—in that she has gone public about her work as a provider. Decked out in bustiers and fishnet stockings, she and her colleagues marched on the Utah state capitol, brandishing posters that say *Your bishop is my best client.* She cofounded The Magdalene Collective, a support group for sex workers, cofounded the Salt Lake chapter of SWOP (Sex Workers Outreach Project, an international organization for sex worker outreach and advocacy), and served in a leadership position for Utah Women Unite, whose platform includes advocacy for the rights of sex workers and their clients. She sits on police department community advisory panels, is a willing interviewee for the news media, and meets often with a state senator to discuss safety and rights for sex workers. "Really," she added, laughing, "all we do is talk." I hadn't asked, but apparently many do, so she no longer waits for the question to answer it.

A year prior to her TEDx talk, Nikki participated with two fellow sex workers in a panel discussion, "Let's Talk about Sex (Work), Baby!", sponsored by the Utah Coalition Against Sex Assault. *Salt Lake Tribune* reporter Jennifer Dobner wrote,

The women are lobbying state lawmakers in hope of shaping future policies that impact the industry. . . . To that end, the group drafted a letter and a petition asking to sit down with Sen. Todd Weiler, R-Woods Cross, a known champion of morality-focused legislation . . . the goal is to better understand the senator's beliefs and motives.

"Our fundamental goals are the same," [Nikki] said. "We all want safe communities, we all want safe children, we all want people to be safe from violence. We can agree on that level."

To his credit, Weiler welcomes the invitation, he told *The Salt Lake Tribune*. "I'm happy to meet with them and consider what they have to say," he said. "Despite what people think, I'm a pretty nice guy and I like to learn."[20]

Not long after her TEDx talk, Nikki learned that her father, the former police officer, had caught wind of the presentation. She braced herself, expecting him to be livid. "Instead," she said, "he was incredibly supportive." He offered to help manage her business affairs and, when the time comes, help with publishing the book she plans to write.

In 2019, working closely with Utah State Senator Paul Ray, Nikki was instrumental in the creation and passage of HB40. The much-needed legislation allows sex workers to report crimes committed against them in the course of their work without fear of being charged with soliciting or prostitution.

"I want to help people heal through sexuality," Nikki told me.

13

Providers plan for the future

You may recall Linda's wholesale auto parts venture designed to give her "something to fall back on when I tire of the game or when I'm no longer hot."

When I tire of the game or when I'm no longer hot. It's a time that every provider knows must sooner or later come. While some may have not given future plans much thought, not a few have already mapped out and begun pursuing the next chapter in their lives.

Boop takes seriously her duties as a mom to her high-functioning autistic son and maintains a trust fund for him. At the time of our interview she was one year away from a second baccalaureate degree and a new career. I asked what career she planned to launch. She smiled and said, "Not going to say. Yet."

Likewise, Betty plans to exit the sex trade in about a year. She will likely return to the mental health services field in which she has multiple degrees and years of experience.

Shortly after our interview, Natalie headed to California to work as a medical assistant and continue her bikini and lingerie modeling career. You may not be surprised to learn that there are more opportunities for lingerie models in California than in Utah.

Tina has diligently saved during the seven years she has worked as a provider. "I don't burn through my money like a lot of providers do," she said. Although she can always return to working as a registered nurse, at 29 she is set to retire—not just from the trade, but retire altogether—within one or two years. I asked what she might do with her free time. "I'm thinking about starting an organization to help rape victims, or maybe single moms," she said, "or maybe both."

Jewel is assiduously pursuing a cosmetology career. Michelle manages a restaurant. Veronica is pursuing a career in the hotel business. Zoe, who spoke with me for only a few minutes, works in a massage parlor and is saving toward opening her own massage business.

This is not to say that they need hurry into a career change. "When I'm no longer hot" doesn't seem to loom close. Most were between 25 and 40 years old, and some Salt Lake area providers continue working into their 60s and 70s. Some have the advantage of looking younger than they are. I guessed that Zoe was 24. Nope. Forty-five. Michelle and Jewel could pass for ten years younger than they are. Alicia looked to me to be about 30. I had guessed exactly 25 years low.

Not one provider I spoke with had compunctions about telling me her real age. At least, I assume they told me their real age. The ages they advertise, that's another matter.

14

I earn a comeuppance

"Why is that so surprising?" Boop asked, visibly peeved.

She had every reason. She had just told me she held a Bachelor of Arts in speech and communication, and, without thinking, I'd blurted, "You're kidding."

Having blurted it out, I couldn't drag it back in, and Boop felt justifiably affronted. I apologized, made some weak excuse, and was relieved when she let it go.

Later on, reviewing my notes from the interview, I thought, *Why* had *it surprised me?* Betty's credentials had surprised me, too, but that was in the wake of my gaffe with Boop, so I'd managed not to show it.

For that matter, it had surprised me to learn that Tina was a registered nurse. It had surprised me to learn that Nikki held three degrees and had 14 years as a successful stockbroker behind her.

Why?

Perhaps had I not known they were providers—had our paths crossed at, say, a social gathering—I'd have experienced no surprise, only admiration, at their education and credentials. Much as I disliked admitting it to myself, I wasn't as enlightened as I had prided myself on being. I was more inclined toward stereotypes than I'd thought.

We all have prejudices. I wonder how many more of my own lie hidden away.

Chapter 6

Mormontown's Asian Massage Parlors

I've encountered so many Western men who, just like the main character of Seeking Asian Female, have "Yellow Fever" or an unusual attraction to Asian women. These men seem to fit a pattern: they tend to be older, white, and yes, creepy.

—Debbie Lum, filmmaker

1

"Any color you want"

The first time I visited New York City, a not terribly hygienic looking man sidled up to me and muttered, "Hey buddy, wanna girl? Getcha any color you want." Tempted as my Inner Smart Aleck was to ask if he had anything in Brunswick green, I said nothing and walked on, not least for fear that he might answer in the affirmative.

His execution erred on the inelegant side, but there was arguable soundness to his marketing strategy. If you're a straight American male of any extraction you're statistically likely to have a thing for women outside your race[1] and, if non-Asian, for Asian women in particular.[2] "The Asian thing," Koko confirmed, rolling her eyes. "Lots of guys want to try an Asian girl. So many guys are fixated. They have to try Asian. It's kind of annoying, but I definitely benefit financially from it."

The "Asian thing" may have something to do with the tendency in the West to view Asian women as exotic, hypersensual, mystical, child-like, and subservient. If that's your impression of Asian women, sorry to disappoint, but you have bought into a stereotype at the expense of reality. A good many Asian women rightly find the stereotype tiresome and harmful, and would gladly disabuse millions of people of it.

They are, however, up against at least two daunting obstacles. One is humankind's propensity to separate into Us and Them. The other is that a number of industries that make a good deal of money from the stereotype do their best to perpetuate it. Examples include Asian dating sites, Asian bride brokers, all-Asian brothels, Asian movie and literary stereotypes, Asian porn, and the subject of this chapter, Asian massage parlors, or AMPs for short.

At the mention of AMPs, one might be tempted to picture a suite of dimly lit, private rooms with massage tables where clients willing to tip for the privilege can receive a hand job or more.

In response to that, I shall now speak out of both sides of my mouth.

One side of my mouth will tell you that to assume that illegal activities go on inside an AMP just because it's an AMP and not a nondescript MP with no *A* is unfair and racist. "Asian massage parlor" needn't mean that hand jobs and possibly more, collectively referred to as "extras," are available within. There are a number of Salt Lake area AMPs where extras are not available. I spoke with Asian massage therapists who refuse to provide extras, even if they work in a place where coworkers happily oblige for the right price. Moreover, extras are not the exclusive domain of AMPs. They are to be found at many a massage business, Asian or not.

The assumption that "Asian" means "extras" can be inconvenient if not dangerous for law-abiding massage therapists who happen to be Asian. A client expecting extras may grope, pressure, and throw a fit when he doesn't get his way. Should the massage therapist press charges, the association of "Asian" with "extras" may prevent police from taking her seriously. Should she be charged with soliciting, the association may lessen her likelihood of receiving fair treatment in a courtroom.

Short of personal safety and law enforcement issues, the assumption has its annoying, hurtful side. No-nonsense Asian massage therapists have told me they cringe when asked at social gatherings, "What do you do for work?" What inevitably follows is a series of only half-kidding jokes that fail to register on the Originality Scale and land nowhere near the Funniness Scale.

I shall now speak out of the other side of my mouth. While it's unfair and racist to paint all AMPs with one brush, the AMP that offers extras is not unusual. In a vicious marketing circle that at once capitalizes on and promotes the Asian woman stereotype, a number of AMPs provide extras because men seek them there, and men seek them there because of the number of AMPs that provide them.

The not subtly named website Rubmaps.ch features user reviews of massage businesses. As I write, users list 23 active AMPs in the Salt Lake City area. Readers are warned that five facilities have been reported as "non-erotic." The site also lists eight non-Asian massage parlors, reporting only one as "non-erotic." Reviewers indicating the availability of extras most frequently mention hand jobs, sometimes with "breast play." I spotted only one AMP review in which the user claimed to have purchased sex. He provided a surprising level of detail including the massage therapist's name, prompting a commenter to warn him not to be specific and remind him that cops routinely search the site.

Many AMPs aren't shy about capitalizing on the male obsession with Asian women, unabashedly adorning their advertising and storefronts with photos of gravure idols.[3] Now and then a reality-challenged man will show up at an AMP actually expecting to find the pictured women working there. He removes all doubt as to his naïveté when he later writes in an online review, "I don't think the girls in the photos were working that day."

A or no A, massage parlors that provide extras make for a convenient, legal venue for a quick, illegal exchange. They are well suited to the man who wants an impromptu encounter, or who draws a line in his moral sand with "hand job" on the side marked "Permissible."

2

What happened in Vegas didn't stay there

When Asian massage parlors began popping up in Salt Lake City, they had a familiar look to them. Where had I seen them before? Ah, yes. They reminded me of AMPs I'd noted in Las Vegas, about 420 miles south of Salt Lake City, where business and vacation send me every two or three years.

I usually drive. There's simply no appreciating the landscape from 30,000 feet the way you can at eye level. Without exiting the freeway, you'll pass majestic mountains, take in some of southern Utah's brilliant red rock country, and, crossing the northwest corner of Arizona, drive through the breathtaking Virgin River Gorge. The final stretch will subject you to about 90 minutes of desert, an impressive sight in its own right.

You wouldn't know it from the movies, but there's more to Las Vegas than the oversized gambling establishments at the south end of Las Vegas Boulevard and the vintage Fremont Street establishments. Indeed, the greater part of the Las Vegas metropolitan business district looks pretty much like that of any other western U.S. city, with two exceptions. One is the row of slot machines, not long ago called "one-armed bandits,"[4] inside nearly every diner and grocery store. The other is what I can only surmise is an ordinance requiring not less than one Asian massage parlor per city block.

After passing the umpteenth strip mall with MASSAGE in big, extra bold, red or green sanserif letters and windows covered with photos of hot Asian women, I figured that either Las Vegas has an uncommonly high incidence of sore muscles or that MASSAGE in big, extra bold, red or green sanserif letters and windows covered with photos of hot Asian women might be code for something more. Stepping inside one of the

AMPs was all it took to find out. A gracious, alluringly dressed Asian woman greeted me, pantomimed what I assumed was the action of running one's hand up and down a baseball bat to check for splinters, and drew the number 100 followed by a dollar sign in the air. It seemed like a lot just to check for splinters.

Legal brothels exist in Nevada, but state law restricts them to counties with fewer than 700,000 residents. Clark County, home to Las Vegas, has that and about a million and half to spare, so there are no legal brothels in Vegas. Not to worry. If you're bent on visiting a legal brothel, you need drive only about 80 minutes to adjacent, considerably less populated Nye County, which has four of them. Don't feel like driving? Free round-trip transportation is available.

Those who prefer to avoid the commute to Nye County may be interested to know that anti-prostitution laws are not equal to the task of keeping under-the-radar providers from operating in Las Vegas. Private entertainers like those I interviewed in Utah, and certainly some trafficked ones, are in more than abundant supply. They advertise online, hang out in casinos, and, as I learned when I was staying at the Park MGM, may appear at your side from nowhere at a hotel elevator bank and offer to help you find your room.[5]

Those who prefer to avoid the commute to Nye County *and* who would rather not contact an under-the-radar provider may find a practical, less expensive alternative in a Las Vegas area AMP. Their not-subtle signage makes them easy to find. They're legal, so you can saunter through the front door without fear of arrest. You stand to receive an excellent massage by an appealingly arrayed, possibly licensed massage therapist. For some men, that's plenty; but if you and your therapist are so inclined, you may agree on a price for a bit more, which is likely to cost considerably less than what you'd spend in a brothel. But then, the AMP's menu of services will be limited by comparison, typically to a hand job and a bit of groping.

Until the early 2000s, Salt Lake City appeared to have no equivalent to the Las Vegas–style AMP. Other large cities had no shortage of them, but Salt Lake seemed the exception. Salt Lake had massage businesses, and in some of them individual therapists provided extras, but the storefront AMP concept was conspicuously missing.

At the time, I wondered if Utah's 90-percent-Mormon legislature had passed onerous regulations making AMPs all but impossible to open, much less operate. If you have ever ordered a drink in Utah, you have seen firsthand how Utah's state legislature excels in hampering recreation they feel a religious obligation to render inconvenient but dare not ban outright. Or, I thought, maybe there was simply not enough demand to sustain AMPs in a state where the majority of residents believe the use of genitals outside of marriage is the third most serious sin.

Silly, naïve me. In the mid 2010s, a few Asian massage parlors looking fresh-plucked from Las Vegas opened in downtown Salt Lake City. I have no idea what took them so long. They were instant financial successes, so more followed. It wasn't long before AMPs popped up in the suburbs as well. Today in the Salt Lake environs you need only drive a few miles to spot an AMP from the road. Following the Vegas model, most of them are located in strip malls with MASSAGE in big, illuminated, red or green sanserif letters. They, too, cover the windows with photos of Asian women, albeit more clothed—somewhat—than their Vegas counterparts. This is Utah, after all.

3

Mormon faithful from throughout the world show up for hand jobs

I asked Lilly how many happy ending seekers she thought were Mormon. She figured 70 to 90 percent. That didn't surprise me; it was consistent with what independent providers reported. What *did* surprise me was a fact that she inserted parenthetically in the midst of an unrelated anecdote: "We're always busiest at conference time."

By "conference time," Lilly was referring to the Mormon Church's General Conference, a semiannual, three-day event in which the church's prophet and apostles deliver sermons and instructions to the Mormon faithful. General Conferences are held in Salt Lake City and broadcast worldwide. The talks are later published in print and posted on one or more of the church's websites, but devout Mormons travel from all over the world to soak up the sermons in the presence of God's anointed.

Lilly's parenthetical comment took me aback. It's one thing, even human, to act out when no one is watching. But Mormons who travel to Salt Lake City to attend General Conference are presumably the most believing of the most believing. They are the ones I would have expected to be on their best behavior at all times, whether or not anyone who knows them is watching. For that matter, like most God-fearing people, Mormons believe that someone is *always* watching, said someone being God and his angels. The angels even take notes.[6] You'd think the mental picture of a supreme being watching while angels jot details would be sufficiently creepy to ruin even the best hand job.

Incredulous, later that day I fired off a text to Tina, whom I'd interviewed only a few days earlier. I asked, *Does business increase at General Conference time?* Less than a minute later she texted back, *It does!!!* The three exclamation points were hers.

4

"Address please happy endings?"

Before I could persuade a massage therapist working in an AMP to speak with me, I would need to find one whose English skills were sufficient for a meaningful interview. This presented a challenge. Fluent English is not a requirement for working in an Asian massage parlor, and my Chinese is limited to three expressions that I'm sure I pronounce horribly: 谢谢, 别客气, and 我爱你— "thank you," "you're welcome," and "I love you," respectively. Not quite enough to get by. Fortunately, a bit of networking introduced me to Lilly.

Lilly agreed to visit over lunch at one of Salt Lake's many Thai restaurants. An attractive, middle-aged Chinese immigrant, she wore a modest, knee-length navy knit dress and sported jet-black, shoulder-length hair. She displayed keen business acumen offset by an impish sense of humor. She spoke English well, knew the AMP business, and was willing to talk about it.

Lilly ordered a salad. I ordered a chicken curry dish. Conversation began as I expected it would, that is, with Lilly exercising caution. "I don't want anyone reading your book to know who I am," she said more than once. "Don't use my real name. Don't use the name I give customers, either."

At first she stuck with textbook answers and volunteered nothing. I understood her caution. For all she knew, I might betray her by intent or ineptitude. Maybe I was an undercover cop wearing a wire. It would be no idle fear. Utah law enforcement keeps an eye on Asian massage parlors.

"I am a professional massage therapist," Lilly said. "That's all. Never give hand jobs. No extras. That's illegal. If a customer asks I tell him to leave. Someone asks on the phone, I hang up on him."

I had already spoken with two of Lilly's therapists, so I knew better than to believe the part about not offering extras. I did, however, believe the part about dismissing people who call or text with sexually explicit questions. Voice calls and text messages can be retrieved and used as evidence. Anyone who asks a sexually explicit question by text or phone is either stupid or working undercover. Lilly had no use for either.

"Seven out of ten ask for a happy ending," she said, invoking the popular euphemism for a hand job. She went on, "Who doesn't want a happy ending? I tell them no. Sometimes they get mad. That's why I don't let the girls who work for me answer the phone. Only me. I worry what they say if a man offers a lot of cash."

Lilly had earlier declined to answer when I asked if she owned or managed the spa, but by this time it was evident that she was the owner of this and at least one other local spa. I later spoke briefly with other AMP owners who, like Lilly, were evasive about confirming their ownership.

"Happy endings are illegal," Lilly repeated. "That's how spas get in trouble. If you don't want to get in trouble, don't do happy endings."

After a while, she began to loosen up. "Sometimes," she volunteered with a coy smile, "I tell a caller I can't answer that. I tell him I'm only the scheduler. I don't say yes but I don't say no." Most callers take not saying no for a yes, and most of the time they're right. If they're wrong, it's not as if they can complain to the police. "A massage therapist refused to give me a happy ending" is not the smartest way to open a conversation with a law enforcement officer.

Lilly's phone buzzed. It was a text from a new customer wanting to set up an appointment. She showed me his message: *Address please happy endings?* Then she showed me her reply: *Hahaha.* With the next text, he offered $200. A few minutes later he upped it to $400. Lilly didn't reply.

Her phone buzzed again. This time the text was from a semi driver nearing Salt Lake. He wanted to know if there was a place near her spa where he could park his semi. She told him there was, gave him directions, and set an appointment with him.

Lilly was a child when her parents left China and brought her and her siblings to Salt Lake. "I won't tell you how long ago. Why do you want to know?" They settled in Salt Lake City because extended family already lived in the area. No large Chinese population awaited them, however. Utah has only about 80,000 residents of Asian extraction, accounting for only 4.4 percent of Salt Lake County's population. So small are their numbers that the state's health department doesn't bother breaking "Asian" into national origins. It lumps Chinese, Japanese, and Filipinos into one group and Vietnamese, Indian, Laotian, and Thai into another.[7]

Lilly became a U.S. citizen. When she was old enough for employment, she went to work in the restaurant business. There, she developed back pains, and massage therapy gave her relief. Lilly went into the business to bring that relief to others. "Besides," she said, "I like people. I like talking with them. I like to make them feel good. And they talk to me. They tell me their problems while I work on them. I'm a massage therapist, but sometimes I feel like a mental health worker. And I like the girls," she said, referring to the young women who work for her. "I like hanging with them. Maybe because I always wanted a daughter."

5

How to ask for a hand job without asking for a hand job

Most massage therapists working in AMPs are prepared to deliver a quality, professional massage. If there is to be a happy ending, the therapist will most likely delay offering it until the massage is nearly over, as the "ending" in "happy ending" would seem to imply.

It would be risky for a client to request extras, and equally risky for a massage therapist to offer them, at the outset of a session. Based on what I gathered from Lilly, other AMP workers, and searching on Tor, what unfolds is a sort of cat-and-mouse ritual of hints and encouragement that lets client and therapist remain technically legal as long as possible. In case either of them might be wearing a wire, they avoid discussing extras aloud. Even that's not completely safe. In Utah, hand signals constitute sufficient cause for arrest.

After paying the typical $60 or $65 dollar massage fee—negotiating for extras comes later—the customer is led to a private room. He is instructed to undress, lie facedown on the massage table, and place a towel over his hindquarters. If he somehow forgets the part about the towel, the ritual has commenced. The massage therapist may or may not place the towel on him when she returns. If she places it on him, it may not be a sign of refusal but of caution. If she leaves him uncovered, it's definitely a sign of encouragement.

"Honey, you want light pressure, medium, or hard?" the therapist will ask. The client chooses his preferred level of pressure. If he wants to drop a hint, he may add ". . . and sensual." Calling the client "honey" may hint at the availability of extras, but it has its practical side as well. It relieves the client of having to give up his name or invent one; and, for a Chinese immigrant whose English skills may be limited, "honey" is easier to pronounce than many an American name.

The massage proceeds like any other. The therapist begins with the customer's back, in time moving to his neck, shoulders, arms, and, finally, his legs, beginning with the calf or feet. Taking her time, she moves her hands up to the thigh. If extras are in the menu, she may move her hands to the towel's hem, or to the place where the towel's hem would be were it not discarded and lying on the floor, and ask, "Is this okay, honey?" If the client agrees that everything is indeed okay, the therapist's hands may wander further. In the unlikely event that he says, "No, that's not okay," she will cease her overtures and hope he's not an undercover cop or an offended customer who will report her to the authorities.

Venturing a little closer, then a little closer, and closer still in what amounts to an agonizingly prolonged tease, the therapist may ask each time, "Is this okay, honey?" The client may elevate his hips just a little, a signal inviting the therapist to reach under, touch, and finally begin stroking. After a while she will ask, "You want to turn over, honey?" Most men, Lilly said with a wink, want to turn over.

About fifteen minutes of the hour remains. By now it's pretty well established that the client wants a hand job and that the therapist is willing to sell him one. "How much you tip?" the therapist mouths, pantomiming a hand job a few inches above his now prominent Item of Principal Interest. At this point in the transaction, it's safe to say that said Item has pretty well taken over the thinking, making it the ideal moment for the therapist to negotiate. The customer names an amount. The therapist may accept it or negotiate for more. She may ask for cash on the spot or trust him to be true to his word and pay up after.

She commences the hand job. Most times, it doesn't take long for the client to climax. The therapist then produces a warm, moist towel to clean off her client and her hands. With the massage thus happily ended, the client dresses and, if he hasn't already, hands over the promised tip. At least, most hand over the promised tip. Some jerks break their promise and scurry out, having paid only the massage fee. They know the massage therapist has no recourse. It's not as if she can complain to the police.

The cat-and-mouse ritual keeps both parties within the realm of plausible deniability until the last minute. If the client skips the ritual, rushes it, or is too vocal in his demands, the more experienced massage therapist will take it as a warning sign and stick to a legitimate massage.

There are, however, massage therapists who dispense with the ritual. I found this out firsthand—no pun intended—when, some months after my interview with Lilly, I visited a competing AMP. The parking lot was empty and closing time was only an hour away, so I figured my chances of securing an interview without having to purchase a massage were good. I walked in carrying my trusty padfolio and expensive-looking pen. Eyes usually go straight to the padfolio, and workers become guarded until I explain why I'm there. Not this time. Before I could speak, the attractive, thirtyish Asian woman who greeted me said in excellent English, "Sorry, honey, I'm closing the shop early and going to a party."

Surprised that she was allowed to close and leave at will, I said, "You must be the manager or owner."

"I just work here," she said. It may or may not have been true. As I said, AMP owners seemed reluctant to disclose their ownership status.

She continued, "My friend is a new grandparent and she's having a party. I'm closing early so I can go. Come see me another time, okay?"

I thanked her and turned to leave. Handing me a business card, she said, "Call for an appointment and ask for me. Bring a condom. One hundred for a happy ending, two hundred for a blowjob, three hundred for sex."

No sign of cat or mouse here, I thought. I walked to my car fairly certain that this particular massage therapist was headed for a not-distant arrest. Not eager to be on the premises if and when, I never returned.

6

The extortionist

While there's no sure way to know when a new customer might be an undercover police officer, not much of a keen eye was required to know that the fellow who walked into Lilly's shop was a cop. A major clue was to be found in the fact that he was in full uniform, gun on hip.

Lilly has no policy against police officers as customers. Some of her best, happy ending–enjoying regulars work in law enforcement, but something about this man put her on her guard. Knowing better than to say outright, "I don't want you for a customer," Lilly chose the more tactful, "We're booked for the day."

"Okay," the cop said, and took a seat in the lobby. And stayed.

Nothing kills a massage parlor's business like an armed, uniformed police officer lingering in the lobby. One after another arriving customer froze at the front door, executed an about-face, and left. Customers emerging fresh from a massage only to find a cop seated in the lobby couldn't hurry out fast enough. After a suitable amount of time watching the man kill her business, Lilly relented and showed him to a room.

When she returned to the room a few minutes later, he lay naked on his back atop the massage table, his centerpiece exposed, extended, and pointed at the ceiling. The good news was that he didn't ask for a happy ending. The bad news was that he asked for—demanded—a blowjob.

He hadn't just omitted the ritual. He had vaulted right over it.

Lilly told him no.

Springing to his feet, the cop grabbed her and forced her onto the massage table. Pinning her with one hand, he tried with the other to pry open her mouth and force himself inside.

We were halfway through our lunch when Lilly recounted this horror story. Unable to remain the detached interviewer, I asked if she'd thought about biting off his dick. "I didn't let him get it in," she said.

A trained police officer twice her weight and standing a foot taller made for a fearsome assailant. But then, no man with a lick of sense would think about assaulting Lilly. She is petite but fit and, I suspect, fierce when she needs to be. She fought him off.

Giving up on the blowjob, he stepped away from the table and told her he had a business proposition. Because, you know, who wouldn't want to discuss a business proposition with a cop who just tried to force his dick into your mouth?

"I want you to talk to the other spa owners," he told her. "I know you know them."

She didn't, but the cop was not to be dissuaded.

"You know I'm a cop," he said.

Yeah, the uniform had kind of tipped her off.

"I know where and when Vice is planning a raid. I know who the undercover cops are. Tell the other spa owners I want $2,000 a month apiece to warn them when a raid is coming."

Lilly declined.

"You don't know who you're dealing with," the cop said. "I have busted a lot of AMPs and forced a lot to close because they didn't do what I wanted."

Lilly declined again, so the cop generously offered to lower his monthly retainer to $1,000. Lilly still said no. The cop issued a final warning and left. As of this writing, he hasn't given up. He calls and drops by, reiterates the extortion bid, and promises there will be hell to pay if she doesn't comply. Nothing has come of it. Hell, it would seem, is not an aggressive debt collector.

I asked if she'd thought about meeting him wearing a wire and turning him in. "No," she said, shaking her head. "He's a cop. I'm Asian. I have an accent. I run a massage parlor. I'd lose."

7

Licensed gangsters

"Sometimes the girls do foolish things," Lilly said. She recalled the time a young massage therapist charged $200 to a customer's credit card—$60 for a massage and $140 for a tip—and then charged to it $300 more for an additional tip. The customer authorized the charges, but that wasn't the problem. The problem was that a judge seeing $200 and $300 in successive credit card charges could easily jump to the not unreasonable conclusion that the transaction had involved more than a massage.

Lilly fired her on the spot. The young woman stormed out of the spa and into the parking lot, where she threw a tantrum. She screamed that Lilly had beaten her. Onlookers called the police. When police arrived, Lilly explained what had gone on. They believed her, ordered the young woman to leave, and filed no charges.

All was well, or so Lilly thought, until a new customer arrived at the spa a few days later. A young massage therapist whom I'll call May showed him to a private room and left so that he could undress, lie face-down on the massage table, and place a towel over his butt as the law requires. A few minutes later, May knocked, entered the room, and commenced working on his back. At some point the man offered her $40 for a hand job. May refused. A little at a time, he increased the offer until it reached $200. May still refused.

Some guys give off a vibe. Maybe they're creepy, maybe they have bad hygiene, maybe there's a hint of underlying violence waiting for expression, maybe they seem police officer-ish, or maybe the therapist just doesn't want to give extras. No matter. The vibe is not to be ignored. Whatever her reason, May said no to the hand job. Not one for subtlety, the customer started masturbating and asked her to watch. Inventing an excuse, May told him that her boss would finish his massage. "I tell the girls if a customer gets pushy," Lilly said, "come get me and I'll get rid of him." As May started to leave, the man stuffed $100 into her hand. Then he produced a badge and told her she was under arrest for accepting cash in exchange for a promised hand job.

A backup officer who had been waiting outside the spa joined him. The two cops searched Lilly's purse and found $400. Then they searched May's purse and found $13,000. Dividing the $400 between themselves and seizing the larger sum for evidence, they arrested Lilly and May on suspicion of prostitution and money laundering.

In court, May maintained that she had not agreed to a hand job. The prosecuting attorney claimed that May's "accepting" the $100 tip constituted an agreement to provide sexual services and that the $13,000 was evidence of money laundering. He made no mention of the $400, quite possibly because the police officers had somehow neglected to tell him they'd stolen it. May, who didn't have a bank account, claimed she had saved the $13,000 for a down payment on a home. There is no crime in storing a substantial amount of cash in a purse, so in the end there was no conviction. The $13,000 was returned to May and the women left the courtroom, badly shaken.

Lilly's $400 was not returned. She told the judge about the theft, but to no avail. The judge took the word of his trusted cops, who swore they hadn't taken and divided her money. That is, if there had been any money to take and divide, which they swore there wasn't.

"Police are worse than gangsters," Lilly said. "In China, when the police bust up illegal gambling, they take the money first, then call in backup and make arrests. It feels the same here. Police are licensed gangsters. Put that in your book."

8

The rapist

One night as Lilly tidied up the lobby after closing, a man stepped up to the locked front door and knocked. Apologizing for arriving after 10 p.m., he explained that he had just gotten off work and really, *really* needed a massage. Waving a wad of cash, he promised a huge tip.

Alone in the shop, a tired Lilly wanted only to close and go home. But the man persisted. His shoulder and back were sore, he said, wincing pathetically as he rubbed his left shoulder with his right hand. Lilly, who had entered the massage business to help people, decided to accommodate him. She unlocked the door, let him in, locked the door behind him, and showed him to a private room with a massage table. "Take off your clothes, lie facedown on the table," she told him. "Cover up with the towel. I'll come back."

After allowing the man a few minutes to undress and settle in, Lilly knocked gently on the door. The man called out that he was ready. She entered and found he had done as he was told, except for the part about covering up with the towel. That much wasn't unusual. It's part of the cat-and-mouse ritual.

"Shoulders and back, right?" Lilly said, working his left shoulder with her strong fingers. On second thought, the man said, never mind the shoulders and back. They weren't sore after all. Instead of a massage, he wanted Lilly to undress.

She told him to leave. Stepping off the massage table, he shrugged, made as if he were about to leave—and then grabbed her and heaved her on the massage table. He tore at her dress and pulled at her panties. Lilly fought back with sharp nails and well-placed kicks until he gave up. Vaulting to her feet, Lilly ordered him out.

The vanquished man ranted. "I'm a cop," he bellowed. "I'm going to bust you for this."

Lilly was pretty sure that he was no cop.

"I mean it," he blustered as Lilly led him to the front door. "I'm going to drag your ass to jail."

She unlocked the door and told him to go.

"I won't report you if you suck my dick," he said.

Now fearless with rage, Lilly didn't just shove him out the door. She followed him to his car. Pulling out her smartphone, she snapped a photo of his car, taking care to capture the license plate.

"Don't come here again," she told him. "I can find you and send people."

He never returned.

The next day, Lilly drove to The Home Depot and bought two-inch diameter wooden dowels. Returning to the spa, she hid one under each massage table. Calling together her young therapists, she recounted to them her experience from the night before. "That happens to you," she said, "you use this stick on him."

9

Was I interviewing a trafficker?

Trafficking is famously associated with Asian massage parlors. I couldn't help but wonder how much trafficking goes on in the Salt Lake City area, whether Lilly and other owners I interviewed were engaged it, and whether the workers I interviewed were victims.

Anti-slavery group Polaris places the number of AMPs in the United States at 9,000. It estimates that in the United States alone, the illegal trafficking of Asian women to work in massage parlors—and perform sexual services—is a $2.5 billion business. Their information

> comes from published sources, intensive interviews with survivors of human trafficking, law enforcement, and service providers as well as from Polaris's historic work in the field and analysis of cases reported to the National Human Trafficking Hotline (NHTH).[8]

The trafficking process begins with recruiters dangling promises of lucrative overseas work in front of women looking to better their lives. Should the women ask what sort of work they're signing up to do, recruiters evade or lie. Only upon arriving on foreign soil do recruits learn that they will be working in a massage parlor and will be expected to provide extras and work an unreasonable amount of hours. If they're paid at all, they likely earn less than minimum wage. They are threatened with arrest, deportation, or shame before their families if they quit.[9]

Polaris reports that most trafficked women are:

- Recently arrived from China or South Korea
- Under extreme financial pressure
- Speak little or no English
- Have no more than a high school education
- Mothers in their mid-30s to late 50s.[10]

The "extreme financial" pressure often appears in the form of debts the recruit has allegedly and unwittingly racked up. She learns that she owes the recruiter for her travel expenses. She learns that she owes rent to the AMP owner for putting her up in an apartment or letting her sleep at the spa. To meet her obligations, she has little choice but to do what it takes to bring in the biggest tips, namely, provide sexual services. Depending on the spa, a hand job may be the least of the services she will be pressured to provide.

Walking out is easier said than done. The recruit may be threatened with personal harm. She may have been brought into the country illegally. If she has a green card or passport, the AMP owner may keep it locked away. Either way, she fears arrest. She most likely knows only a handful of words and phrases in the language of her new country. There's even a good chance that she doesn't know that what is happening to her is illegal.[11]

I asked Lilly how she finds her workers. She explained that agencies recruit the "girls," arrange their travel to the United States from China, help them obtain licensing, and place them in spas. She maintains that the operation is legal and legit, that the girls opt in voluntarily, and that they are free to leave or take time off when they want. Some may have entered the profession under pressure from home, but neither the agency nor Lilly forced them to work or misrepresented to them the work they would be doing upon reaching the United States.

Would Lilly put me in touch with an agency so I could interview them? "They won't talk to you," she said. Not a good sign.

I resolved to look for signs of trafficking. Here's a summary from a list that Polaris publishes on its website:[12]

- Prices significantly below market level (e.g., $40 for a one-hour massage in a city where $80 is the norm)

- Women report that they need a large tip (e.g., for expenses, food, family), sometimes even expressing distress if they do not receive a tip

- Women typically work excessive hours or are on call at all times
- Women appear to be living in the business or in a trafficker-controlled secondary site (e.g., apartment, house)
- Serves primarily or only male clientele
- Locked front door; customers can only enter if buzzed in, or through back or side doors that are more discreet
- Regular rotation of women; new women coming in every several weeks
- Advertising on commercial sex websites like Rubmaps.com, Backpage.com, or aampmaps.com
- Is not free to leave or come and go at will
- Is under 18 and is providing commercial sex acts
- Is unpaid, paid very little, or paid only through tips
- Owes a large debt and is unable to pay it off
- Was recruited through false promises concerning the nature and conditions of his/her work
- High-security measures exist in the work and/or living locations (e.g., opaque windows, boarded up windows, bars on windows, barbed wire, security cameras, etc.)
- Experiences verbal or physical abuse by their supervisor
- Is forced to meet daily quotas
- Is fearful, anxious, depressed, submissive, tense, or nervous/paranoid
- Exhibits unusually fearful or anxious behavior after bringing up law enforcement or immigration officials
- Shows signs of substance use or addiction
- Shows signs of poor hygiene, malnourishment, and/or fatigue
- Shows signs of physical and/or sexual abuse, physical restraint, con-

finement, or torture

- Is not in control of their own money, financial records, or bank account

- Is not in control of their own identification documents (ID or passport)

- Is not allowed or able to speak for themselves (a third party may insist on being present and/or translating)

- Claims of just visiting and inability to clarify where they are staying/address

- Lack of knowledge of whereabouts and/or do not know what city he/she is in

- Appears to have lost sense of time

- Shares scripted, confusing, or inconsistent stories

- Protects the person who may be hurting them or minimizes abuse

I encountered two Salt Lake AMPs that deserved checkmarks next to a good number of the above-listed warning signs. The first showed no business name, displayed no licenses, and posted no hours. In a darkened front room, two men lazed on couches in front of a TV, sipping hard liquor. Looking up from the TV, one of the men asked, "Hour or half-hour?" Without waiting for me to say, "Um, no, I'd like to do an interview," he called out in a language I couldn't identify. Three glassy-eyed, not-very-covered-up young Asian women hurried into the room. Legitimate massage facilities, Asian or otherwise, assign therapists to walk-in customers on a rotation basis, but here customers were invited to take their pick. It seemed less like a massage business and more like a Nevada-style brothel where a madam summons a lineup. I had my doubts that the young women were 18 years old.

Intuition can mislead, but there are times when listening to it is the best if not the only option.[13] This was one of those times. Not bothering to open my padfolio much less bring up the possibility of an interview, I got the hell out of there. The place simply looked and felt creepy, a far cry from the spas where I'd lingered long enough to conduct an interview. I thought about reporting the place, but then, what, exactly, would I report? I had witnessed nothing that I could affirm was illegal. A few weeks later, police raided the place and booked the men on trafficking charges. And, yes, the young women working there were underage.

I had an eerily similar encounter with the second, which also was subsequently raided and similarly charged. From details reported in the news, I'd say rightly so. I am grateful for the sake of the victims that the raids took place, and grateful for my sake that they didn't take place when I was visiting. Though there's nothing illegal about standing in a lobby while holding a padfolio and looking ill at ease, there are better ways to make a positive first impression on a vice squad.

The other Salt Lake area AMPs I visited struck a sharp contrast. Their front rooms were well lit, and most were tastefully appointed. Hours were posted. Licenses hung on the walls. The women were not summoned to a lineup. They remain open and have not been raided. This is true even for spas where individual therapists have been busted for offering extras. Either these AMPs are not involved in trafficking, or undercover operations have yet to prove that they are.

With help from Google Translate,[14] I was able to question a number of AMP workers in hopes of getting a handle on how their situations stack up against Polaris's list. Here's an excerpt from the transcript of a Google Translate conversation with a therapist who came to the United States seeking political asylum:

> ME: When you came to the United States, did you want to be a masseuse?
>
> MASSAGE THERAPIST: No. I want to come to the United States to teach Chinese children Chinese, but I have not found a job. I was too tired to work at a restaurant, and I still have less salary. There is no way to change jobs in order to earn money.

ME: I asked because I heard that sometimes Chinese women come here to do different jobs and are forced to become masseuses. Then they can't leave.

MASSAGE THERAPIST: Why can't they leave? This is my choice.

ME: Good.

MASSAGE THERAPIST: I can leave.

The workers I spoke with said they were not tricked into the business and appeared baffled at the notion of coercion or entrapment. They entered the trade willingly, and were soon astonished at the money they could make in tips if they provided extras. Some came to the United States to work as massage therapists, while some came to teach, open a restaurant, work in a nail salon, or simply look for work. I spoke with two who entered the United States seeking political asylum.

Tips ranging from $40 to $200 for extras are not unusual. Of the workers who admitted to providing extras, most claimed to limit extras to hand jobs. Many send money home to children, aging parents, or both. And not a few spend the money on themselves. I met five therapists who owned their own vehicles. Four drove luxury SUVs. The fifth drove a Subaru wagon.

Some AMP therapists found menial work upon arriving in the United States and switched to the massage business once they saw its income potential. Most in Salt Lake had worked in massage parlors in other cities, usually New York or Los Angeles, before choosing to locate here, where they'd heard that people are nicer. They tended to agree with that assertion, but those who had worked in Southern California also tended not to be terribly fond of Salt Lake's winters.

AMP workers who provide hand jobs aren't necessarily eager to do so. Nina, for instance, is college educated. Forty-five years old, petite, and five-foot-two, she taught Chinese, physics, and math, all at the high school level in China. Divorced, indebted, and supporting her aging parents, she came to the United States in hopes of earning more money, faster. Reality dashed her dreams almost as soon as she arrived. With her limited English, her professional skills were of no use. She took a job as a server in a Chinese restaurant, but it paid poorly. Having heard she could make good money in the massage business, she obtained a massage license, yet her earnings were paltry until a coworker let her in on happy endings as the secret to making good money. The coworker demonstrated the technique for Nina on a client who was more than pleased to offer his apparatus for practice. "I'm a teacher, but my English is no good so I can't teach here," Nina told me, unhappiness evident in her voice. "I give a good massage. I don't like this," she said, pantomiming a hand job, "but that's how you make money. I cried for three months. Then my boss said stop crying because it makes me look scary to customers." She still prefers not to do hand jobs and avoids offering them, but gives in when a customer requests and persists.

Alicia, who owns an AMP in downtown Salt Lake City, fell into the massage business through happenstance. She is 56 years old. Eager to move to the United States and obtain a green card, she paid a man living in the northwestern United States $20,000 to marry her.[15] That was four years ago. My surprise at the amount must have showed, for she quickly added, "I know. It was a bargain. It's usually $50,000." They divorced shortly after she obtained her green card. In the meantime, she had loaned a considerable amount of money to a friend who owned an AMP in Salt Lake. Strapped, the friend offered the AMP as payment in full, which Alicia accepted. That was how Alicia came to Salt Lake City and became an AMP owner.

The fact that Alicia could afford a $20,000 marriage deal—and drove a brand-new Lexus SUV—suggested to me that she was far from destitute when she arrived in the United States. She confirmed as much, adding that she owns several homes in other states. For her, the massage business is not a trap but a cash cow. Her plan is to sock away as much from it as she can for another three years and then retire.

It is true that Utah AMP owners exercise a good deal of control—perhaps undue control—over workers' lives. Their therapists work from opening till closing time, usually 10 a.m. to 10 p.m., seven days a week, during which time they're not to leave the premises. Most live in and share rent for an apartment owned by or leased to the boss. Workers who live on their own seem to be the exception.[16]

AMP workers, strippers, and Nevada brothel workers are contractors, not employees: they are neither salaried nor paid by the hour. AMP workers generally receive 50 percent of the $60 or $65 house fee and keep 100 percent of their tips. The arrangement obviously favors owners, freeing them from paying minimum wage, paying overtime, managing payroll and withholdings, and observing equal employment laws.

A former employer myself, I'm aware of IRS rules for designating workers as contractors versus employees.[17] I decided to quiz my CPA about it. His considered, professional opinion was that AMP therapists, strippers, and brothel workers qualify for employee status. I asked, "So how do these businesses get away with calling them contractors?" His considered, professional answer was, "I don't know," and he said I could quote him. My further research suggested that, while federal and local governments initiate some audits, more often investigations are prompted when workers complain or former workers file for benefits. Neither is likely in the case of immigrant AMP workers, since most are probably not familiar with U.S. labor laws and not apt to file for benefits.[18]

But are AMP workers trapped? The workers I met took hours off for shopping and days or weeks off for travel, often to visit family in another U.S. city or in China, willingly returning to work. They were free to quit, free to leave one spa for another under separate ownership, and free to move away from Utah. They are arguably "trapped" in the sense that there is little else they can do to make like amounts of money in the United States. But then, golden handcuffs are not unique to AMPs.

I allowed two Asian massage therapists to stay in one of my spare bedrooms for a few days on separate occasions when they were looking to change spas. Nina was one of them. By this time I had paid and tipped for more than my share of massages-turned-interview, so this was a welcome, low-cost opportunity for more conversation. Both explained that they wanted to switch spas because the one they worked for wasn't busy enough. One moved to a spa in Los Angeles. The other tried various Salt Lake locations before moving to a spa in Sacramento. Both owned cars. From our conversations, it was clear that they had control over where they worked. Neither sought to leave the massage business, but neither liked it, either. To them, massage was no more nor less than their best option for earning money given their limited English. Most notably, neither was working through an agency. They sought out and connected with spas on their own.

I met two nonowner therapists who are naturalized U.S. citizens, own homes, and are raising children in Utah (and two others who have applied for citizenship). Like many, they were divorced, had few career options, and had worked as restaurant servers. They eventually sought work in Asian massage parlors for the money. As citizens with their own homes and cars, they have more liberty than their peers. They still work daily 12-hour shifts, but they sleep at home and take time off as they please. They provide happy endings, allow touching, and make a good living at it.

As far as I could determine, no therapist I met was *required* to provide hand jobs or other extras. To be sure, owners turn a blind eye to hand jobs. Extras are a sure route to generous tips for workers and to repeat business for owners. Yet plausible deniability matters to owners. They make it emphatically clear that workers will be fired if they're caught doing hand jobs. It is no idle threat: workers who did hand jobs implored me not to tell the boss. It seemed understood that hand jobs will be offered, but it's equally understood that the owner must not *officially* know.

The chart below lists my observations alongside Polaris's warning signs. It's important to keep in mind that by no means did I conduct an investigation or anything that would remotely qualify as one. We're talking first impressions from one-hour encounters—when owners and workers would present themselves at their best—and information I picked up from review sites.

Signs of Trafficking per Polaris	My Observations
Prices significantly below market level (e.g., $40 for a one-hour massage in a city where $80 is the norm)	Salt Lake AMPS charge $60 or $65 for a one-hour massage, which is in line with what other massage businesses charge.
Women report that they need a large tip (e.g., for expenses, food, family), sometimes even expressing distress if they do not receive a tip	Workers freely talked about tips, but "need," "distress," and coercion did not come up.
Women working excessive hours or being on call at all times	Hours are typically 10 a.m.–10 p.m. Workers were not available outside of those hours.
Women appear to be living in the business or in a trafficker-controlled secondary site (e.g., apartment, house)	Most of the AMP workers I met lived in an apartment owned by or leased to the spa owner, splitting the rent among themselves. A few maintained their own apartments, and two owned homes. I saw no evidence of workers living in a spa, but then, I wasn't shown to the back. Lilly, who maintains an apartment for her workers, said she has "permitted" workers who prefer not to pay rent to sleep in the spa.
Serves primarily or only male clientele	Primarily male clientele.
Locked front door; customers can only enter if buzzed in, or through back or side doors that are more discreet	One of the creepy spas I described had a darkened entrance that faced away from the main street. Other spas (including the other creepy one) had prominent, well-lit front doors. A few had a back door as well. None had locked doors with buzzers, which are common AMP features in other cities.

Signs of Trafficking per Polaris	My Observations
Regular rotation of women; new women coming in every several weeks	Some spas indeed seemed to have a revolving door. I know that at least some workers, as indicated, have a say as to where they are placed. I also met therapists who have worked in the same spa for months and in some cases years. Some moved from spa to spa, job-hopper style, of their own volition. (One worker told me, "This spa isn't busy enough. I'm thinking of quitting here and going to another one.")
Advertising on commercial sex websites like Rubmaps.com, Back-page.com, or aampmaps.com	Yes, most advertised and/or had online reviews.
Is not free to leave or come and go at will	Workers routinely request and are allowed hours, days, or even weeks off.
Is under 18 and is providing commercial sex acts	With the exception of the two creepy spas, I encountered no one under the age of 25. Most were in their 30s, 40s, and 50s. "Commercial sex acts"—in the form of hand jobs only—were on the menu for many but not all.
Is unpaid, paid very little, or paid only through tips	Workers receive 50 percent of the $60–65 massage fee and keep 100 percent of tips.
Owes a large debt and is unable to pay it off	Workers whom I asked directly and indirectly about this reported not being in debt to their spa owner or placement agency. Some told me they have legitimate debts such as car loans.
Was recruited through false promises concerning the nature and conditions of his/her work	Every worker I spoke with said she had opted into the business.

Signs of Trafficking per Polaris	My Observations
High-security measures exist in the work and/or living locations (e.g., opaque windows, boarded up windows, bars on windows, barbed wire, security cameras, etc.)	No barred windows, barbed wire, or boarded-up windows. I disagree that opaque windows is a sign of trafficking, as most massage businesses cover their windows. Most have a security camera in the entryway, but this too is not unusual for any business, not just massage spas. (My business has one.)
Experiences verbal or physical abuse by their supervisor	Not that I'm aware of.
Is forced to meet daily quotas	Not that I'm aware of.
Is fearful, anxious, depressed, submissive, tense, or nervous/paranoid	Not that I'm aware of.
Exhibits unusually fearful or anxious behavior after bringing up law enforcement or immigration officials	Not that I'm aware of.
Shows signs of substance use or addiction	Not that I'm aware of.
Shows signs of poor hygiene, malnourishment, and/or fatigue	Good hygiene seemed to be the rule.
Shows signs of physical and/or sexual abuse, physical restraint, confinement, or torture	Not that I'm aware of.
Is not in control of their own money, financial records, or bank account	The women I met controlled their own money.
Is not in control of their own identification documents (ID or passport)	Unknown overall, however, three workers carried and showed me their driver's licenses.
Is not allowed or able to speak for themselves (a third party may insist on being present and/or translating)	Not that I'm aware of.

Signs of Trafficking per Polaris	My Observations
Claims of just visiting and inability to clarify where they are staying/address	Not that I'm aware of.
Lack of knowledge of whereabouts and/or do not know what city he/she is in	Not that I'm aware of.
Appear to have lost sense of time	Not that I'm aware of.
Shares scripted, confusing, or inconsistent stories	Not that I'm aware of.
Protects the person who may be hurting them or minimizes abuse	Not that I'm aware of.

So, was I interviewing a trafficker? I don't think so. The individual therapists I interviewed, as far as I could tell, were not trafficked.

But then, like anyone, I can be fooled. There is no easier mark for the skillful liar than someone who "cannot be fooled." As Mark Twain put it, "It's easier to fool people than to convince them that they have been fooled."

Speaking of being fooled, there's no record of Twain's having said or penned that.[19]

10

Spurious claims of trafficking

I'm about to challenge some—*some*—of what we see and hear in the media on the subject of trafficking. Before I do, permit me to go on the record as acknowledging the existence of and speaking out against human trafficking in all of its forms.

Yet even Polaris concedes that not all AMPs are trafficking operations. A Salt Lake area police detective who asked not to be identified confirmed as much to me. His off-the-cuff estimate was that as many as one-third of local AMPs do not engage in trafficking. From my own not terribly deep dive, I would say that *most* AMPs in the Salt Lake City environs do not.

Confusion over the meaning of *trafficking* doesn't help. The mention of sex trafficking conjures up visions of Liam Neeson's character's daughter in the movie *Taken*: minors and adults who are kidnapped, transported to a new location, and forced into prostitution. "Sex trafficking is not just prostitution, which is engaging in sex with someone for payment," according to the *Brigham Young University Journal of Public Law*, "but is the enslavement of unwilling people who are coerced into a condition for sexual exploitation."[20]

Yet United States Code gives sex trafficking a much broader definition, making it more or less a synonym for prostitution:

> The term "sex trafficking" means the recruitment, harboring, transportation, provision, obtaining, patronizing, or soliciting of a person for the purpose of a commercial sex act.[21]

Federal law also stipulates that anyone under the age of 18 who provides sex for pay is "a victim of a severe form of trafficking in persons," coercion or no coercion.[22]

The sweeping federal definition lets law enforcement, crusaders, and the news media get away with invoking *trafficking* with every prostitution bust without regard for—or perhaps motivated by—how the term lands with everyday people. Besides the type of kidnapper portrayed in *Taken*, a drug-addict who pays for his habit by suggesting his girlfriend enter into prostitution is a trafficker; so is a pimp who recruits women of any age; so is anyone who drives a provider to an appointment; and, in fact, *so is anyone who pays or offers to pay for sex.* A john who pays for sex with someone a day shy of 18 years old, knowingly or unknowingly and even if she is a willing participant, is a "severe" trafficker.

Lumping all of the above practices under "sex trafficking," though legally legitimate, creates a false impression. Every time the media reports a bust as "potentially connected with trafficking," it's easy to imagine a large-scale *Taken*-esque operation. The majority of those busts are nothing of the sort. The media, law enforcement, and the justice system do not appear eager to distinguish one form of trafficking from another. Certainly that's due in part to the fact that allowing the T-word to conjure the most horrifying picture possible serves more than a few interests. Invoking the T-word preempts criticism in the form of "Why are police wasting valuable resources busting harmless women instead of going after violent street crime?" Brandishing the T-word positions crackdowns on prostitution as rescue operations and makes damsel-rescuing knights of vice cops.

Take, for instance, a reportedly "large-scale human trafficking sting" carried out in November 2019 in Utah County. The accused, unaware that they had been online with police officers, allegedly thought they had arranged and were showing up for sexual encounters with minors. Heinous as that is, *intent to commit statutory rape* might seem a more apt term than *trafficking*, since neither coercion nor payment was involved and—since this was a sting—*no one had actually been trafficked*. Utah County Sheriff's Sgt. Spencer Cannon appeared to have chosen his words carefully in order to bring trafficking charges: the men, he said, were acting in "the role of a pimp." Meanwhile, participating law enforcement agencies surely basked in headlines like, "26 Suspects Arrested in 3-day Human Trafficking Sting in Utah County."[23] Readers could be forgiven for picturing caravans pouring into town with hordes of women in shackles.

Outside of law enforcement, organizations whose raison d'être is to combat prostitution also find the T-word useful. Linking trafficking to all forms of prostitution motivates government and the public to support their cause with kudos and funding. It makes a target for shaming of anyone who suggests the existence of opt-in sex workers who enjoy what they do.

According to Lilly, massage parlor owners work under constant threat of being charged with trafficking, deserved or not. Police have been known to spend up to eight months investigating an AMP, she said.

The goal is to build a case one massage therapist at a time. That surprised me. Why not bust the therapist the moment she agrees to a hand job and be done with it? "Because," Lilly explained, "they don't want the girls. They want the owner."

Here is Lilly's account of how law enforcement may go about implicating where implication may not be due. A young massage therapist who offers an undercover cop a happy ending, Lilly explained, is small pickings. If police can nail the owner, they can close the spa and send a message to other owners. The process, she said, is to haul the terrified young therapist to jail. The rapid-fire questions and accusations, which with her limited English she cannot follow, only deepen her terror. But suddenly there's a ray of hope. She learns that they'll let her off with only a wrist-slap—this time—if she cooperates. The terrified young woman need only change *I work twelve-hour shifts* to *my boss forces me to work twelve-hour shifts against my will.* She need only change *my boss lets me stay at the spa* to *my boss doesn't let me leave the spa.* And how does your boss exercise this control over you? *I . . . I don't know . . .* Is it because you owe her money and she won't let you leave until you pay it back? *Yes, it's what you said.* Do you do hand jobs? *No.* Your boss makes you do hand jobs, right? *She makes me do hand jobs.*

I want to be clear: Trafficking *is* real. I neither claim nor wish even to imply that all reports of trafficking are unwarranted, or that the situation Lilly described goes on with the detention of all or even most massage therapists. Utah law enforcement agencies have raided and shut down bona fide, beyond-question trafficking operations and, in the process, rescued and aided bona fide, beyond-question trafficked women, minors, and, to a lesser extent, men. But it's nonetheless important to acknowledge that police have incentives to invoke the T-word without waiting to find out if its use is warranted.[24] "We may have broken up a major trafficking operation" are magic words that make heroes of cops and stave off accusations of wasting precious resources on victimless crimes.

Some Salt Lake area police departments invite the local news media to accompany them on stings and raids. Footage of police hauling handcuffed men out of massage parlors draws large audiences and increases advertising revenues. And law enforcement agencies seize the opportunity to use the T-word on camera.

The officially expressed goal behind publicizing busts is to scare men away from seeking extras in AMPs. There is evidence that it does, though the effect is usually only temporary. I am aware of one instance in which news coverage *increased* an AMP's business. When an undercover cop arrested a woman in a downtown Salt Lake AMP for offering sexual services, several local news media published her name, mug shot, and the name of the spa. Almost immediately, new clients began calling the spa, requesting her by name—not the American name she used for work, but her real Chinese name, which they could only have obtained from news reports. I spoke with her a year after the arrest. New requests for her by name were still pouring in. She hated having a record but admitted that the "publicity" she'd received from her arrest had significantly increased her earnings.

I later ran Lilly's and other AMP workers' comments along with my own observations by former Salt Lake County Sheriff Jim Winder.[25] He would have none of it. He suggested that Lilly was either "lying or delusional," and that if the workers I'd spoken with were not there against their will, they were exceptions.

Winder's experience is not to be dismissed lightly. But it's important to consider that illicit spas inevitably come to the attention of police officers more often than licit ones do, which will inevitably bias their view.[26] And Winder seemed to confirm that *Taken*-esque trafficking in Salt Lake differs from what the media convey. "When I was sheriff," he said, "we created a human trafficking detection machine. We'd arrest prostitutes in local motels, try to gain their confidence, and offer them protection to get out. We dealt almost exclusively with drug-addicted females drafted by a boyfriend, a brother, parents, or other family members. The view that we're talking about women trafficked from Asia or Russia is bullshit. The typical local trafficked prostitute lives here. Imports are rare."

11

Swan song for a texter

"It's scary," Lilly said. "I have helped a lot of girls in their twenties who want to come to the U.S. by giving them work and letting them stay at the spa. They need the money and they want to work, not be on welfare. They send money home to support a family, some of them. We come here, we work hard, and we stay off welfare. And the cops want to put us in jail for a hand job."

We sat silent for a moment. "What's wrong with happy endings?" Lilly mused. "Men have needs. They come here, we take care of them. Then they go home to their families, they stay with their families. Happy endings save a lot of families."

Our lunch and interview concluded, I took care of the check and we stood to go our separate ways. We shook hands as I thanked her for the interview. "Just a sec," she said. Her phone was buzzing again.

Digging the phone from her purse, Lilly laughed and showed me the text. The man who had texted at the outset of our lunch had just increased his bid for a hand job to $700. Evidently, the deeper meaning of Lilly's *hahaha* was lost on him.

"I'm not going to see him," Lilly said, putting the phone back in her purse.

Interlude

Busted Mormons and Fuzzy Lines

Do what you (and everyone else) does when it comes to church advice, counsel, policy and commandments that are disagreeable. Pretend they don't apply to you.

—*Salt Lake Tribune* columnist Robert Kirby

1

A Utah provider outs a Utah politician

On February 6, 2018, Republican John Stanard[1] resigned from the Utah House of Representatives to spend time, he explained, with his terminally ill father. Friends, colleagues, and constituents expressed understanding and sympathy.[2]

Two days later, the British tabloid *Daily Mail* ran an exclusive story with this opener:

> A married Republican lawmaker who voted for stricter laws against prostitution has abruptly resigned after an escort claims he met her twice for sex. Call girl Brie Taylor claims John E. Stanard paid her for sex during two business trips to Salt Lake City, Utah, in 2017.[3]

If you're at all familiar with the *Mail*, you will not be surprised to learn that the story featured full-color photos of a buxom, lingerie-clad Taylor. If you didn't know better, you might think the *Mail* was exploiting her sexy photos to sell papers.

For Stanard, there was no denying the allegations. Taylor produced damning text exchanges she'd had with Stanard, the latter's phone number in plain sight. In a show of surprising naïveté for a public figure, Stanard had used his personal cell phone to contact Brown and set up their encounters.

Lucky for Stanard, not too many people in Utah read British tabloids. Unlucky for Stanard, even Utah has the Internet. The story found its way across the ocean in minutes, where Utah's local news media lost no time in picking it up. This included the Mormon Church–owned daily newspaper *Deseret News*.[4] That's really something, because the *News* tends to shrink from stories involving sex, not least because running them might mean having to print the word "sex." Unlike the *Daily Mail*, the *Deseret News* omitted Brown's alluring photos.

The part about Stanard's ailing father was true. He had terminal cancer. Still, the impending *Daily Mail* story surely helped Stanard with his decision to resign. I am reasonably sure he knew the story was about to break. His first clue might have been the *Mail's* contacting him for comments.

A longstanding sexual services provider with pages of online reviews, Taylor understood the importance of screening. Well before Stanard showed up at the Salt Lake hotel room she had rented to entertain clients that day, Taylor had googled his phone number. She knew his name and that he was a state representative. She told the *Mail*, "I was surprised that he was using his real phone number. I thought that was kind of stupid but I knew he wasn't a psycho so I met him."

Taylor described Stanard as a "nice gentleman." When he arrived, she offered him a libation, not an unusual courtesy for providers to extend. Stanard declined. He was a practicing Mormon visiting Salt Lake City as a representative from St. George, Utah, and good Mormons don't drink alcohol. Not drinking alcohol is so strong a part of Mormon culture that many a Mormon man sneaking off to a strip club makes damn sure to order only soft drinks. This is not a little ironic, given that while Mormon doctrine holds that God is not keen on booze, it holds that he is even less keen on sexual acting out.

It was after their second meeting that Taylor learned that Stanard had made a name for himself in the Utah House of Representatives as one of the most vocal champions of "traditional marriage" and "family values." If you missed the speeches where he said so, you could have logged on to his website and read them for yourself. Could have. For some unfathomable reason, Stanard deleted the website shortly after the news story broke. In any case, it said, "I am a strong advocate for conservative family values. I am pro-life, as well as for traditional marriage."[5]

Stanard's public record certainly said as much. He was known for doggedly pursuing and helping to pass increasingly tough penalties for prostitutes and johns. In this case, "johns" means "people caught doing what Stanard was secretly doing." He voted for a bill that took soliciting a prostitute from a Class B to a Class A misdemeanor. He supported a resolution declaring pornography a public health crisis. He helped ease evidence requirements for arresting and convicting prostitutes and johns. He voted for increasing the fine for soliciting sex from $300 to $2,500.

Call her a stickler, but when Taylor saw the vengeance with which Stanard went after people like her—and like his own secret self—it struck her as a tad hypocritical. "I was surprised when I found out that he voted in favor of stricter laws," the *Daily Mail* quoted her as saying. "It is hypocritical because he is supporting laws that make it stricter for other men who do what he does."

So she contacted the *Mail* and outed him.

I don't know why Taylor contacted a UK tabloid instead of any of a number of Salt Lake City news media, but I can guess. The *Mail* actively solicits first-hand salacious stories, especially from women 30 and older, a description Taylor happens to fit. Oh, and lest I forget to mention, the *Mail* pays for such stories.[6] Now, I cannot say with certainty that the *Dai-*

ly Mail paid Taylor. When asked about that, the *Mail* reporter who wrote the story replied, "I don't really see how that's relevant." So, officially, your guess is as good as mine. Unofficially, "I don't really see how that's relevant" sounds a lot like what you'd say when you want to avoid lying by saying "No" but would rather not tell the truth by saying "Yes."

Providers take confidentiality seriously. "It's part of what the client pays for," Tina told me. "It's included in the price." Every provider I spoke with echoed the sentiment. Which is why what followed Stanard's exposure was not just a media feeding frenzy but also a good deal of animated online discussion among providers and hobbyists.

In a matter of hours, Taylor's outing of Stanard became a hot topic in online provider-client forums. Within two weeks, one post on the subject garnered 3,354 hits and 126 comments. I tallied the comments. For every one that praised Taylor's action, two condemned it. No one disagreed that "the hypocritical SOB" deserved to be exposed; disagreement was found only in whether it was right for a provider to have done the exposing. Comments ranged from "He's an asshat but that doesn't mean his confidentiality should be violated" to "I say she's a damn fine whistle blower, a patriot and an American hero."

I don't condemn Taylor, but I lean toward viewing her exposure of Stanard as an unfortunate if not outright wrong move. I might lean less in that direction if I thought his exposure had made a positive difference. It did not. All that Taylor accomplished was the punishment of one man for hypocrisy and the infliction of cruel and needless consequences upon his family. It wasn't as if the Utah State Legislature was going to convene a special session to pass the Frank Stanard Memorial Prostitution Decriminalization Act. Odds are legislators chalked up the incident to the devil's having ensnared their poor colleague and steeled their resolve to pass stricter laws for keeping the devil in check. It's equally likely that some legislators resolved to be smarter the next time they set up a rendezvous with a provider.

2

A bishop works the stupidity angle

In a sting operation on Valentine's Day, 2019, police arrested 51-year-old Utah resident David N. Moss on "suspicion of exploiting a prostitute, patronizing a prostitute, two counts of lewdness and sexual battery." Moss had walked into a sting operation after unknowingly soliciting a pair of female undercover police officers posing online as sex workers.

That much wasn't unusual. Prostitution stings and busts aren't exactly rare, even in Utah, but this case made the front page in the local papers and showed up in the national news media. Even *Newsweek* ran the story, giving it nearly 500 words.[7]

More than one factor went into making big news out of what otherwise would have been a routine arrest. First was that Moss was a former St. George, Utah police lieutenant. He had headed the department's vice squad and been forced to resign due to "allegations of sexual misconduct." That lent the story a hypocrisy angle, since he was busted for doing what he used to make a living busting others for doing.

There was also an irony angle. In text and in person, Moss bragged to the undercover officers that, as a former vice cop, he could teach them how to avoid arrest. Indeed, if anyone had known how not to blunder into a sting operation, he should have. "It's kinda cutting edge stuff that go [sic] against the norm," he texted, "but those that use it like it."

Finally, the news story had—and I hope you won't mind my resorting to a technical term here—a stupidity angle. Convinced that he was face-to-face with real providers, Moss grabbed the hand of one of the detectives and placed it on his crotch. Then he unzipped his pants and whipped out his genitals. And that, he explained, is how you make sure you're not dealing with an undercover cop. The undercover officers found him so creepy that they repaired to the restroom to "change into something more comfortable," locked the door, and summoned fellow officers who were waiting outside to haul him away.

Moss had offered to manage the women as prostitutes, claiming to have managed others in the past. "When we work together, I book and you entertain. I offer protection, I train you on how to act so we get repeat/regulars and higher paying," he reportedly texted. After his arrest, Moss claimed that "managing" sex workers was not the same thing as "pimping."[8] The nuance is lost on me.

All of the above made for delicious journalistic sensationalism, but in local gossip circles, another aspect of the case played even bigger. Moss was at the time serving as a Mormon bishop in the city of Lehi, Utah, about 30 miles south of Salt Lake City. To its credit, the church relieved Moss of his bishopric within a day of his arrest. The church spokesman who announced it added, "The behavior alleged in this incident is completely unacceptable and unbecoming of any member of The Church of Jesus Christ of Latter-day Saints, and especially of someone serving in a position of local leadership."[9]

Most local headlines and TV news promos led with the former cop angle, leaving the bishop angle for the body of the story. Not a few critics raised a social media ruckus about that, accusing the media of going easy on the church. Others accused the church of pressuring the media to bury the bishop angle in hopes that people skimming only headlines would overlook it. Nonsense. The Mormon Church wields a good deal of power in Utah, but it doesn't have the power to tell media not owned by the church what to put and not to put in a headline. In a state with over 4,000 bishops and only a handful of vice cops, the vice cop angle was the more newsworthy one.

3

The fuzzy line

It came as no surprise to me that a Mormon state representative and a Mormon former vice cop would pay for sexual services. By the time these particular cases hit the fan—and there have been many more like them—I had conducted enough interviews to know that johns number among every social, business, government, and church position.

But let's be honest. At times we are all hypocrites to one degree or another. Though there may be a difference in scale and potential for harm, each of us has indiscretions, mishaps, shortcomings, or flaws we would prefer not to see featured in the *Daily Mail*. I cannot tell you how grateful I am that no one at the *Mail* knows about the *Playboy* magazine I shoplifted from a grocery store when I was 12. I really don't want that getting out.

Most sex-for-pay forum participants readily admit to hypocrisy. They advocate for the hobby, but only online and only behind aliases. They text providers from burners[10] and use fake names. They meet providers in hotels a good distance from their business and home. They look for massage parlors with rear parking and back doors. When the topic of prostitution comes up, they remain silent instead of raising a hand and saying, "I pay for sex, and I think it's great."

Society demands a certain amount of hypocrisy. We are taught from birth to try to look better than we really are. Most of us know not to admit publicly to enjoying gossip, peeing in the shower, or actually liking marshmallow Peeps. If we led with our shortcomings, most of us would never go on a second date. There is a fuzzy line between hypocrisy and prudence.

A business associate and I were driving together to an appointment when, in what deserves a nomination for Non Sequitur of the Year, he said, "I would never tell my wife if I cheated on her." He considered himself a good Mormon, which all who knew him well considered a stretch.

He had made no secret to his associates of his lust for two particular women, so I interpreted *I would never tell my wife if I cheated on her* to mean either *I'm already cheating on her* or *I'm planning to cheat on her soon*. He continued, "It would hurt my wife deeply. It would break up our family. I think not telling her would be the moral thing to do."

I had plenty of reasons for holding the man in low regard, but this was not one of them. There was something to his reasoning. If we take as givens that he was going to proceed (acknowledging that the obvious alternative would be not to proceed); that he loved and didn't want to lose his wife and children (he said as much and I believed him); that he was capable of having his fun without changing his behavior at home (I'm not so sure he could, but let's go with it for the sake of argument); and that disclosing his activity would have devastated his wife and torn to shreds his family (of a certainty); then not disclosing it made a certain amount of sense. I contented myself with holding him in low regard for ample other reasons.

I don't presume to know enough about anyone's personal life to endorse or condemn sex outside a once agreed-upon exclusive relationship, much less the decision to disclose or keep quiet. Both are conversations to hold with one's conscience. The rest of us need only to stay out of it.

Chapter 7

Male, Once-Mormon Sex Workers

No matter how little virility a man has to offer, prostitutes make
him feel for a time that he is the greatest man in the world.

—Malcolm X

1

Manhunting

The alert reader will have noticed that, to this point, my narrative has focused on straight cisgender females. I had no luck lining up interviews with transgender and other noncisgender providers. Some advertise in Utah, albeit infrequently. Perhaps more visit than live here. I'd also had no luck finding male providers until it occurred to me to return to Tor and search "male escorts" instead of just "escorts." Up popped websites like friendlyboy.pro, mintboys.com, and rent.men. Typing "Salt Lake City" in their respective search boxes yielded pages of beefcakes flexing to impress. And impress they did. I suspect the average bigot would think twice about making homophobic remarks within striking distance.

Scrolling through headlines like "Italian Stud Who Loves to Have a Good Time," "Hung Young Lad," and "Your Jock Next Door," I set about trying to sort real providers from scammers and police decoys. I passed on the beefcakes in favor of men with more believable, everyday looks, awarding extra points for amateur photos. I passed on men who were willing to be flown in but didn't actually live in Salt Lake. In short order, I had a list of male providers who appeared to be local and real.

Since approaching female providers via text had failed spectacularly for me, I decided to test the popular definition of insanity—doing the same thing over and over expecting different results—and sent text messages to the men. I adapted the note I'd sent to the women:

Hi—

I'm wondering if you might have an interest in being interviewed for a book.

I assure you that I'm a published author and on the level—you can verify it by googling me and by visiting my websites. Also I can give you names and numbers of providers who will vouch for me.

The book is about sex work in Utah. It's sympathetic to and told from the provider's viewpoint. To date I have interviewed only female providers; I'd like to balance it out by speaking with a few men. Fwiw I'm straight, and I'm not suggesting anything illegal. Just a conversation, that's all. No one will be outed.

So—any chance you'd be willing to speak in person or by phone?

Interviews usually take 60 minutes or so. The providers I've interviewed have enjoyed being able to share their stories. Some have said it's like therapy.

Any interest? Please email or text me. I'm hoping to hear from you soon.

Two men, both former Mormons, responded within the hour. There's no telling if the quick response was luck of the draw or if male providers are simply more eager to share their experiences. Either way, Kent and Gene could not have been more different in their personalities, stories of coming out, and attitudes about their work as providers.

2

Beginnings: Kent

I interviewed Kent by phone about an hour after he received my text. He assured me the photos in his ad really are of him. He needn't have. One of the reasons I reached out to him was that, in stark contrast to those of his competitors, his photos were obviously not shot by a professional. Handsome and well-built, he stood smiling and shirtless, revealing a tattooed chest. He sported short-cut dark brown hair and fashionable stubble. His write-up had a feel of honesty to it, creating the impression of a friendly, unassuming person.

He came out to himself at eleven but knew better than to come out to his parents. "I come from a well-to-do, strict, very intolerant Mormon family that moved around a lot," Kent said. "They talked about 'fruit-cakes' and 'faggots,' that sort of thing." Unfortunately, he managed to keep his orientation from his parents only for two years. "When I was 13, my father searched my phone and found messages from older men. I got the shit beat out of me. Later that night I tried to commit suicide. I wasn't successful, obviously. I told myself, *I'm 13. I've got to get through these next couple of years living with dad, and I know I'll be okay.* I toughed it out. My father has come around on the gay thing, but we're not on talking terms."

Kent was living with his parents in Arizona when, soon after high school, he decided to move to California. "That's where I got in the business," he said. "It opened Pandora's box. At home, I didn't quite fit in. I was condemned by my LDS[1] family. I was a bit overweight. Away from home I was willing to do anything for acceptance. I got into sex work because of an illegal drug. It was a way to get paid, get paid well, or get free drugs. I got addicted to drugs and to men's attention. Having men pay for your attention, it's almost like a double-edged sword. I was obviously trying to fill a void."

While all sex workers must mentally deal with breaking one of society's biggest taboos, certainly society makes it worse for gay men in the trade, and Mormon society makes it exponentially worse. "My family doesn't know what I do. My friends don't know either. It's very shaming, especially for a man. To be proud of it, it took a long time to get over the guilt and the shame. Especially meeting with married men. I felt like a home-wrecker. I don't ask my clients if they're married and I prefer they don't tell me, because I don't want to know."

Kent found a life partner, but in 2017, an accident took his partner's life and left Kent seriously injured. He quit the sex business and moved back in with his parents, who by this time had relocated to Salt Lake City, while he recovered from his injuries. "A few months later, my dad kicked me out. I have a day job but I don't make a lot of money with it. So in 2018, I got back into the business."

In a follow-up text exchange, I learned that Kent had lost his day job. As of this writing, he is back in the sex trade full-time.

3

Beginnings: Gene

A few days after speaking with Kent, I met Gene for lunch. With my permission and encouragement, he brought along his driver, whom I'll call Stanley, and his friend Rose, a female provider you've already heard from in these pages. That meant I'd be paying for four instead of two lunches. It was worth it, and it was a fraction of what Gene would have charged for a session.

"Coming out to myself was hard," Gene said, after the server had taken our orders. "I didn't want to be gay. I wanted to be straight, marry, and have kids."

In his early thirties, Gene is fit, has short, strawberry blond hair, and has a rugged handsomeness about him. Like Kent, he grew up in a Mormon family that moved around. He went to high school in a town north of Salt Lake City. After that, he graduated magna cum laude from a "top-tier university" and went directly to work as a financial planner in California.

"I couldn't have asked for a better post-ed job," he said. "I did it for a bunch of years, and I was successful at it. I was good at persuading people to entrust their funds to an inexperienced kid. Trouble was, I spent only four hours a day face-to-face with clients and the rest of the day on the computer. If I'd wanted to spend my career staring at a monitor, I'd have been an accountant. I was just coming off a relationship, so I felt cooped up and became depressed. So I quit."

Single and unemployed, Gene returned to Utah for a quick visit. A "weed-related DUI" turned the visit into an extended one. When we met, he was waiting to complete his probation before he would be allowed to leave the state.

The idea of becoming a provider came from a friend already in the business. "I wouldn't feel right taking a real job with a company since I plan to leave when my probation is up. But I was freshly single, gay, and promiscuous, so I thought, *If I'm going to sleep around, I might as well get paid for it.* I was already doing anonymous hookups. The only difference was the money."

Unlike Kent, Gene is open and unabashed when it comes to being a sex worker. "Before I went into it," he said, "I asked friends and family what they thought. They said, 'If I had your youth, build, and looks, I'd do it.' Even my LDS family knows. All they say about it is 'be careful.'" That surprised me. Mormon families are not known for accepting children who come out as gay, much less as gay sex workers.

His first client, who found him online, was his junior by a few years. "I like older men," Gene said, "so it wasn't what I was looking for in a sexual experience." The second warned Gene in advance "that he would be coked out of his mind and wouldn't be able to talk." The man hadn't exaggerated. "All he could manage was a weird, indistinguishable, open-mouth, open-throat noise, and he kept doing it."

Both clients enjoyed their session with Gene and wanted to see him again, but he turned them down. "By then I knew who I wanted and didn't want for clients, and I spelled it out in my ad. I want 45 and older. I won't take younger guys. I like to get acquainted with a client, get a feel for him on the phone or by texting, before agreeing to meet. And I never see two clients in the same day. I think every client deserves my full effort, and I can't give it if I'm tired after seeing someone else."

4

Kent: "It can be very lonely sometimes."

"Do I enjoy it? No," Kent said. "It's just for the income. It can be very lonely sometimes. It's a false sense of connection. Someone's paying you to do these acts."

Kent charges $250 for short encounters, $500 to spend the evening, and $1,000 to stay overnight. "I'm studying to become a lawyer," he said. "I'm not making as much as I'd like. Any little bit helps. There's not enough business here. There was a lot more in California. And there are a lot of no-shows. I think a lot are first-timers and get cold feet at the last minute."

He finds clients online and at popular gay pickup locations. "There are quite a few cruising spots in Salt Lake," he said. "Oxbow Park is notorious. So is Exit 111 off of Interstate 80 on the way to Reno. It's out in the middle of nowhere. You can see guys just parked there, sitting in their cars, waiting to meet someone. There are sex workers there and guys just looking to get off. Sometimes they're paid, sometimes it's just hookups. I make sure I get paid. There's a lot of outdoor sexual activity with men who get off on being watched. If you get caught you can get in a hell of a lot of trouble."

I hadn't heard of either hangout, so I decided to visit them. Oxbow Park is in West Valley City, a Salt Lake suburb. It sits adjacent to the Jordan River Parkway, a paved bike and pedestrian path running alongside a river that the Mormon pioneers named, and you may have seen this coming, the Jordan River.[2] It might have made for the ideal pickup spot if Salt Lake County hadn't built its Oxbow Jail but a half-mile away. According to Kent, police have been cracking down there of late. "One time they came through on horseback," he said. "Scared the hell out of me."

Exit 111 truly is, as Kent said, in the middle of nowhere. Six miles west of the Salt Lake City International Airport, it dumps you onto a stretch of road surrounded by flat, barren desert. Turn right from the exit and in a few hundred feet you'll come to a dead end. Sure enough, there I saw men waiting in their cars, engines idling to keep the air conditioning running, a must under Utah's baking summer sun. Turn left and after a few hundred feet the pavement gives way to a dirt road that no street vehicle with an ounce of self-respect would attempt. There, too, sat men in idling cars. As I drove by, they peered at me and I at them. My interest in doing interviews warred with a hunch that this was not the ideal time or setting. The hunch won. I drove back to the freeway and headed home.

Exit 111's middle-of-nowhere status is about to change. As I write, the State of Utah plans to build its new prison there. With Oxbow Park near a county prison and Exit 111 soon to be near a state prison, it would seem that the gay community hasn't had the best of luck when it comes to choosing pickup sites.

I asked Kent to describe his clients. "Most if not all are LDS," he said. "Married, LDS men. I get ward secretaries, genealogy specialists, first and second counselors, high councilors, young men's presidents, bishops, stake presidency members." How does he know? "They tell me. One of the first things they say when we meet is, 'You can't tell anyone, I'm a bishop and it would ruin me.' Of course I won't tell. I don't want to hurt anyone. A person's privacy is very important. People tell me their life story when they meet me."

He added, "I get a lot of white collar, accountants, bankers, guys who own their own companies, some very, very successful people. Lawyers and doctors are big here. Haven't gotten any politicians. A lot of news anchors. A lot of ethnicities, too, but mostly white guys. Also, big company conventions bring in a lot of men from out of town, especially in summer."

5

Gene: "After someone has had their dick in my mouth they open up."

Gene's attitude about being a provider could not have been more different from Kent's. "Best job I've ever had," he enthused. "It's awesome. I'm
enjoying the experience of meeting people, getting to know them. I have
learned a shitload about people. I have made a lot of friends. Plus I like
to observe human behavior. It intrigues me, how two similar men can
process the same experience differently, have a different reaction. After
someone has had their dick in my mouth they open up. I feel like I'm a
therapist for men dealing with being gay, doing a gay act, cheating on
their wives."

Gene started out charging $150 for a session, but soon raised his
price to $250 and sometimes $350. "One guy in from Miami paid me
$850 for three hours," he said, his astonishment evident. "But I'm in it
as much for the fun as the money. I made a lot as a financial planner, so
I'm financially secure. I can be choosy about who I'll see and how often."

Gene said that most of his clients are businessmen from outside of
Utah. As for local clients, he said, "Half are openly gay and the other half
are latent, married Mormon men."

"Hang on," I said, "I want to write that down."

"Latent, married Mormon men. Make sure you get *latent*."

Continuing, Gene said, "If they're LDS is usually the first question
out of my mouth. When they're LDS it's a big turn-on for me. I have
never done a Mormon bishop. I would love to. That would be a huge
turn-on. I see financial planners, car salesmen, attorneys. Attorneys are
my most frequent, paid and unpaid. I see artists, business owners, some
blue-collar men, warehouse workers, insurance agents."

I asked Gene if police officers numbered among his clients. "No,"
he said, "but that's okay. All cops have small dicks." I laughed. "I'm not
kidding," he said. I had already lined up interviews with police officers. I
made a mental note not to ask.

Gene told me of receiving a text from a man claiming to be completely immobilized. "I wondered if I was being punked," he said. He agreed to see the man, but arrived mentally prepared for his friends to jump out, yell *gotcha!* and have a good laugh.

It was no gag. Gene arrived at the specified address, let himself in as instructed, and found a wheelchair-bound man who could neither speak nor move any of his limbs. The man could muster enough of a facial expression to answer a yes-or-no question; more than that required the use of a laser gadget and computer.

Gene asked, "Do you know why I'm here?"

Yes.

"Do you understand what's going to happen?"

Yes.

The client was apprehensive, nervous about how Gene would receive him or react to him. "I found out he's Mormon," Gene said. "He's a return missionary,[3] a BYU graduate, married, and has kids. His wife doesn't know about this. But he said he and his wife have freaky sex sometimes."

He paused, shrugged, and said, "What's freaky in Utah?"

"Beats me," I answered.

Resuming his narrative, Gene choked up a little. "I totally serviced him while he just sat there. He loved it. He came twice in 45 minutes. Paying for sex should be legal, especially for the handicapped. They have thoughts, they have desires, and they can't do anything about it. I walked out of there feeling great about myself. I cared about this guy. I felt like I'd been added to his medication, that I was part of his support staff."

Hearing about the experience made me a little misty-eyed, too.

Gene said, "I saw him later for a second session. It was just as good as the first. I think there will be another one."

6

Special requests: Kent

"Some of these men," Kent said, "they ask the weirdest things. One of the things I get often, especially in Salt Lake, a lot of requests that I dress like a woman. You know, panties and bra. I won't do it. It's not who I am, not what I like. I have turned down $500 for it."

Sometimes getting men to pay for his services is a challenge. "There are a lot of flighty men, a lot of men who will give you problems, they don't want to pay. They'll say, 'Well I can just go get this for free,' even when they're calling from my ad. I tell them then go get it for free and leave me alone."

Kent has his boundaries. "Sometimes a guy will ask me to watch him have sex with his wife, and then have sex with him while his wife watches. I won't do that. And I won't do his wife. Sometimes they want that, too. No way. I had one encounter with a woman, and that was enough for me. I will never do that again."

It's not unusual for Mormon men to ask Kent to arrive wearing garments, referring to the Mormons' sacred underwear. "I tell them I don't own any, but if they have a pair, I'll put them on when I get there." (Gene has fulfilled garment requests, but not for paid encounters.)

"Client requests can be a little worrisome at times," Kent said. "We're talking married, LDS, white men. They have kids. They hold priesthood authority.[4] When they meet up with me, it's almost like they say anything goes. Do they use protection? You can't take their word for it. They're quick to take your word for it that you're clean. A lot of them don't seem to care if you're clean. The kind of behavior they engage in, considering they have kids at home, it's mind-boggling. No matter who it is, I just assume that everyone has something."

It sounded to me as if Kent sometimes forgoes protection. Incredulous, I asked if I'd misunderstood. I hadn't. "Protection? Yes and no. Most men out there doing this don't use it. So sometimes I tell them okay, never mind. I've gotten an STI twice. Nothing that can't be cured. I get tested every two months. Once I didn't have symptoms but tested positive."

Kent takes TRUVADA for PrEP,[5] a prophylactic pill that drastically reduces the likelihood of getting HIV-1 through sex. I later spoke with a pharmacist who confirmed that PrEP is highly effective.[6] Kent said, "A lot of sex workers including myself are on it. It protects against AIDS but not other things like warts, herpes, syphilis, gonorrhea, things like that. But a lot of people are very ignorant here, gay, straight, or whatever. They think if I'm on PrEP then I'm clean, and that's good enough for the average married guy. One of the goals I have—I do a lot of volunteer work on the side—is to educate people on this issue."

7

Special requests: Gene

Gene entertained one woman for payment and, according to his ad, is open to entertaining more. But it wouldn't be his first choice.

"I will try anything once if it's pleasurable for someone else," Gene said. "Well, almost anything. Some guys have pedophile fantasies, where they want me to play the little boy. I won't do it. I almost called the cops on one guy I suspected wasn't just fantasizing. I won't do blood and scat. I'll pee on them if they want, but I won't let them pee on me. And I'm not into BDSM. I guess I'm pretty vanilla."

Gene won't dress like a woman either. "Except," he said, "I have a blond wig. I'll wear that if they want."

One of Gene's clients gets off on being called Sarah. "He kept saying 'Call me Sarah,'" Gene said.

"*Call me Sarah*," I mused. "When you write your memoir, there's your title."

Another of Gene's clients, a Mormon and a regular, became obsessed with Stanley, Gene's driver who also happens to be his roommate. He's straight, but that didn't deter the client from peppering Gene with questions about him during sessions. "Is Stanley around? What's he doing right now? Has he ever had a man? Do you think you could get him to watch?" Later, the client met Rose and shifted his obsession to her. "What's Rose doing? Is she here? Think she'd watch us?"

Across the table from us, Rose said, "I'm willing."

"I'm not," Gene replied.

Continuing, Gene said, "One guy wanted me to bite his dick as hard as I could. I started gentle and the guy encouraged me to step it up. I tried it later myself, having a guy bite me, except with less pressure. I liked it. Also, I get a lot of feet stuff. Massage their feet, suck on their toes."

Some clients, Gene said, are in denial about being gay. He forwarded to me a text from a new client. Here it is verbatim:

> I want to play like we're neighbors. You invite me over to hang out. You tell me you're a nudist but since you've injured your shoulder, you need my help getting out of your clothes. Get the idea? I want us both to say "Not to be gay but . . ." a lot. "Not to be gay but since I hurt my shoulder can you help me out of these clothes?" . . . "Not to be gay but can you tickle my back" . . . etc.

One preferred activity took Gene by surprise, and it was entirely unwelcome. The man punched him. "Maybe it was a turn-on for him," Gene said, "but not for me. I assaulted him big-time and threw him out. I was done."

Unlike Kent, Gene is strict about protection. "I caught a guy trying to sneak off the condom. I warned him and made him keep it on. A minute later I caught him trying to sneak it off again. I kicked him out and kept his money."

8

"Sorry, but right now I'm busy fantasizing about Rose."

As lunch wound down, Gene began rhapsodizing about the pleasures of gay sex, of being on the bottom, and of the experience of male-on-male prostate stimulation. Short of experiencing it for myself, he said more than once, I simply couldn't imagine how great it is. He repeated it often enough that I was becoming uncomfortable. Was I flattering myself, or was he floating an invitation? Just in case, I decided to deal with it before it progressed further. "I realize that gay versus straight isn't a binary, but a continuum," I said, "and that people land everywhere along that continuum. I'm about as pro gay rights as you can get, but orientation-wise, if I were any closer to the end marked 'straight' I'd fall off the continuum."

Gene quieted. It seemed to me that he looked sullen, even brooding. I worried that I'd misunderstood and insulted him. Or, that I'd understood perfectly and insulted him. Rose and Stanley carried the conversation for a few minutes. Finally, to my relief, Gene brightened and rejoined the conversation.

After lunch, Gene sent me a text. *You were clear about being straight, but if you're curious to try being on the bottom, I'm your man.*

So I hadn't misread him after all. I replied, *Lol, I'm flattered. If I ever want to try it, I'll know who to call.*

He forayed again.

And again.

And then again.

I kept my replies courteous and light. He was beginning to annoy, but I didn't want to be ungracious toward someone who had just been generous with his time and candor. Searching for a not-unkind way to emphasize that I wasn't kidding about being straight, I texted, *Sorry, but right now I'm busy fantasizing about Rose.*

Unfazed, he texted, *Just to be clear, I'm not talking about for payment.*

Seeking to be unambiguously firm without being outright mean, I replied, *Thank you. I understood as much. Aaaaaand now it's time to move on.*

That seemed to do it. He texted only once more, this time to give me Rose's number.

I thought about that exchange. I don't think Gene's persistence was so much a gay thing as a male thing. It occurred to me that I'd just had the smallest taste of what women routinely endure from men who won't take no for an answer. I suddenly understood the dilemma of wanting to be clear while not wanting to be rude. I experienced not wanting to offend even though Gene was offending with his persistence. I felt my frustration grow as each *no* was batted away, treated not as a decision to be respected but as a quaint protest to be overcome. I understood worrying about being unkind, even with so gentle a rebuke as "it's time to move on."

I would have been within my rights to say, *Look, I said no, and no means no. Now leave me the hell alone.* Yet I don't think he was trying to be inappropriate. Perhaps he was convinced that in some part of my psyche I was tempted, that he was only trying to help me surrender to what I really wanted. We have seen it, after all, in movie after movie: one actor wrestles another into a kiss, and the scene ends not with "No means no, dammit" but with the second melting into the first's arms. If in the movie *Goldfinger* Pussy Galore had kicked James Bond in the nuts as he deserved,[7] I bet Bond could still have found a way to save Fort Knox.[8]

Chapter 8

The Mormon John

*There is great safety for a shy man with a whore . . . there is none
of the horror of the possible turndown which shrivels
the guts of timid men.*

—From John Steinbeck's *East of Eden*

1

Who are the Utah men seeing providers?

When I asked providers about their clients, I was careful to specify that
I wasn't after names. I needn't have. No provider would have given them
to me anyhow. Only once was the no-names line inadvertently crossed.
A provider shared two details about a man "high up in government and
church." She could not have known that I knew the man, much less that
disclosing one of his past private-sector jobs and letting slip the first
name of his wife—whom I also happened to know—would instantly
identify him to me. These details would have meant nothing to anyone
who didn't know them as a couple.

The revelation floored me. "High up in government and church"
approached understatement. I was surprised that a man at his level of

public exposure would risk all by routinely seeing providers—for, this provider told me, he saw others besides her. One slip of the tongue to the wrong person would ruin him. Lucky for him, I wasn't the wrong person.

. I do not judge him for indulging. That's between him and his conscience. What bothered me was that his career and church service put him in a position to prosecute and excommunicate providers, whom he solicits or solicited, and johns, who do what he does or did. I regret the knowledge. I wish I could erase it.

Every provider I interviewed rattled off a roster of clients that included white- and blue-collar workers, CEOs, judges, prosecutors, attorneys, physicians, business owners, and students and professors from local colleges and universities. "People you'd least expect," Tina said. Jewel used to see "a criminal lawyer with a coke habit. His wife divorced him because he kept cheating on her."

Rose said, "I had a cop client who broke every rule. Drugs, lots of drugs. We had sex in his cop car. Then he started stalking me, pulling guys over for following me and then grilling them. I had to drop him as a client."

Most providers I spoke with estimated that 80 to 98 percent of their clients are married men, with 70 to 90 percent being Mormon and having married in a Mormon temple. Of course, fairness demands not putting too much stock in the estimates. It's not as if providers keep a tally, and providers, like anyone, are subject to hindsight and selection bias. Either way, what's clear is that a good many men in the Salt Lake area who see providers are married, active participants in the Mormon Church.

Every provider I spoke with had entertained rank-and-file Mormons as well as leaders at ward, stake, and higher levels. At first I wondered how providers would be privy to a client's church affiliation much less his church calling. The answer is that it's not unusual for clients to talk openly with providers about their personal lives. And something of a clue is to be found when a Mormon man disrobes and reveals his sacred white underwear. "We see a lot of Mormon white underwear," Boop said. "Some guys try to hide it as they undress, which of course can't be done.

I'm like, come on, dude, I know you're Mormon and I don't care. Let's fuck."

Koko told me of a Mormon client of some authority within the church hierarchy who contracted a sexually transmitted infection. At the time he'd been having unprotected sex—which the providers I spoke with refuse to do—with both a sex worker and a mistress. He wasn't sure whether the sex worker or the mistress had given him the infection, but, whichever one it was, he was pretty sure he'd passed it to the other. He refused to seek treatment for fear his wife would find out. "He was a jerk," Koko observed, as if it weren't already understood.

A one-time client presented Tina with a copy of the Book of Mormon at the end of their session. He solemnly testified to her that if she would ask God in prayer, the Holy Ghost would "manifest its truthfulness" to her. I asked Tina, who considers herself "super Christian," what she did with the book after the man left. "I handled it with napkins," she said. "I felt it was too sacred to handle with my bare hands after sex." But, I said, non-Mormon Christians don't accept the Book of Mormon as scripture. "It's sacred to Mormons," she replied. "I don't think it's okay to bash any religion."

All of my female interviewees entertain clients in the military and in law enforcement. One police officer, a department head, smuggles cocaine seized in raids out of the station to share with his provider. All have clients who are medical professionals, such as physicians and dentists. Veronica said, "I had an endodontist as a sugar daddy for a while."

Like Boop, Tina has entertained "some gorgeous guys. Guys you'd think wouldn't have to pay for it. I think some guys feel powerful knowing they can pay a girl for sex if they want. It's a turn-on for them."

Betty and Boop have noted a surge of clients who work in information technology. I wasn't surprised. The Salt Lake metropolitan area earned the nickname Silicon Slopes for its explosive growth in high-tech arenas, boasting facilities for Micron, Intel, Adobe, Facebook, Amazon, SanDisk, eBay, and even the National Security Agency (NSA). "It's a whole new demographic," Boop explained. "They work seventy-hour weeks at a desk all day, so they don't have a social life and, besides, their social skills are terrible. So how and where are they going to meet women? But they have money."

Jewel particularly likes clients who pay her to be their travel companion. "It's great when guys buy me a plane ticket to visit them out of state. I put in about an hour a day with them, and then I have the rest of the day to enjoy where I am. I've had clients fly me to Texas, Florida, and California."

2

Finding johns

Tracking down providers, male and female, was a piece of cake compared with tracking down johns. Providers need to be findable if they are to remain in business, whereas johns have a vested interest in *not* being found. It seems they have a thing about preferring to avoid fines, jail time, and arrest, and about not wanting to lose their marriage, their children's regard, their community and church standing, and possibly their employment.

I'd naïvely hoped providers might persuade a john or two to contact me. No such luck. Looking back, I doubt that any secrecy-minded client would respond positively to hearing from his provider, "I just spoke with a stranger claiming to be writing a book. You should speak with him too."

Next I tried reaching out to johns through EroticMonkey.ch, one of a few websites still accessible from within the United States where providers advertise and clients submit reviews. I visited its forum and posted this message:

> Hey Utah hobbyists, I'm a published author at work on a book about the trade in Utah. I take the point of view that the hobby can be a good thing and should be legal or at least decriminalized. I have interviewed a number of providers but would love to chat with a few clients. Anonymity assured. If you'd be interested in being heard, please send me a

private message. I'll provide info so that you can see for yourself that I'm on the level.

After leaving the post up for a month, I counted the replies. Counting was easy, since the total of replies was zero. I waited a few more weeks and finally deleted the post.

I had about given up on speaking with johns when, thanks to my uncanny ability not to keep my mouth shut, I lucked into interviews with four of them. At a social gathering, I mentioned that I was writing a book about prostitution in Utah and hoped to speak with johns. It turned out to be quite the conversation starter. Later, as people were leaving, a man approached me and quietly said he'd be willing to talk on condition of anonymity.

"How about I call you 'John' in the book," I said. I figured that not to call at least one john "John" would constitute a crime against dad jokes. He was all for it.

Three more johns approached me in the ensuing months, making a total of four. I have decided to call one of them "Jack," which you probably know is a nickname for John, though how "Jack" is any more convenient to say than "John" is beyond me. Continuing with the theme, I shall call the others "Jonathan" and "Ewan," the latter, according to some, being a Scottish variation of "John." I'll pause while you roll your eyes at your humble author who thinks he's clever.[1]

3

"How I became a john"

John is in his late 40s. Nice looking and pleasantly plump, he is a manager at a large local company. He is married and has kids. He and his family are active members of the Mormon Church. He is a ward clerk, tasked with counting attendees at sacrament meetings and recording various other data, the Mormon Church being big on tracking and reporting.[2] His wife teaches lessons for the Relief Society, which is the women's organization of the Mormon Church.

John happened upon the hobby while shopping online for a car. "I was checking out used cars on Backpage when I saw the Escorts section and thought, hey, this looks interesting." He was referring to classified advertising site Backpage.com, which is no longer in operation. In January 2017, the U.S. government forced the site's owners to eliminate the Escorts section in response to a National Center for Missing and Exploited Children finding that "nearly three-quarters—73 percent—of all suspected child sex trafficking reports it receives from the general public through its cyber tip line are linked to one Web site—a single Web site. That Web site is called Backpage.com."[3] Providers—and traffickers—simply moved their ads to the Body Rubs and Massage sections, so in April of the following year, the U.S. Justice Department shut down Backpage for good. A grand jury indictment swiftly followed.[4] In the wake of the shutdown, a number of other adult services websites immediately ceased U.S. operations. Many nontrafficked providers objected to the wave of shutdowns.[5]

"I clicked on Escorts and started looking at ads," John continued. "There was this one that just, I don't know, her pictures grabbed me. I went back and forth. Should I call, should I run. But you know where this is going. I called. I'd never done anything like that before and I was nervous. She picked right up. We set a time, and I went to see her at her hotel room. She looked exactly like her pictures. My gosh![6] We made out like teenagers. We started taking off our clothes. She put a cover on me with her mouth. I didn't know you could do that. Then we had sex. It was amazing. Like meeting back up with an old girlfriend."

He was the only one of the four johns who had been busted. "Walked into a sting," he said. "I had to pay a $300 fine,[7] get tested for STIs, and get counseling for a year. I had a Class B misdemeanor on my record for five years until I could get it expunged. I was incredibly lucky. They mail you a summons. I was home when it came. Snagged it so my wife never saw it."

I asked if getting busted scared him away from the hobby. "For a while," he said. "Mostly, it taught me to be more careful. I was pretty stupid that time. I should have known something was up when she kept asking 'what else do you want to do.' Soon as I said the wrong thing, two cops came into the hotel room and wrote me up. I was lucky. They could have impounded my car and made me spend a night in jail. They told me that's what they'd do if I tried to warn anyone on my way out of the hotel."

Jack, a Millennial, looks quite fit. His real name, dark hair, and olive complexion suggest a Mediterranean heritage. He works as a "well-paid computer programmer." Like John, he is Mormon, married, and has children. His first experience with paid sex occurred when he was a massage client. "I injured my back rock climbing and was getting massages for it," Jack said. "Legit massages. Always saw the same girl. My third appointment, she started moving her hands closer and all that, and then she pulled down the towel and went to town. Before I knew it, I was getting one hell of a hand job."

I recognized the name of the spa. I was surprised, for it has a solid reputation as a legitimate, no hanky-panky place. Extras, I learned, can be available at spas I'd assumed were strictly no-nonsense. It depends on the individual massage therapist and on how much vigilance management chooses to exercise.

"Took me totally off guard," Jack continued. "It just happened, and I'll tell you, I let it. I wasn't going to stop her. It's not like I was using my big head any more. Later I thought, *What the hell? I'm married. I'm not doing that again.* Then I was back a week later. Things went from a hand job to a blowjob, to a blowjob with touching, to both of us naked and having sex on the massage table." In time, Jack moved on to seeing independent providers.

Unlike John and Jack, Jonathan didn't stumble into the hobby by accident. He went looking for it. "I had an urge and thought I'd check out Personals in the *Trib*'s classifieds." He was referring to the independently owned *Salt Lake Tribune*, one of Salt Lake City's two dailies.[8] That he had been looking for providers in a daily newspaper identified Jonathan as a long-time hobbyist. His initial foray would have taken place a good two or more decades ago, before the Internet took its toll on printed classi-fieds. "Mid- to late fifties," he said when I asked his age. He asked me not to describe him, and to withhold information about what he does for a living. "I don't mind if you say I'm married," he said. "And I'm Christian. Not Mormon. I believe in the Jesus the Bible teaches."[9]

He found more than he'd hoped for in the *Tribune*. Besides Personals, there were classifications for Escorts, Private Dancers, and Private Mod-els. But a drawback of pre-Internet classifieds was the absence of photos. "My first experience wasn't all that good," Jonathan said. "I wouldn't have picked her if I'd seen pictures. Just not—I don't know. I felt guilty right after, which didn't help. Next lady I saw, she was awesome."

I asked Jonathan why his guilt didn't sour him, why he tried again. "I got over it," he said, with a shrug.

"But," I persisted, "your first encounter disappointed. Why try again?"

He replied, "I didn't like my first beer either."

Besides independent providers, Jonathan enjoys visits to AMPs. I asked if he worried about police raids, which happen in the Salt Lake area with some frequency. He didn't. "I have a system for not showing up when there's likely to be a raid," he said.

"Are you buddies with a cop who tips you off?"

"Nope."

"You have a police scanner?"

"Nope. It's psychological. Behavior modeling, sort of."

He agreed to tell me his "method" on condition that I not describe it in the book. "You publish it," he said, "it won't work anymore, because the police will be on to it."

I am only too happy not to publish his method, mainly because I think it's bogus. To him, however, I put it more tactfully. "I'm not too sure about your method," I said.

"It works. I've never been busted."

"Lots of people have never been busted," I replied. "Ever heard of randomness?"

4

Feeling conflicted

John, Jack, and Jonathan are married and religious, so it's not surprising that they all experienced guilt at the outset of their hobbying. They no longer do. They exercise discretion not because they believe they are doing wrong, each assured me, but to protect their marriages, avoid hurting their spouse, and avoid the condemnation that society stands at the ready to dish out.

Nonhobbyists may have trouble wrapping their minds around the idea that a man could see a provider and still be happy at home and in his marriage and still love his wife. While it would make sense that some johns are unhappy at home, no shortage of other factors can motivate johns, including happily married ones, to see providers. There's lust. There's the thrill of the risk. There's the thrill of violating the ultimate taboo. There's the need to talk with a provider in the role of therapist. There's the desire to explore fantasies that are off-limits at home. There's the marriage that's happy and fulfilling except for the sexual aspect. There's the need to unwind, to let a provider take the place of a good stiff drink.

And there's the desire for variety. Jack explained, "You know restaurants that advertise home cooking? Home cooking isn't what I want when I go out. I want something I don't get at home. It doesn't mean that I don't like my wife's cooking. It just means I want something else. It's the same with seeing hookers. You go out to get something you can't get at home. You get it and then you go home."

"It's safe, mutually satisfying, no one needs to know," John told me. "The value proposition is that it will never go beyond. No dating, dinner, calling at night, or anything beyond like that. Did I ever feel conflicted? At first, yeah. You think, *What am I doing? Come on. Dude, you gotta put a lid on this thing.* That would last a few weeks. Then I'd think, *I wonder what so-and-so is doing,* and I'd text her. Or she'd text me. *Hi.* Never more than that. Just *Hi.*"

Over time, John's inner conflict abated. "It's not wrong," he said. "We just have a society where everyone says it's wrong. In a country where, what, half of married men cheat? Come on. Why is it worse when you pay for it? I think paying for it is better. I'm not having an affair. It's not love. I'm just getting laid and my family doesn't suffer."

I asked Jack if he experienced inner conflict from a religious standpoint. "Yes and no," he said. "I had this inner dialog going on. That barometer that you know what you're doing is wrong. By wrong I mean dangerous, how much damage it would cause if somebody found out. What if my wife found out. What if my kid was driving down the street and saw me go into an apartment. Otherwise, no harm, no foul. If there's no risk, if no one for certain ever finds out, I'm fine with it. But there's always that what-if factor. I love my wife and my kids. I know that sounds weird since I see hookers, but I don't want to lose them."

Jack described precautions he takes to keep his wife from suspecting. "You don't want to come home with smells," he said. "Not just if the girl you saw was wearing perfume. Most of them don't wear it anyhow, they know not to. But maybe she smokes, or just the smell of another person rubs off on you. Have to watch for that. One time I knew I smelled like the girl I'd just been with, so on my way home I picked up a packet of mustard and rubbed it around my mouth. When I kissed my wife hello she said, 'Busted.' That scared me. Then she said, 'You had a hotdog on your way home.' Whew."

I read an account on The Erotic Review website by a man who'd showered at a provider's place of business before going home. That night as he and his wife snuggled into bed, she nuzzled him and whispered tenderly in his ear, "That's not our shampoo." With that, she rolled over and went to sleep. I can't tell you what happened next, because that's where the writer ended his story. I shared the story with Jack. "Yeah, that," he said, "you need to bring your own shampoo. Soap, too. And you need to wait a few hours. If you smell too fresh, that's suspicious."

Jonathan has a gym membership, which gives him an excuse to shower before coming home. "I tell her I was working out," he said. "I guess in a sense that's true."

Jonathan seemed the most conflicted. "I've got no worries about going to hell," he said, "because I've accepted Jesus. We all sin. We're saved by faith, not works. I've gone a period of time keeping it clean, but it's a weak point. Pre, during, and immediately after I was good with it. In the act I could justify it. Hours later, I'd think, *Dammit. What am I doing? I'm gonna get caught, someone is going to know me, see me.* You can rationalize anything, you just can. You know stealing is wrong, but if you're hungry enough, you'll do it. You're married, you've taken vows, but at home you're not getting laid. You can rationalize it. Remorse sets in. Why does remorse set in? The upbringing. It's knowing how much damage it would do if somebody found out."

John said, "I don't accept that monogamy should be a rule. As long as my wife doesn't know, because it would hurt her. Short of that, nothing wrong with it. At first I felt guilty as hell. I crossed that line, I couldn't uncross it. But now I'm good with it. It's not an affair. I still love my wife. I'm not going to leave her and the kids. Once I sorted it out, gave myself permission, I quit feeling bad. I'm not hurting anyone." He paused before going on. "And I still treat her really well," he said. "That's important. Some guys start treating their wives different. That's like a major clue they're up to something."

5

The morally tortured Mormon john

I have no idea what percentage of johns are mentally and emotionally comfortable in the hobby, but I reasoned that there must surely be johns struggling to reconcile "I'm seeing a sex worker" with "I'm a good person," and especially with "I'm a good Mormon." The Mormon Church condemns extramarital sex in no uncertain terms. Given that and society's constant and often hypocritical moralistic barrage, one can hardly blame a john for experiencing warring emotions.

It didn't surprise me that I was unsuccessful in tracking down morally tortured Mormon johns to interview. A man who berates himself for his behavior is hardly likely to jump at a chance to parade his guilt in a book. Yet, as neuroscientist David Eagleman observed, all people need to unload.

> Psychologist James Pennebaker and his colleagues . . . discovered that when subjects confessed or wrote about their deeply held secrets . . . there were measurable decreases in their stress hormone levels[10] . . .
>
> The main reason not to reveal a secret is aversion to the long-term consequences. A friend might think ill of you, or a love might be hurt, or a community might ostracized you. This concern about the outcome is evidenced by the fact that people are more likely to tell their secrets to total strangers; with someone you don't know, the neural conflict can be dissipated with none of the costs. This is why strangers can be so forthcoming on airplanes, telling all the details of their marital troubles, and why confessional booths have remained a staple in one of the world's largest religions.[11]

I doubted that morally tortured johns would prove the exception. The problem for them would be their limited options as to potential unloadees. A friend or relative might condemn or, worse, blab. Religious leaders are supposed to keep confidences, but because they're human they might condemn, blab, or both. A mental health therapist might or might not be a good option, depending on the therapist, and depending on the extent to which religion influences the therapist's advice. It's not unusual for Mormon therapists, consciously or not, to push clients toward solutions found within church doctrine, policy, and activity.[12]

The guilt-ridden Mormon man faces challenges beyond the need to unload. His religion clearly states that the third most serious variety of sin is sexual sin. If he dies unrepentant, severe consequences await him in the hereafter. Angels will shout his sins from the housetops.[13] He will languish in Spirit Prison, where ". . . your sufferings be sore—how sore you know not, how exquisite you know not, yea, how hard to bear you know not."[14] He will not be allowed to dwell in eternity with his wife, for there she will be given to a worthier man. If the worthier man already has a wife, mainstream Mormon doctrine holds that she will become one of his eternal polygamist wives.[15] As for his children, in eternity they go with the mother. Meanwhile, here on Earth, the man compounds his sin each time he enters a Mormon temple, receives the sacrament at church,[16] or lies in interviews when asked if he obeys the Law of Chastity.

Repentance offers the means of erasing the sin, but repenting of big sins in the Mormon Church is no piece of cake. In many religions, a repentant john need only ask God for forgiveness and then he's good to go. In the Mormon Church, that much is good for small sins like, say, downing a Mojito on New Year's Eve, but when it comes to big sins, asking God for forgiveness is only the start. It's also necessary to obtain the church's forgiveness, which can be done only by confessing face-to-face to an official representative of the church, which is to say, to a bishop, stake president, or both. Per church policy, the bishop and stake president will likely require the john to confess to his wife. If the wife has harbored no suspicion, the confession can deal a devastating blow that could easily have been avoided had the john simply ceased his extracurricular activities and kept his mouth shut. The confession can and often does lead to divorce, estrangement from children, and the public shaming that is disfellowshipment or excommunication.

With confession an essential part of repentance, the morally tortured Mormon john might feel all the more keenly the need to unload on someone. The risks of confessing to a bishop or stake president may explain why so many johns choose to unload on providers.

The role of unloadee isn't always pleasant for the provider. After doing your best to give a client a wonderful experience, there's nothing quite like having him gaze deeply into your eyes and tenderly whisper, "I feel awful."

One provider who responded to only a few questions by text, said, "Afterward, sometimes they lean back and cover their face with their hands. They start in with how terrible they feel. 'I can't believe I did this again,' 'I'm such a jerk,' 'This is immoral and wrong,' 'I swear this is the last time.' Hello, I'm right here. Does he think about how it makes me feel when he says he feels like scum thanks to me?"

She isn't the only provider who experiences a jab to the heart when a john berates himself and, by extension, her. The more a provider enjoys connecting with clients, the more hurtful his unleashed guilt-gush can be. As another provider put it, "He might as well say, 'A decent guy like me would never see a dirty slut like you.' Then he's back a week later."

According to Rose, post-coital guilt is not unusual for first-timers. One john, she said, sank back onto the bed after climaxing and, a few seconds later, lamented, "I can't believe I let you ride me while I had my garments on." Rose shook her head and smiled. "Dude just cheated on his wife, and his big worry was that he had his Mormon underwear on."

Jewel is well acquainted with post-coital client remorse. "I get, 'Oh my god, I can't believe I did that,' 'What will people think,' 'You can't tell anyone,' 'I've sinned,' 'I'm married,' 'I'm Mormon,' 'I don't usually do this,' 'Please don't message my phone,' things like that. I try to put them at ease, assure them I won't tell, that no one will know."

Betty said, "They usually make the excuses before they fuck. I hear a lot of 'My wife doesn't fuck me anymore.' Lots of 'my wife is sick' stories. I don't know if they're trying to justify or play the pity card. It's like they're saying, 'Don't judge me.' It's a little ironic."

By contrast, Boop's experience is that most men save the excuse-making for after. "I feel like I'm supposed to do an absolution," she said.

6

Creative loopholes

Confession and self-berating aren't for everyone. A popular guilt-avoidance technique is to come up with a divine loophole, one that God apparently overlooked, that makes it possible to see providers while remaining technically within the rules of the faith. The loophole usually takes the form of "It's okay as long as . . . " The approach requires considerable

mental gymnastics, but then, many prefer mental gymnastics to intro-
spection and self-honesty.

Not to be overlooked is the role that religious apologetics plays in
training Mormons to make the unpalatable palatable. Merriam-Webster
defines "religious apologetics" as *a branch of theology devoted to the defense of the divine origin and authority of Christianity,*[17] but I prefer my
own definition: *the art of making two plus two equal nine if an answer
of four would mean your religious leaders or your holy book got something wrong.* Apologetics is a necessary part of believing in any religion,
but it is more so in faiths like Mormonism that pile on more doctrines,
claims, and requirements than less exacting faiths. Sooner or later, every
Mormon must come to the defense of their church that instituted but
now excommunicates for polygamy,[18] barred African Americans from
the priesthood until 1978,[19] taught that dark skin was a curse,[20] honors
a founding prophet who conned farmers into paying him to divine for
buried treasure,[21] and more. Anyone who can reconcile the above would
certainly emerge with reasoning skills sufficient to justify seeing providers.

A favorite loophole is to play with definitions. There's rarely much
disagreement as to what constitutes sex, adultery, or masturbation—until the need to claim innocence arises. Thus Ling, who works in a legal
brothel in Elko, Nevada, hears from a regular who makes the drive from
Salt Lake three or four times per year, "It's not adultery as long as I'm
paying you."

A married Mormon man explained to Tina that it's okay for him
to touch her, kiss her, go down on her, and let her give him a blowjob,
as long as he doesn't penetrate her. Penetration, he told her, would be
adultery. Another man told her that as long as he climaxes by rubbing
his dick with the flat of his palm instead of wrapping it in his fingers, it's
not masturbation.

One of Lilly's regulars maintains that orgasm marks the line between
the faithful and the unfaithful husband. It is, therefore, a line that he will
not cross. "He tells me he can't cum because he's Mormon and has a wife.

'You make me feel good but not cum, that's enough, it's not cheating.' That's what he said." He has given Lilly specific instructions to stop the hand job when he reaches the brink of orgasm. It took a few tries before she had the timing down. "When his leg spasms," she said, "he's almost there, so I stop."

Tina entertains a client who claims that seeing her is less costly than divorce. "He pays fifteen hundred a session," she said, "and tells me it's cheaper than alimony and child support. There's no sex or even touching. Just a hello and a goodbye kiss, nothing more. He says it's more honest that way." Another of Tina's clients sees her for conversation and nothing more. "He says seeing me is cheaper than seeing a marriage counselor." I don't doubt that he said that, but I do doubt his math. Tina charges a good deal more than Salt Lake marriage counselors.

You may recall the john who left Tina with a copy of the Book of Mormon and testified to her that it contained the word of God. I cannot but wonder if he had in mind the Mormon teaching that "missionary work has a redemptive effect for the missionary as well as the convert."[22]

A more unusual means of relieving guilt is to make the provider responsible for your actions. "Sometimes they try to get me to seduce them so they can give in," Jewel said. "That way they can tell themselves it wasn't their fault." You have to hand it to someone who can search online for a provider, rent a room, arrange to meet her there, pay her to get naked with him, and then tell himself that nothing would have come of it if that damned provider hadn't put the moves on him.

On an anonymous online forum for Mormons seeking advice, a woman said her husband had confessed to her an encounter with a provider, but in defiance of church policy refused to confess to their bishop and stake president. He "felt in his heart" that God had forgiven him, he told her, so confessing to his wife should be enough. When she didn't go skipping from the room delighted at the news that he had been cleansed of his sin, he told her that *she* was now the sinful one—for not forgiving and forgetting.

Like most Christian churches, the Mormon Church teaches that sins can be erased through repentance and faith in Jesus. It even prescribes specific steps: recognize that you've sinned; sincerely regret it; apologize to those your behavior may have harmed; undo the damage if you can (e.g., if you stole something, give it back); and ask God, those you have harmed, and, in some cases, church leaders for forgiveness. While the intent is to offer those who err a means of setting things aright, some Mormons would twist repentance into a sin-now-pay-later plan. More than one provider told me of Mormon clients who acknowledged they were breaking a serious commandment from God but weren't worried because "they could always repent."

Tina seemed to show something of a willingness to make excuses for clients on their behalf. "I think cold wives kind of push their men in that direction," she said. "I was raised never to tell my man no. Even if you're not in the mood, you can at least give him a blowjob or ask him if it can be quick." Something bothered me about painting wives as de facto responsible for husbands' sexual acting out. With due respect for her up-bringing, I responded, it is certainly every woman's right to say no, and exercising it needn't send a man into the arms of another. Ultimately, it is the man who decides to stray or not to stray. Tina did not disagree, and offered a case in point. "This one really handsome guy I see," she said, "he admits his wife treats him great. And she's gorgeous—he showed me a picture. They're like Barbie and Ken. I asked so why does he come see me. He shrugged and said, 'I'm a dog.'"

We agreed that there was something to be said for his candor.

7

The single and lonely john

On a Saturday afternoon as I was putting finishing touches on this chapter, or so I thought, I received a call from Ewan. Late one night, he had sat relaxing in one of Salt Lake's many excellent microbreweries,[23] downing beers with his buddy, the above-referenced Jonathan. As conversation waxed increasingly open, a not-unusual phenomenon where serious beer consumption is involved, Ewan confided to Jonathan that he had seen providers. "You don't say," Jonathan replied. They spent the next couple of hours trading stories. His interview with me fresh in his memory, Jonathan persuaded Ewan to contact me.

Ewan is in his 40s. He is single, putting him in the minority as far as johns are concerned. He describes himself as a disaffected Mormon. "My wife divorced me because I quit believing in the church," he said. "Religion is a big thing in a Mormon marriage. I think we had a good marriage. Love, mutual respect, all that. Thing is, church was everything to her. We had a gospel-centered home. When I had my faith crisis, she said she didn't want a husband who didn't honor his priesthood, who wasn't going to the Celestial Kingdom."[24]

When you're an actively participating Mormon, church consumes much of your life. When you're an actively participating Mormon living in Utah, it consumes even more of it. Most of your neighbors, friends, and coworkers are Mormon. Your religion and your participation in it provide the foundation of what you have in common. If you leave, it is inevitable that you will feel ostracized to one extent or another.[25] Devout friends have long heard from the pulpit that the reason people leave the faith is that someone hurt their feelings,[26] or that they just couldn't go another day without, say, having a beer.[27] You are dubbed an apostate, someone who puts pride, coffee, tea, alcohol, porn, or adultery before the Lord and before family. You're branded the kind of person members of the church are counseled to avoid.[28]

As a newly minted ex-Mormon, you're likely to end up feeling lonely until you manage to build up a new circle of friends. That's where Ewan finds himself now. "I lost my wife. I have five kids. They think I'm suddenly this bad person. Some of my Mormon friends aren't sure it's okay to associate with me anymore. Mormon women don't want to date me. The ones that do want to change me, to bring me back into the fold."

He finds solace in providers. "Sometimes I crave physical affection, even if I have to pay for it. Sometimes you just want to be touched. To feel wanted."

Even so, Ewan admits that paid affection has its limitations. "I think my ATF likes me well enough," he said, *ATF* being an initialism for *all-time favorite*. "She makes it feel real. But I don't kid myself. I know that's her job. Deep down, I know that. When I get depressed or I'm feeling alone, I can't just call her up like she's a real girlfriend. I can't just say, 'Let's go to a movie' or 'Let's go for drinks.' You have to set that stuff up ahead of time. And you have to pay for her time, and I can't always afford it. That's when it hits me, reminds me, I don't have a real girlfriend. Not really. I hate it. I get lonely and I hate it."

Ewan doesn't want his family or church acquaintances to know he sees a provider. "They already excommunicated me," he said, "so I'm not worried about that. It's just that everyone will say, 'Oh, that's why he quit the church.' It's not. I quit because the church is bullshit. But they'll say, 'He wants to sin, that's why he says it's bullshit. Look, he even sees prostitutes.' They'll think that's why I left."

He paused for a moment before adding, "I just don't want to give them that."

I asked, "You left the church before you started seeing providers. How do you feel about practicing Mormons who see them?"

"You know," he said, "all religions go on about 'don't judge.' Then they judge. I'm not going to do that. I've been hurt by former friends who judge me, not for seeing providers, which they don't know about, but for not believing. So I think I'll take a pass on that question."

8

Can a john truly be a believing Mormon?

Ewan, the former Mormon, said, "You have to wonder if these Mormon guys paying for sex really believe in their religion." I hadn't wondered, but now I did. I put the question to various believing Mormon friends who, as far as I know, do not see providers. Most averred that anyone who sees providers couldn't possibly truly believe—because anyone who truly believes wouldn't see providers. The astute reader may detect in that a bit of circular reasoning.

I'm not so sure it's that simple. There are people who smoke but believe smoking causes lung cancer, people who text while driving but believe that texting while driving is irresponsible and deadly, and dieters who order dessert but believe they should swear off dessert. Certainly there is room for the Mormon man who believes God has said providers are a no-no but, for any of a number of possible reasons, continues seeing them nonetheless.

Forbidden fruit didn't get to be forbidden by being easy to give up.

Chapter 9

A Police Officer and a Gentleman

Home is heaven and orgies are vile,
But I like an orgy, once in a while.

—Ogden Nash

1

The outspoken police chief

I wanted to round out my perspective with a police officer interview, but I wasn't sure how eager a cop would be to speak with me, much less how much candor I could realistically expect. Over coffee, a friend suggested giving Jim Winder a try. He pointed out that when the former Salt Lake County Sheriff resigned his position in 2017, he hadn't been shy about sharing his thoughts with reporters. Perhaps Winder would agree to an interview and speak openly.

Lean and fit, over six feet tall with a full head of close-cropped gray hair, Winder was elected to the county sheriff's office at the age of 44 in 2006, handily winning reelection in 2010 and 2014. Over time, Winder found himself increasingly at odds with the Salt Lake County Council. On May 30, 2017, Winder announced that after 32 years in the sheriff's department, which included 10 years as sheriff, he was leaving to accept a position as chief of police in Moab, Utah.[1]

With a population of 5,300, Moab is about 240 miles southeast of Salt Lake City, and 20 miles from the Utah-Colorado border if you happen to be a crow. Thanks to a pair of mountain ranges in the way, it's about twice that distance if you happen to be a car. Yet Moab is no sleepy town. It's a world-renowned destination for sightseeing, hiking, rock climbing, cycling, and rafting. More than a million outdoor enthusiasts pour into Moab every year, a transient population roughly equal to Salt Lake County's permanent population.

The town's popularity has much to do with its proximity to two world-famous national parks, Arches and Canyonlands. Know it or not, you have seen both, probably many times. If you have ever seen a film or photo of a towering rust-colored arch carved by the elements from solid rock against a backdrop of a rust-colored desert mountain range, chances are you were gazing upon Delicate Arch, the most famous of more than 2,000 arches in the fittingly named Arches National Park. In the opening sequence of *Indiana Jones and the Last Crusade*, it is Arches National Park into which River Phoenix stumbles out of a cave, pilfered relic in hand. You would have seen Canyonlands National Park in 2013's *The Lone Ranger* with Johnny Depp and Armie Hammer, with that breathtaking landscape arguably being the movie's only redeeming quality. Adjacent to Canyonlands is Deadhorse Point State Park, which in the 1991 movie *Thelma and Louise* stood in for the Grand Canyon when the titular characters soared off a cliff in their Thunderbird convertible. The Grand Canyon has a stunt double. Who knew?

Calling Winder's resignation from the county sheriff's department "a surprise move," Utah's *Gephardt Daily* reported:

> Winder . . . said that Salt Lake County is in need of change, and he did not feel that his proposals were being taken seriously, or even inspiring dialogue of other possible solutions to problems, including crime levels in downtown Salt Lake City and overcrowding in jails, among other is-

sues. . . . "You bet I'm frustrated," [Winder] said. "In my opinion, many in the county are, too."[2]

Not shy about sharing his thoughts was right. "One of the nicest things I can say about him is he will never be accused of being a politician," declared a local in a letter to Moab's *The Times-Independent*.[3]

Winder sounded like my kind of guy—that is, outspoken and direct—so I emailed him an interview request. Three weeks passed with no reply. I didn't blame him. Spending an hour on the phone with some guy writing a book about prostitution probably doesn't top the average busy police chief's priority list. I sent a follow-up request, figuring that if I didn't hear back from him this time, I'd leave it at that. Winder replied less than an hour later. "I apologize about the delay in responding," he wrote. "Happy to have a conversation with you either in person or by phone."

2

"If there's no coercion, I fail to see the issue."

I have no regard for writers and filmmakers who hoodwink interviewees by hiding or misrepresenting their intent. I wanted Winder to know where I was coming from should he wish to guard his comments or, for that matter, bail. "I have been interviewing women who work out of apartments they rent for the purpose," I opened. "They are neither trafficked nor pimped. A few are former addicts but are clean now, or at least that's what they've told me. They charge from $200 to $600 for a session. They keep the number of visitors low so as not to draw neighbors' attention. I am writing from the point of view that what they do is harmless and shouldn't be illegal, but I'm open to your turning me around on that. Also, I am happy to keep this interview anonymous if you prefer."

Winder said I was welcome to use his name. Having read some of his prior interviews, that didn't surprise me. What did surprise me—pleasantly—was that Winder didn't unleash what I'd braced myself for, namely, an unqualified earful about the evils of prostitution. "The demographic you're describing," he said, "those who are not trafficked as you described, that's hard to argue with. I agree with you. The women are engaged in it from a business perspective. If there's no coercion, I fail to see the issue. We struggle because of the puritanical view. If we allowed it, rather than forced moral compunction, we'd probably have a lot less societal problems. Puritanical punishment methods don't work."

I asked Winder if he was a Mormon. "I'd rather not say," he replied.

The type of provider I interviewed, Winder said, was largely outside his experience. "Three hundred dollars is pretty Sam's Club," he said. "It's not what we typically see. I applaud you. You have gotten into a group that's clean, nonaddicted. That's great. They are filling a niche."

Winder expressed admiration for the sex worker business model that exists in some European countries. "A woman can apply for a business license as a sex worker," he said. "She pays taxes, pays a fee, has health checks, and engages at rates that she sets and that the market will bear. She remains in control and has the same protections as any other business owner. That's okay."

I said, "You'd be okay with that in the U.S.?"

He replied without hesitation, "Absolutely."

Winder is no two-dimensional thinker. "Like homelessness," he said, "people approach prostitution from a monolithic perspective. You can't talk to them about the gradations. I had a family member who migrated into the trade, so I'm very familiar with it from both sides of the equation. They start as an escort, which is legal, but it's a question of time before someone wants sex and offers too much money to turn down."

Police officers deal more with providers at the extremes, he said, who are more prone to attract attention. At the lower extreme are "drug addict types" offering unprotected blowjobs and sex for ten to fifteen dollars, which is just enough to pay for the next meth hit. "You'll see them in parks and parking lots, in plain sight, leaning against or bent over cars," he said. He talked about the risk of disease and violence involved with prostitution at that level. "It's nutty. The whole thing is just beyond."

I shuddered at the mental picture. The extreme Winder described was a world apart from the women I interviewed. Knowing a thing or two about how price relates to the perception of quality, I wondered, *Who on earth would risk being with a fifteen-dollar provider?* I answered myself about as fast: *Probably someone equally broke, equally desperate, equally high on meth. Probably someone who cares no more than the provider about picking up or passing along bugs, assuming any bugs remain that either of them hasn't already picked up.*

I ached at the thought of human beings whose lives have spiraled downward to that point. No one sets sights on landing in those circumstances. I wondered what combination of environment, genes, bad luck, wrong turns, and events beyond their control had brought them there. There's no telling who among the rest of us might be a butterfly effect away from a similar fate.

At the high end of the price continuum are what Winder called "circuit girls." They travel the country working and attending various events, such as Utah's Sundance Film Festival, charging $1,500 or more for their services. Like the women I interviewed, circuit girls tend not to cause disturbances and rarely have run-ins with the law. That police rarely have to deal with circuit girls and are largely unaware of "Sam's Club" providers lends credence to my suspicion that typical research into prostitution overlooks a significant percentage of providers. "Circuit girls" and "Sam's Club girls" draw no notice and cause no stir. They're not streetwalking or bent over cars in parking lots. They don't cause complaints, attract police, or check into public health clinics with sexually transmitted infections (STIs). All of which makes them invisible to typical research methods.

I ventured that not much prostitution makes its way to Moab, that the trade is confined more to bigger cities. Not so, Winder told me. Moab has prostitution, "but largely in a different way. While higher-end call girls may accompany a tourist visiting Moab, what we see here is more narcotics-oriented. It's hideous. Addictions or family members may force them into prostitution. Say you have someone working a minimum wage job and is hooked on meth—there's less of a heroin problem here—she will sleep with anyone to obtain drugs or for money to obtain them. Or their boyfriends traffic them to get drugs. The line between trafficking and drug abuse is very vague."

It's possible for smaller towns not to know the extent of local drug abuse that is linked to prostitution. "Some smaller departments in smaller communities don't have the resources to follow up on every complaint. Not following up means they don't know what's going in their jurisdictions. They're missing the boat on working effectively with their communities. Because you'll find abuse, neglect, and crime-crime-crime you wouldn't have otherwise found."

He continued, "So do I care [about the type of provider you described]? Only enough to prove or disprove if there is an ongoing criminal activity in which there's a victim. Is it trafficking? Is someone getting ripped off? Otherwise I don't care. Neither is taking place with the high-end call girl. Resources are so finite that if we are wasting our time on victimless crimes, then shame on us."

3

Vice advice

Winder said that police receive few complaints about suspected prostitution in apartment complexes. Unusual traffic in and out of an apartment more often leads neighbors to suspect a drug dealer in their midst. In fact, the offender usually turns out to be a user, not a dealer.

In the event of a complaint, police show up and have a look around. "If we're talking about a busy drug dealer, it will usually be obvious within a day or two from the constant traffic. If it's prostitution you'll see less traffic in and out of the apartment, maybe three or four per day, but vehicles will be an indicator. These are typically mid-range apartments where residents drive Ford trucks and Camrys. If you see Jags, BMWs, and Range Rovers, chances are it's either prostitution or mid-level drug dealing."

When police believe they have a drug dealer in their sights, they dispatch a Neighborhood Narcotics Unit (NNU)—plainclothes officers in an unmarked car—to surveil.[4] When the suspected dealer climbs into a car and drives off, NNU will instruct officers in marked cars to keep an eye. Suspicion of drug activity doesn't justify a pullover, but a legitimate traffic violation does. Sooner or later there's a good chance that a roll-through, broken taillight, improper lane change, or expired license plate will provide the needed excuse. That much doesn't grant authority to search a vehicle, so the officer will run the driver's name through the system and look for anomalies in plain sight, such as weapons or drugs. In the absence of a record and suspicious anomalies, the suspect is free to go. Provided, that is, the suspect is smart enough to keep quiet. Most dealers are smart enough, Winder told me, but many a user is not.

The next step is a "trash cover" in which plainclothes cops obtain a warrant and go through the apartment dumpsters.[5] If they find an overabundance of wine bottles, condoms, lube, and sex-toy boxes, there's a good chance a prostitute is working in one of the apartments. "Then the next question," Winder said, "is whether it's prostitution alone or prostitution with dope. One of two courses of action might follow. We might execute a knock-and-talk." A *knock-and-talk* is exactly what it sounds like: officers knock on the apartment door and, if it opens, initiate a conversation with the occupant. "If it's a drug user, you'd be amazed at how often they say, 'Yup, you got me.' If it's a prostitute and no drugs are involved, she'll probably calmly say, 'No, no drugs going on here.' About 30 percent sign a voluntary waiver allowing police to go in and search. If they find no dope, the officers leave."

It's not unusual for the person who called in the complaint to follow up and ask what police found. "If there has been no arrest," Winder said, "the best we can say is that we have not found any criminal activity. If they persist and ask, 'Then what is going on?' we'll say it's noncriminal. If they press it, we might say it's none of their business."

I was well aware from interviewing providers that many public figures from religion, business, and politics carry on secret lives as clients. Had Winder ever apprehended but chosen not to arrest a public figure?

He drew a breath, paused a beat, and then with his typical candor said, "Yes. I have encountered probable cause and then made a determination not to arrest for all kinds of people. It doesn't matter whether or not it's a public figure. When I'm wearing my law enforcement hat, it doesn't matter who they are. But we can't make predetermined judgments. We're not in a position to turn a blind eye. If we get a call we have to investigate."

I asked about the practice of releasing the names of busted johns to the media for publication, as some law enforcement departments do. "I don't agree with that," he said "Shaming is morally repugnant. It leads to a host of secondary unintended consequences—suicide, divorce, impact on kids. The scarlet letter affects all. I think it's weird."

When it comes to deterring prostitution on the client side, Winder prefers john education programs to shaming. This was the first I'd heard of *john schools*, a now widespread program that began in San Francisco. It provides johns a harrowing look at the trade from the point of view of underage, trafficked, and abused providers. Apprehended johns may attend as part of sentencing or in exchange for leniency. Data concerning results of the San Francisco program are disputed,[6] but Winder is sold on them. "They're better, very informative," Winder said. "A john can speak with a call girl, understand what he's really doing, what she's really going through, what and who has pressured her. He can see that to her it's just a job, that he's no Don Juan."

4

Undercover cops: rules and myths

I was eager to discuss the rules for undercover work, not least because of the myriad "sure-fire" methods of detecting undercover cops that providers shared with me. Providers would see through many of these methods if they gave them a bit more thought. For instance, a surprising number of providers believe a cop must answer truthfully when asked point-blank, "Do you work in law enforcement?" This myth isn't difficult to debunk. No statute or departmental policy requires undercover officers to answer that question in the affirmative.

Another popular "method" for would-be arrest evasion is the use of coded language. Some providers ask for a "donation" instead of a fee. Some ask for "200 roses" instead of "200 dollars." Some offer "full service," meaning sex, or a "GFE," short for "girlfriend experience," believing they are within the law as long as they don't utter the word "sex." But if their meaning is clear to a client, it will be clear to a judge, too.

Some providers instruct the client to place "the donation" on a table or dresser. The idea is that if she doesn't touch the cash while he's there, then she didn't legally accept it. They fail to realize that, either way, cash has been exchanged.

Some providers look for clues. Some take nervousness as a sure sign they're dealing with a cop, while others take it as a sure sign they're not. Some told me that overconfidence is a sure sign of a cop, while others told me it's a sure sign of an arrogant jerk who isn't a cop. Some, apparently unaware of the existence of sensitive hidden microphones, told me that a man speaking in a loud voice is probably wearing a wire.

Quite a few providers said, "I can just tell." This one made Winder chuckle. "An undercover cop's success depends on acting skills," he said. "Some are great at playing drunk or acting nervous. I'd say the vast majority of these girls can be fooled."

Not to be overlooked is the previously discussed "LE check," short for "Law Enforcement check." A provider may ask the client to expose his genitals or to touch hers, figuring cops aren't allowed to comply. I asked Winder if undercover cops are permitted to proceed with sexual contact.

"What drives prostitution investigations is more at the policy than the statutory level," Winder explained. "Some agencies have written policies allowing officers to penetrate females," he said, not hiding his disgust. "A surprising number think it's okay. They're allowing officers to commit rape and sexual abuse." Here Winder was emphatic: "So in some cases, yes they can, and no they should not."

To Winder's point, Broadly.vice.com reported, "In many US states, it is technically legal for undercover cops to have sex with sex workers during the course of anti-prostitution sting operations. Advocates argue this is nothing less than institutional rape."[7]

As recently as early 2020, the *Salt Lake Tribune* reported that at the conclusion of a session in a Salt Lake area massage parlor, a Unified Police Department of Greater Salt Lake officer motioned to his masseuse "that he wanted a sex act, he later wrote in a 2018 police report."

> The woman complied, removing a small towel that was draped over his waist, and began touching his genitals.
>
> "I stood up and removed [her] hand," he wrote, " . . . and told her I needed to use the bathroom immediately. I gave the bust signal" . . .
>
> Unified police officials say this was not unusual; about half of their undercover operations targeting so-called massage parlors involve the masseuse touching an officer's genitals before an arrest is made. It's necessary, they say, to show that the employees are engaged in sex acts because it can be difficult to communicate with workers who do not speak fluent English.
>
> Some experts say tactics like this are outdated, inappropriate and, often, not necessary to prove a criminal case in Utah.[8]

Like Winder, a former Salt Lake City police chief had nothing good to say about the practice, his unfortunate choice of idiom notwithstanding:

> "There is no bone in my body that says that is the right thing to do," said Chris Burbank, a former Salt Lake City police chief who now works with the Center of Policing Equity. "You, in fact, committed the crime and then arrested the other person for that crime."[9]

I wondered, but didn't ask Winder, if there's a correlation between departments that allow undercover cops to have sex with providers and the percentage of cops who volunteer for vice duty.

The point of undercover work is to establish innocence or to obtain sufficient evidence for an arrest and conviction. The problem is with that word *sufficient*. To bring to a halt the practice of police going too far in pursuit of that elusive standard, Winder and other departments coordinated with the Utah legislature to come up with workable standards short not just of penetration but also of touching and exposing. "In Utah," he said, "the threshold was lowered about three years ago. Probable cause is not difficult to obtain. In essence, they can articulate that she is engaging in activities designed to indicate prostitution. If there's a fee or the functional equivalent of a fee, it counts. Offers, agreement, drugs, cash, consideration, ten bucks on the table, arranging through advertising, agreeing to meet in an arranged place for sexual activities—these all count. You go in and you're speaking flirtatiously, either of you suggest bed and it's agreed upon, you're under arrest. No warrant needed."

I said, "So essentially the standard is, if it would make a judge or jury roll their eyes and say, 'Oh, come on; it's prostitution,' it's enough to make an arrest."

Winder replied, "Exactly. It's enough to arrest. Conviction is harder."

I was pleased to learn that convictions are harder to obtain. What would make a judge or jury roll their eyes and say, "Oh, come on," is not the most objective of standards. In discussing this project, I came across quite a few people who would do an eye roll and utter, "Oh, come on," with no more than a glance at a woman's dress, shape, heritage, body language, or color. "You don't need hard evidence when you can just *tell*," one acquaintance whom I hope is never selected for jury duty told me.

I asked if busted johns ever agree to work undercover for law enforcement in exchange for lighter sentencing. Winder said it can happen, but it's infrequent. I asked if police ever "turn" providers to help with client stings. "That happens less so," he said, adding that a fair number of providers are confidential informants on other matters, "such as reporting someone who boasts about having beaten someone, someone who is one of Utah's most wanted, or someone the provider believes has committed a serious crime." He said they are not at risk of arrest when they report. "They might not call police headquarters, but they might communicate regularly with cops." He quickly followed up, "And not necessarily on a quid pro quo basis." The *necessarily* in *not necessarily* wasn't lost on me. Every provider I spoke with except Gene has clients who are cops.

Though we didn't discuss it, the issue of entrapment as a defense bears mention. Police officers who pose as providers and johns are not guilty of entrapment as long as they do it right, and most police do. If out of the blue a police decoy approaches you and cajoles you into a paid sexual encounter you'd had no intention of seeking, that's entrapment. But if you initiate the transaction and the decoy plays along, good luck claiming the decoy made you do it. If you sit down next to a decoy at a bar and offer her cash for sex, if you approach a decoy on the street and ask how much for a blowjob, or if via text you arrange to meet a decoy advertising online, it doesn't matter how much you think her appearance exuded "I'm a sex worker." You weren't entrapped. You were careless, unlucky, or both and, most important, you initiated the transaction.

5

We discuss trafficking

Our only point of disagreement had to do with trafficking. It began when Winder said, "Some Asian women come here to do manicures and pedicures. It's coercive in that they need the money or they're being trafficked. They're kept under poor conditions. They're charged for everything—lodging, lights, etc. They can't earn enough, making them like indentured servants. This often migrates into prostitution."

That happens, but I believe from my research that what Winder described doesn't apply to Salt Lake area Asian massage parlors across the board. I shared with Winder details from my conversation with Asian massage parlor owner Lilly regarding how her workers were recruited and treated.

"I think she's delusional," Winder said. "She's not being honest with you. They pay for everything. Indentured servants. Once here, they're in a pickle."

As noted earlier, I described individual workers with whom I visited who appeared to be working of their own free will. Winder was tactful enough not to suggest I'd been duped, though surely it crossed his mind. Instead he suggested that the women I'd met were exceptions.[10]

6

"You get older, you mellow."

I liked Winder. He was forthright, unpretentious, and courteous. I felt instantly comfortable with him. We carried on an easy, genial conversation, moving from topic to topic and from anecdote to anecdote as old friends might do. When we disagreed he was eminently civil. He struck me as genuinely committed to the good of the community. He is not out to enforce technicalities just because he can.

I asked if his attitudes and perspective make him unique in law enforcement. "I think I'm probably in the minority," he said. "Also, it's an age thing. You get older, you mellow. But I'm not an expert in any sense."

As our conversation wound down, Winder waxed philosophical. "But I think it's sad, even the type you have described. What is sex? It's not just a physical thing. There's the emotional connection. Paying for it? I just don't get it."

Chapter 10

Should It Be Legal?

Selling is legal. Fucking is legal. Why isn't selling fucking legal?

—George Carlin

1

The art of turning fun into shame

Sorry, Marvel Universe fans. *The Amazing Spider-Man*'s Uncle Ben wasn't the first to say, "With great power comes great responsibility." The expression has been around in one form or another since the French Revolution,[1] and for all we know the French imported it from another culture. Regardless of who said it first and when, today's Highly Moral Lawmakers (HMLs) seem to think it needs an addendum. Their version is more along the lines of, "With great power comes great responsibility, and with great responsibility comes an obligation to prevent people from having too much fun, especially if it makes us envious." This version most certainly did not originate in France, since not once in the history of word-association games has anyone ever responded to "puritanical" with "the French."

Aware that outlawing fun could justly make them look like a bunch

215

of killjoys, HMLs set about rebranding every form of fun they found objectionable, which was pretty much every form of fun, as *vice*. It was a marketing and public relations coup. "Outlawing vice" has a certain "for the public good" ring to it.

HMLs next turned their attention to the banning or controlling of any activity that so much as remotely smacked of fun, such as alcohol consumption, recreational drug use, gambling, birth control, blasphemy, profanity, and all things sexual. They were careful to avoid discussing *dosage*, for that would have necessitated acknowledging that any of the above in harmless doses can be, well, harmless. Even drinking too much water will kill you.[2]

In their zeal to foster a fun-free environment, HMLs lost no time in getting their hands on our genitals. Over time they mapped out precisely how, when, where, why, and with whom we were and were not to use them. Thanks to their dedication, most societies today have laws that seek to ban or control masturbation, porn consumption, sex toys, strip clubs, transsexualism, sex talk, sexy attire, contraception, abortion, sex education, marital sex, premarital sex, extramarital sex, nonmarital sex, gay sex, and the insertion of unauthorized objects into unauthorized orifices for unauthorized purposes. Adding cash to the equation makes forbidden encounters all the more forbidden.[3]

It should come as no surprise that Mormon-dominated Utah has had more than its share of HMLs throughout its history. Even when the above are not expressly illegal, the Mormon Church is vigilant in forbidding them.

Not to be outwitted, determined fun seekers have found creative ways to walk right up to but not step over the legal line. Paid encounters with full or limited nudity and with limited mutual touch are legal in Utah provided there is no sexual contact. Examples include strip clubs, private dancers or models, escort services, sensual massages, and the fast-growing cuddling industry. There is, of course, little that HMLs can do to control what escorts and cuddlers choose to do behind closed doors. That's why law enforcement agencies conduct the occasional sting operation.

Millennia of seeking to ban and control fun have not been in vain. Government intrusion into our personal lives has yielded a wealth of useful information. Just look at what we have learned:

- People tend to enjoy fun. This is not a little circular, since *fun* is kind of implicit in the word *fun*.

- Outlawing fun tends not to eliminate fun but to drive it underground.

- As with any commodity, where there is sufficient demand for fun, supply is inevitable.

- Where fun is illegal, suppliers can get away with inflated prices, making the business of supplying illegal fun immensely profitable.

- Driving fun underground creates business opportunities for organized crime, whose natural habitat happens to be the underground.

- Dealing with organized crime isn't the safest thing you can do.

- Illegally purchased fun comes with no assurance of quality or safety.

- People harmed as a result of selling or purchasing illegal fun have little to no legal recourse.

- Arrests and prosecution for victimless illegal fun divert focus from nonvictimless crimes, and they place a financial and practical burden on law enforcement and overcrowded jails.

- Banning vice deprives governments of potential licensing and tax revenues.

- The for-profit prison industry profits handsomely from, and actively lobbies for, incarcerating people for criminalized fun.

We have also learned a thing or two from governments that have experimented with making fun legally permissible. Namely, that many of the above harms diminish or vanish. Consider that the repeal of Prohibition largely removed organized crime from the alcohol business.[4] States with legalized marijuana have experienced a drop in violent crimes.[5] Likewise, as we're about to see, making prostitution legally permissible has had its share of positive outcomes, including greater safety for providers and clients, reduced disease transmission, and a reduction in sex crimes.

2

Okay versus not okay prostitution

I believe that voluntary, safe, discreet sex work among consenting adults, which herein I'll refer to using George Washington University sociology professor Ronald Weitzer's term, "indoor prostitution,"[6] should be legally permissible. If that surprises you, either you haven't been paying attention, or you just opened this book for the first time and happened to start reading on this page.

The legal permissibility of sex work is a heated topic in which bias and zeal drive research and conclusions, leaving plenty of fodder for any stance anyone wishes to take. If you want to oppose legally permissible prostitution, you need only google "why prostitution should be illegal." Within seconds, you'll be greeted by an endless list of seemingly sound arguments. On the other hand, if you want to support legally permissible prostitution, you need only google "why prostitution should be legal." Within seconds, you'll be greeted by an endless list of seemingly solid arguments.

As I make my case for legally permissible sex work, I want to be clear about something. I'm not arguing that *all* prostitution is okay. Child prostitution is absolutely vile. Forcing people to provide sexual services against their will is absolutely vile. Trafficking in the commonly understood sense is absolutely vile. As global human rights organization Amnesty International policy advisor Catherine Murphy put it, even while arguing for the decriminalization of sex work, "Trafficking is an abhorrent abuse of human rights and must be criminalized as a matter of international law."[7]

Nor is streetwalking okay. Not least among objections is the fact that many people prefer not to have sex workers showcasing their wares, or clients consuming them, in front of their home or business. Also, people are not fond of finding their sidewalks and lawns littered with condoms and needles. In addition, streetwalking seems to bring with it other harms beyond the reach of a regulatory environment. Weitzer reports that New Zealand, the Netherlands, and New South Wales, Australia, have experimented with legal streetwalking zones, but have had little luck curtailing the associated problems.[8]

It is not okay that there are people who wish to exit prostitution but for any of a number of reasons cannot. Perhaps they are coerced. Or perhaps they cannot obtain other employment due to a criminal record, lack of other jobs skills, or impaired self-esteem. These are people who deserve help, not prosecution.

As I have stated often enough that by now you may want to chuck a shoe at me, the providers I present in this book are neither trafficked nor pimped. They are of age. They willingly choose sex work not for lack of options but for money, enjoyment, or both. Many have college degrees, marketable skills outside of sex work, and a solid résumé. They practice safe sex. They advertise online and never solicit in public. They charge from $200 to $600 or more for an encounter. They meet clients in the privacy of hotel rooms, apartments rented for the purpose, or clients' homes. They exercise discretion, rarely if ever drawing notice. That is the type of sex work that I'm calling "indoor prostitution" and arguing should be legally permissible.

3

The demonizing of sex work

An oft-cited 2017 study by John Potterat estimates that there are 23 prostitutes per 100,000 people in the United States.[9] That would put the total number of prostitutes working in the United States as of this writing at about 75,506. By contrast, Havocscope, an organization that researches black market activity, estimates that there are about a million prostitutes working in the United States.[10] That's a 924,494 difference of expert opinion.

Utah accounts for roughly 1 percent of the nation's population, so from the above numbers we might estimate that Utah is home to 756 (Potterat) or 10,000 (Havocscope) working prostitutes. We might further estimate that 605 (Potterat) or 8,000 (Havocscope) of them work in the Salt Lake City metropolitan area, since that's where 80 percent of Utah's population reside. I am no statistician, so perhaps I'm not qualified to make the following observation, but I shall throw caution to the wind and risk suggesting that there's something of a gap between 75,506 and 1,000,000; between 756 and 10,000; and between 605 and 8,000.

Counting sex workers and clients is not as easy as, say, counting vehicle registrations. Unlike vehicle owners, prostitutes and johns tend not to register with the state. Anonymous surveys help, but not much. Even under protection of anonymity, people are loath to level about personal matters, not just with researchers but also with themselves. If you don't believe me, send out an anonymous survey asking people what percent of the time they wash their hands after using a public restroom. Then hide in a public restroom and count how many people wash when they think no one is watching. The difference might just make you swear off shaking hands.[11] But it should also tell you something about people's reluctance to be honest about their personal habits, especially when it comes to sensitive matters. As H. L. Mencken stated in response to Alfred C. Kinsey's study on men's sexual behavior, "All men lie when they are asked about their adventures in amour, [and] pedagogues are singularly naïve and credulous creatures."[12]

With no direct means of counting sex workers, researchers must resort to indirect means. This, too, can be tricky. Havocscope, for instance, arrived at its numbers from "security services estimates, reporting by public health programs, and other monitoring data from global criminal justice programs.[13] I'll grant that these data make for a reasonable starting point, but—at the risk of sounding a bit circular—I would point out that people who work for security services, public health programs, and global criminal justice programs only know about the prostitutes they know about and have absolutely no idea about how many prostitutes they don't know about. They are left to infer the whole from a slice that may or may not be representative. Most of the prostitutes I interviewed have never been identified by law enforcement or health services of any sort. They and the many like them are all but statistically invisible.

Potterat's figure of 23 prostitutes per 100,000 citizens impresses in its specificity. But Potterat's point of departure, too, is public records—specifically, the figure is "based on a capture-recapture study of prostitutes found in Colorado Springs, CO, police and sexually transmitted diseases clinic records between 1970 and 1988."[14] It's doubtful that public records in Colorado Springs provide any better of a snapshot than the public records Havocscope reviewed. They might even provide a less accurate one, for it's doubtful that the population of a picturesque town nestled in the Colorado Rockies is a perfect representation of Americans overall, even if demographic characteristics and sexually transmitted disease rates there are representative of the United States as a whole. Nothing against Colorado Springs, mind you. I spent several days there and loved it. I recommend a visit. Book your room at The Antlers.[15]

I'm not done identifying the challenges in this type of research. In a separate report that relies, in part, on Potterat's earlier study, researchers attempted to get a handle on the number of clients per known prostitute in Colorado Springs: "In the first interview, 98 adult prostitute women reported a mean of 347 male sexual partners in the last 6 months."[16] That would be useful information if we could rely on it. I'm not certain we can. I doubt that Colorado Springs providers use tally counters (that's the technical name for those clicky things ushers use to count people entering a venue). In other words, the providers guesstimated, and you can bet that their guesstimates were not bias-free. It is human to bias answers, wittingly or unwittingly, toward what you think your questioners want to hear. It is even more human to do so when your questioners happen to be arresting officers with some say over your sentencing.[17]

To be fair, such challenges are not news to researchers, who try to adjust their findings accordingly. The trouble is deciding whether to adjust numbers up or down, and by how much.

Speaking more generally, another huge reason I'm loath to accept popular data about prostitution as prima facie reliable has to do with the ultimate objective of the research. While I have no reason to doubt the integrity of individual academics who take a scholarly interest in the subject, many of the organizations that fund this type of research—or that pursue and promote their own internal research—have their own agendas. In some cases, they are out to eradicate prostitution, and they intend to use data to that end.

When it comes to sensationalized reporting about the sex trade, retired sex worker Maggie McNeill penned this for the *Washington Post*:

> In fact, many of those who represent themselves as sex work researchers don't even try to get good data. They simply present their opinions as fact, occasionally bolstered by pseudo-studies designed to produce pre-determined results.[18]

None of this is to suggest that all or even most researchers and those who retain their services are insincere or dishonest.[19] It is to suggest that even the best researchers are human, and they can be blinded to their own biases. And because researchers rely on and compete for funding, they cannot always easily escape the influence that comes with knowing that certain sources of funding will reward those who, say, come up with the highest numbers they can justify and the most horrifying, sphincter-puckering case studies they can dredge up. And because we're often talking about observational studies, the methods used to eliminate bias in controlled studies do not apply.

Chances are that willing providers who enjoy the trade often do not show up in finished reports. If they do, they will likely be trivialized in a footnote or discounted as anomalies. Take, for example, a comment that appears in Lenora C. Babb's article, "Utah's Misguided Approach to the Problem of Sex Trafficking: A Call for Reform":

While there are certainly women and men who enter sex work as a choice, many if not most are brought in and kept in the industry through violence, coercion, and manipulation.[20]

Note the glib qualifier "many if not most," which means but doesn't sound like it means "we don't know how many." I can use "many if not most" with the best of them. For instance: *Many if not most opponents to legally permissible sex work engage in liberal use of all-or-nothing rhetoric and irresponsibly jump to claims of "many if not most."* A prime example is found in this observation on Laws.com's "The Prostitution Statistics You Have to Know"[21]:

It is extremely clear that persons engaged in prostitution are not happy with their unfortunate choice of profession. Countless studies report that over 80% of prostitutes say they wish to get out of prostitution. This information does not explain why women do not get out of prostitution. There is [sic] plenty of statistically based studies on prostitutes reporting reasons why they do not quit their jobs and do something legitimate.

Never mind that "extremely clear" is redundant, used for effect. To infer that "persons engaged in prostitution are not happy" from interviews with arrested sex workers is to make an irresponsible leap; arrested sex workers will be motivated to say what they perceive arresting officers want to hear, whereas never-arrested sex workers might tell an entirely different story. "Countless studies" is a neat way not to cite a real number and to avoid acknowledging contradictory studies. Note the use of prejudicial language such as "unfortunate choice of profession" and "why they do not . . . do something legitimate," which serves to elicit a nod of unthinking agreement from those who already buy the subject as black-and-white.

Again, I don't wish to imply that all professional researchers pull their data from a certain bodily crevasse that Nature was kind enough to place within easy reach. But some do. So while to preemptively dismiss professional estimates would be irresponsible, not to challenge them would be equally so.

4

Thinking that can get you into trouble

Opponents of prostitution use estimates to horrify people into supporting efforts to eradicate the sex trade. "Look how widespread it is," goes the argument. "We must wipe it out." You can hardly blame prostitution opponents for making that argument, because the public tends to buy it. And you can likewise hardly blame the public for buying the argument as long as you don't think about it very hard. Too much thinking about it could lead you to realize that "we must wipe it out" doesn't follow from "look how widespread it is." Consider other widespread activities, such as stopping for red lights, eating scrambled eggs with ketchup, and remembering to say "please" and "thank you." Oddly enough, no group has mobilized to bring them to a halt despite how widespread they are.[22]

The moment you realize that "wipe it out" doesn't follow from "widespread," you might wonder why no one points that out. Perhaps it's that people raised in a society that condemns prostitution are likely to assume that "we must wipe it out" is a given. Any who don't take it as a given may be inclined not to speak up. Imagine raising your hand at an anti-prostitution rally and saying, "Actually, I think some forms of prostitution might be harmless, maybe even beneficial." You might find yourself labeled a degenerate[23] or, worse, have to explain to your significant other on the way home from the rally why you were sticking up for prostitution.[24]

But you wouldn't be wrong.

Those who mobilize against prostitution aren't necessarily out to mislead, even when that is in effect what some are doing. Their ranks include mental health professionals, medical professionals, law enforcement professionals, former prostitutes, and concerned citizens—all people who have witnessed firsthand or are otherwise aware of the horrors that are too often part of the sex trade. The whole of their experience is worst-case scenarios. It's no wonder that they cry "Heresy!" at the suggestion that prostitution could ever be harmless, much less healthy or helpful, or that the solution to associated ills might be to address the ills rather than prostitution itself. The sex workers I interviewed may be so far outside critics' sphere as to have escaped their notice.

5

When governments ease up on prostitution

There is some debate among proponents as to whether sex work should be *legalized* or *decriminalized*. I won't presume to tell you which term is correct or preferable, in part because not even legal experts seem to agree on their definitions. The more I researched and the more attorneys I spoke with, the more definitions I accrued. I shall remain out of that fray by dismissing *legalized* and *decriminalized* in favor of *legally permissible*.

If you agree with me that indoor prostitution should be legally permissible, you're not alone. One-quarter to one-half of U.S. citizens agree with you.[25] That is, one-quarter to one-half dare say so, and only in confidential surveys. Add in those who don't dare say so along with those who aren't honest with themselves, and the number will likely be higher.

The evidence seems to show that making indoor prostitution legally permissible leaves sex workers as well as the community better off. Legally permissible indoor prostitution allows for safety regulations, health requirements, zoning, and licensing, the last having the potential of providing an economic boon to communities. It gives sex workers legal recourse in the event of hobbyists who are physically abusive or leave without paying, and it gives hobbyists recourse against scammers and muggers. Providers privy to crimes can come forth as witnesses without fear of self-incrimination. Not least, providers have an easier time moving into other careers when prostitution doesn't show up as a crime on a background check.

The World Health Organization has gone on the record in favor of making sex work permissible:

> Modelling studies indicate that decriminalising sex work could lead to a 46% reduction in new HIV infections in sex workers over 10 years; eliminating sexual violence against sex workers could lead to a 20% reduction in new HIV infections.
>
> WHO supports countries to address these structural barriers and ensure sex workers' human rights as well as implementing a comprehensive package of HIV and health services for sex workers through community led approaches.[26]

The WHO goes on to recommend "supportive legislation, policy and funding" and "addressing stigma and discrimination."

Amnesty International also supports legally permissible sex work:

> We have chosen to advocate for the decriminalization of all aspects of consensual adult sex—sex work that does not involve coercion, exploitation or abuse. This is based on evidence and the real-life experience of sex workers themselves that criminalization makes them less safe.[27]

It is an easy matter to look at the positive effects in cities, states, and countries that allow sex for pay. As Jennifer Wright, political editor at large for *Bazaar*, observed:

> There are a great many countries where sex work is legal, such as New Zealand, which decriminalized sex work in 2003. The results of the Prostitution Reform Act have been beneficial for sex workers. A study from the Christchurch School of Medicine found that "90 percent of sex workers believed the PRA gave them employment, legal and health and safety rights. A substantial 64 percent found it easier to refuse clients. Significantly, 57 percent said police attitudes to sex workers changed for the better." Prostitutes also reported being able to go to the

police when they were hurt or threatened, and one sex worker success-
fully sued a brothel owner for sexual harassment.[28]

In an article published by *Time*, Reason.com staff editor Elizabeth
Nolan Brown reported on the effects of making prostitution permissible
in New Zealand:

> so far sex workers and the New Zealand government have raved about
> the arrangement. A government review in 2008 found the overall num-
> ber of sex workers had not gone up since prostitution became legal, nor
> had instances of illegal sex-trafficking. The most significant change was
> sex workers enjoying safer and better working conditions. Research-
> ers also found high levels of condom use and a very low rate of HIV
> among New Zealand sex workers.[29]

Even in places where indoor prostitution is only implicitly legal, sex
workers have been able to better their lot by means of organizing. Northeastern University law professor Aziza Ahmed wrote:

> Already, trade unions of sex workers have launched in the United
> Kingdom and other European countries, and New Zealand has applied
> labor protections to the sex industry. Advocacy groups have also begun
> to use courts to defend their labor rights. In South Africa, an appeals
> court ruled in 2010 that a sex worker who said she'd been unfairly fired
> from a massage parlor . . . had a right to a hearing before a government
> body that settles labor disputes.[30]

Some who view sex-for-pay as evil oppose improved safety conditions for sex workers, seeing the dangers as useful deterrents. I haven't
much patience with that point of view. All people, including people who
do things of which one may disapprove, deserve protection from disease,
violence, harassment, and theft. If humanity fails to persuade, perhaps
the potential of sparing yourself or someone you love from rape might

do the trick. (More on that in a moment.)

Weitzer examined outcomes where governments have legalized and now regulate prostitution. "Counties [in Nevada] hosting legal brothels have near-zero illegal prostitution," he wrote.[31] On the other hand:

> Crackdowns on indoor prostitution can have the unintended result of increasing the number of streetwalkers, thus exacerbating the most problematic side of the prostitution trade. Closures of massage parlors and other indoor venues have had precisely this effect in some cities.[32]

Permissible indoor prostitution can have a positive effect on the local economy. Author and sex therapist Marty Klein made this interesting observation about the encouraging economic effects of decriminalized prostitution in, of all places, Baghdad:

> Nightclubs have reopened, hotels are busy, the streets are less scary. And so women are back to selling sex, men are buying, and life goes on.[33]

But let's be fair. To bring a little balance to the conversation, let's take a look at . . .

6

Arguments against permissible sex work

Despite nearly daily revelations of the vocal "family values" crusaders caught not family-valuing, I accept that most opponents of permissible prostitution are well-intended. Their arguments, though not new, are most likely sincere and deserve a fair hearing. The most common objections more or less consist of one of the following:

- Imagine it was your daughter.
- Sex workers are trafficked or otherwise in the business against their will.

- Making prostitution legally permissible will increase the number of prostitutes.

- Our community doesn't support that kind of thing.

- Sex work should be illegal because it's immoral.

- Prostitution brings with it a host of related crimes from drug dealing to mafia involvement.

- Prostitution risks the spread of STIs.

- Legally permissible prostitution will result in an increase in the incidence of rape.

- Legally permissible prostitution will increase trafficking.

- Sex workers are exploited.

- Sex work demeans women.

The above arguments often pass without challenge. While it's not difficult to dispatch the better part of them with facts and sound reasoning, facts and sound reasoning often prove powerless to change minds when it comes to topics with a strong emotional component, which prostitution has. If you have ever tried using sound reasoning and facts to persuade your best friend that the person he or she is dating is a louse or your in-laws that they're wrong about anything at all, you know what I mean.

In the hope that you number among those who are not impervious to facts and sound reasoning, I shall take the anti-legalization arguments one at a time:

Imagine it was your daughter. This argument doesn't pretend to be factual or reasoned, only emotional. It's one thing to argue for a woman's right to sell access to her body, the rhetoric goes, but quite another if we're talking about someone dear to you. To this, Jennifer Wright penned a response I can only envy: "I tried this experiment and discovered that I do not like to imagine my family members having sex of any kind, paid or unpaid." After listing several professions she would prefer an imaginary daughter not enter, Wright summed up,

You can agree or disagree with me that I'm right to not want a daughter to enter into those professions. The fact remains that, regardless of how I feel about them, my future daughter has a perfect legal right to pursue them.[34]

Sex workers are trafficked or otherwise in the business against their will. A wealth of books and blogs by sex workers as well as my own research attest to the existence of willing sex workers. To deny their existence is to indulge pure stubbornness. Moreover, this is a conversation about *legally permissible* prostitution, and under no circumstance would coerced sex work be legally permissible.

Making prostitution legally permissible will increase the number of prostitutes. That has not been established. In fact, according to the above-cited *Time* article by Elizabeth Nolan Brown, New Zealand's experience flatly contradicts that claim ("A government review in 2008 found the overall number of sex workers had not gone up since prostitution became legal . . . "). For that matter, the unstated premise that an increase would be a bad thing has not been established either. But if permissibility would cause an increase in the number of prostitutes, it would mean that a substantial number of people are standing at the ready to join the profession the moment it ceases to be illegal. I doubt that, and I bet you doubt it too. Otherwise, you'll have to give up the next argument.

Our community doesn't support that kind of thing. If that is so, you have nothing to fear. Where there is no demand, there will be no supply. A community that doesn't support "that kind of thing" is destined to remain blissfully free from it. But, back to the prior paragraph, if you think legally permissible prostitution means more people will enter into prostitution, you're admitting that your community supports that kind of thing after all.

Sex work should be illegal because it's immoral. This is an argument that holds up well—as long as everyone is agreed that sex work is immoral. As you may have gathered by now, not everyone is agreed on that one.

Prostitution brings with it a host of related crimes from drug dealing to mafia involvement. I am hard-pressed to imagine a more elegant argument against *illegal* prostitution. As discussed, *legally permissible prostitution* tends to obviate such problems.

Legally permissible prostitution risks the spread of STIs. Sex of any sort risks disease transmission. But where prostitution is legal there tend to be condom laws, making it considerably less likely than illegal prostitution to spread STIs. Nevada provides a good case study. It was none other than Nevada's legal brothel owners who lobbied their legislature for a condom law. A host of other regulations apply to Nevada prostitutes, including requirements to pass a background check, undergo weekly health exams, and submit to monthly STI tests.[35] Despite alarmist claims to the contrary, latex condoms provide an "essentially impermeable barrier" to particles the size of STI pathogens.[36] Although nothing guarantees safety from STIs, latex condoms significantly reduce the risk.[37] Perhaps that's why, when Harvard immunology student Alexa Albert conducted her 2001 study, there had never been a reported case of disease transmission in a legal Nevada brothel.[38] More recent reports focus more on the prevalence of STIs among prostitutes than on transmission to clients and show a significantly lower STI incidence among legal prostitutes.[39]

Legally permissible prostitution will result in an increase in the incidence of rape. The opposite happened in Rhode Island's inadvertent, natural experiment:

> One recent study of data from Rhode Island—where a loophole allowed legal indoor prostitution in 2003–2009—found the state's rape rate declined significantly over this period, especially in urban areas. (The gonorrhea rate also went down.)[40]

Similar declines correlate with legally permissible prostitution in 25 Dutch cities.[41] Even in New York City, where the practice remains illegal, researchers correlate a decline in rape with increased access to indoor sex workers.[42]

Legally permissible prostitution will increase trafficking. In fact, it seems to reduce it. Writing for the *Daily Beast*, Cathy Reisenwitz noted:

> While prohibitionists claim that legalizing prostitution has increased
> human trafficking in the country, the data don't support them. In fact
> the opposite happened. Germany legalized sex work in 2001. Between
> 2001 and 2011, cases of sex-based human trafficking shrank by 10 per-
> cent.[43]

Sex workers are exploited. This is absolutely true. To pay anyone to
do anything is, by definition, exploitative. It exploits Chris Hemsworth
to pay him to bare his upper body when he plays Thor, it exploits Gene
Simmons to pay him to stick out his tongue, and it exploits Stephen King
to pay him to keep cooking up ways to scare us. As Eric Sprankle, a Min-
nesota State University associate professor of clinical psychology & sexuality studies, tweeted, "If you think sex workers 'sell their bodies,' but coal
miners do not, your view of labor is clouded by your moralistic view of
sexuality."[44] The better question is whether the exploitation is *coerced* or
unfair. Independent adult sex workers who set their own prices, can quit
when they want, and are free to decline undesirable clients are far from
coerced. Jewel's earlier-cited comment comes to mind: "It's my body, and
I set my own price. Nobody can tell me what to sell it for."

Sex work demeans women. In many ways a restatement of both *sex
work should be illegal because it's immoral* and *sex workers are exploited*,
this is an eye-of-the-beholder thing. Sex work demeans women only if
you find sex work demeaning. Most of the women I interviewed find it
empowering. But suppose I concede the point (which I do not). If sex
work is demeaning, then you have an argument for disliking but not dis-
allowing it. It is not government's job to keep us from demeaning our-
selves. That is why puns, karaoke, and bad toupees remain legal.

But, as I said, reasoning and facts tend to accomplish little toward
persuading entrenched opponents of permissible indoor prostitution to
reconsider. Which brings me to . . .

7

Let's get real: Why people *really* oppose legalization

Pimping, trafficking, disease, drug abuse, and crime are not the real reasons people oppose permissible indoor prostitution. Those are straws that opponents grasp while watching with horror as society slowly awakens to the fact that no one has any business dictating what consenting adults do in the bedroom. Eliminate pimping, trafficking, disease, drug abuse, and organized crime from prostitution, and most who claimed to oppose it for those reasons will still oppose it. That's because their opposition to prostitution is not built upon evidence; quite simply, the very notion of prostitution *offends* them. The offense they take may be rooted in emotion, culture, religion, or some combination of these factors. But since "I think prostitution is disgusting" and "God disapproves" tend to prove insufficient for policymaking, opponents reach for what they consider to be more defensible arguments, like those presented in the last section. As the *Montreal Gazette*'s Stuart Chambers wrote:

> Historically speaking, "unnatural" sex has always been problematic for moral crusaders. For example, masturbation and homosexual acts were previously depicted as "harmful" to individual and collective health; yet such claims proved not only to be unfounded, but dangerous. This, however, has not stopped the perfectionists among us from endorsing a new cause: the present obsession with prostitution . . . the lessons of history are once again ignored by crusaders.[45]

Or, as Reisenwitz put it, "some people see sex that makes them uncomfortable to think about as wrong for other people to have."[46]

If we're going to ban activities solely because some of us find them personally repugnant, I suggest we start by outlawing haggis and disco. If we're going to ban indoor prostitution because organized crime engages in it, perhaps we should ban bank lending because loan sharks lend, too.

If your opposition to permissible indoor sex work is emotional, visceral, or religious, I promise not to make you engage with a sex worker. But your emotions, viscera, and religion are no reason to control what others choose to do.

Chapter 11

A Mormon Was Naughty. So?

In our home we grew up thinking we were
Mormons first and human beings second.

—Sonia Johnson

1

One fine day in Nashville

On August 13, 2019, in an H&M clothing store in a mall in a Nashville, Tennessee, Alondra Alcala picked out five outfits to try on. A helpful male H&M employee directed her to a fitting room, where she commenced undressing. Looking up, she happened to notice the corner of a smartphone—specifically, the corner where the camera lens resides—poking over the wall from the adjacent fitting room.

Not by coincidence, the phone hastily retracted the moment Alcala looked up and spotted it. This was immediately followed by the sounds of someone hurriedly exiting the adjacent fitting room. Initially frozen with shock, Alcala now leapt to action. She jerked her clothes back on, bolted from her room, and spotted the man who had shown her to the fitting room.

"I was kind of cornering him," she said, "kind of grabbing his arms, and I did watch him delete photos of me on his phone. Thankfully I was able to slap it out of his hand and take it and run out."

As Alcala called out to a fellow customer to call 911, the offending H&M employee's wife approached her, imploring her not to notify police.

I obtained all of this information from Salt Lake City news station KUTV's website. Now, you may be wondering why the man's wife happened to be on-site during her husband's shift at H&M, and, perhaps more so, why a Utah TV station bothered picking up a story about a random act of perversion that took place some 1,600 miles away. It turns out that the man wasn't really an H&M employee. He was vacationing with his wife in Nashville from their home town of Holladay, Utah, a suburb of Salt Lake City. Even so, a Utah peep in Nashville would hardly have grabbed headlines all the way back home—if the offender hadn't happened to have held a leadership position in the Mormon Church. The 55-year-old man was serving on a Mormon high council, an esteemed governing body of 12 men just under a stake presidency in authority.[1]

And yet—so? As of this writing, the Mormon Church has 596 stakes, 4,824 wards, 322 branches, and ten missions in Utah alone.[2] Throw a stick in downtown Salt Lake and you're likely to hit a dozen bishopric members, half a dozen high councilors, and two or three stake presidency members. Moreover, heinous as the peeping high councilor's action was, it pales in comparison to the growing mountain of abuse accusations directed at Catholic priests, televangelists, and other religious leaders. How is it that in Utah a Mormon high councilor caught peeping in Tennessee can command as many column inches as more than 300 Pennsylvania Catholic priests accused of molesting 1,000 children?[3]

2

A certain *je ne sais quoi*

"Whenever or wherever a Latter-day Saint is mentioned in a news story," wrote Mormon Church First Presidency member N. Eldon Tanner in 1981, "whether it be for appointment to high government office or for law-breaking—the 'Mormon' connection is usually mentioned. Other denominations rarely receive that distinction."[4]

Tanner spoke too soon. Nowadays it's difficult to log on to Facebook, open a newspaper, or turn on the news without learning of religious leaders from a growing number of denominations caught embezzling, committing sexual assault, engaging in homosexuality while condemning it, or carrying on an affair. But then, Tanner had a point. Especially in Utah, a Mormon leader caught with a hand in the naughty jar makes for bigger news, and for bigger gossip, than, say, a Catholic, Presbyterian, Lutheran, Muslim, or Hindu leader caught in like circumstances. Even Mormons who aren't in leadership positions tend to receive more attention than non-Mormons. Hang out near the average Utah office water cooler and you may hear, "Orson cheated on his wife. And he acts like he's such a good Mormon." You will be less likely to hear, ". . . and he acts like he's such a good Episcopalian."

What's up with that?

Out of many possible answers, I suggest that one is to be found in the Mormon Church's pervasiveness and influence in Utah, and another in the way the church continually holds itself up as a beacon of morality. For those outside the fold, those two factors deliver a one-two punch that can grow tiresome if not downright insulting.

Consider a discourse delivered by Thomas S. Monson as president, prophet, seer, and revelator of the Mormon Church in October 2015. The occasion was one of the church's semiannual worldwide conferences. Stepping up to the podium in the imposing Mormon conference center across the street from the famous Mormon temple and tabernacle in downtown Salt Lake City, television cameras capturing every moment, Monson told members of the church at large:

> As the world moves further and further away from the principles and
> guidelines given to us by a loving Heavenly Father, we will stand out

from the crowd because we are different. We will stand out because we dress modestly. We will be different because we do not use profanity and because we do not partake of substances which are harmful to our bodies. We will be different because we avoid off-color humor and degrading remarks. We will be different as we decide not to fill our minds with media choices that are base and demeaning and that will remove the Spirit from our homes and our lives. We will certainly stand out as we make choices regarding morality—choices which adhere to gospel principles and standards. Those things which make us different from most of the world also provide us with that light and that spirit which will shine in an increasingly dark world."[5]

More recently, Monson's prophet-successor Russell M. Nelson, in an address to the Brigham Young University student body, said:

You are the children whom God chose to be part of His battalion during this great climax in the longstanding battle between good and evil—between truth and error. I would not be surprised if, when the veil is lifted in the next life, we learn that you actually pled with our Heavenly Father to be reserved for now. I would not be surprised to learn that premortally, you loved the Lord so much that you promised to defend His name and gospel during this world's tumultuous winding-up scenes. One thing is certain: You are of the House of Israel and you have been sent here to help gather God's elect.[6]

To Mormons, speeches like Monson's and Nelson's inspire, motivate, and validate. To non-Mormons, they can be a slap in the face. People are not fond of hearing that they're immodest, profane, drunk, obscene, addicted to porn, and devoid of light by virtue of not being Mormons. They grow weary of being reminded that they are not the ones whom God reserved to defend his name and that they do not number among God's elect.

Nor were Monson's and Nelson's comments anomalies. Any honest churchgoing Mormon will affirm having been raised with a steady diet of:

You are a chosen people.[7]

You are a light and an example to the world.[8]

Do not associate with people who do not share your values and standards.[9]

Go ye out from among the wicked.[10]

You're a member of the Mormon Church because before the world was made you were more valiant than other people.[11]

The Lord held you in reserve to come forth in the last days because you were among the most valiant spirits in the pre-mortal world.[12]

If you're Caucasian, it's because you were more valiant in the pre-mortal world than people born non-Caucasian, your ancestors were more righteous than non-Caucasian people's ancestors, or both.[13]

When people learn that you're Mormon, they'll be impressed because they know you have high standards. It's your job to set a good example for non-Mormon friends and neighbors.[14]

You are to be a savior on Mount Zion.[15]

Members of other churches have some truth, but only the Mormon Church has the whole truth; it is the one true church.[16]

You're a Mormon because you know the shepherd's voice.[17]

People who aren't Mormons aren't truly happy.[18]

People who leave the Mormon Church do so because they're oversensitive, confused, misled, not valiant, or because they just plain want to sin, sin, sin.[19]

Your destiny is to become a god just like God the Father.[20]

In the last days, the United States Constitution will hang by a thread, and it will be none other than the Mormons who step in and save it.[21]

Mormons are told they have a God-given duty to bring in converts.[22] An important first step, they are taught, is "to set a good example."[23] It follows that Mormons believe they live better lives than their non-Mormon neighbors. The idea is that outsiders will see in Mormons a certain *je ne sais quoi* and want some of that *quoi* for themselves.

3

"We're better than you"

If you believe your lifestyle is so exemplary as to make people want to emulate you, it follows that you see yourself as standing on higher ground. When messages like the above filter out, it's little wonder that outsiders begin to feel that the attitude of the Mormon Church and its members is, "We're better than you."[24]

Putdown aside, "we're better than you" finds its way into action. Where Mormons are the dominant demographic, they are known for disdaining and excluding non-Mormon neighbors. There are Mormons who don't allow their children to play in the homes of non-Mormon kids, or to play with non-Mormon kids at all. There are grown Mormons who believe they shouldn't associate with non-Mormons. Many Utah Mormons hardly know their next-door non-Mormon neighbors.[25] Non-Mormons newly arriving in Utah often find their new Mormon neighbors' initial interest in them fades the moment it's clear they're not interested in converting.[26]

Now, there are plenty of Mormons who neither think nor act like that. They're real. They're not stuck on themselves. They don't think they're better. They make great friends and neighbors. Indeed, Mormons are people like any other people. There are good, bad, friendly, unfriendly, fair-minded, bigoted, principled, and unprincipled. Mormons are found at every point along the Lovable-to-Asshole Continuum.

Which is precisely why the ongoing "we're better than you" message gets tiresome.

The problem lies not in urging Mormons to be better people but in

Mormons treating their moral superiority as a *fait accompli*. If Mormons worked toward bettering themselves without implying having arrived at the goal, and if they were less exclusionary, there would be no more reaction to Mormons caught with their pants down than, say, to Presbyterians, Episcopalians, or Congregationalists caught with theirs down.

All that's needed is a bit of conscientious tweaking to the attitude, which, in time, would find its way into the rhetoric, which, further in time, would find its way into the behaviors.

Even remarks like Monson's aren't beyond saving. Here, at the risk of presuming to edit a prophet, I offer this modest rewrite:

> I plead with you to be strong. Dress modestly, don't use profanity, don't consume harmful substances, avoid off-color humor and degrading remarks, don't fill your minds with the base and demeaning, and seek to have the Spirit in your homes and lives. But for Pete's sake, don't go around thinking these things make you better than others, make people look up to you, or make you too good to associate with others. The goal is not to be better or exemplary. It is to be our best selves.

Until the attitude-tweak happens, non- and former Mormons will continue letting out a triumphant, schadenfreude-indulging "Aha!" every time another Mormon is caught being just as human as anyone else.

Postlude

"Well, This Is Creepy."

I'm just a musical prostitute, my dear.

—Freddy Mercury

The buzzer sounded, signaling a client's arrival. In the cramped employee lounge in the back of the office suite, Lexie took one more drag of weed before handing the pipe back to her coworker. "My turn?" she asked the coworker. The latter nodded. Standing up, Lexie checked herself in the mirror. The woman looking back at her could have could have stepped straight from the easel of pinup artist Alberto Vargas. Large blue eyes looked out from under blond tresses. She wore a denim mini and a loose-fitting top with a plunging neckline.

You may recall that Lexie had declined an offer to appear in *Playboy*.[1] Though the money was tempting, she wasn't comfortable posing naked for the world to see. But a paid "private conversation," that she could handle.

"Save me some of that," she said, gesturing toward the pipe, and headed down the hall toward the small front room where the newly arrived client waited.

The private conversation business was one of many creative workarounds that inevitably arose in response to Utah's rules for strip clubs. Utah law permits nude dancing only where alcohol is not served. As a result, not long ago in Utah you would have found all-nude strip clubs serving soft drinks, and all-nude-except-for-pasties-and-panties strip clubs serving alcohol.

But individual Utah cities and counties can ban live nude entertainment outright if they wish, and by now most have. As of this writing, Utah has no all-nude strip clubs. Clubs serving soft drinks must now follow the same rules as their alcohol-licensed cousins. If that surprises you, you're not alone. Many people are surprised that Utah issues alcohol licenses.

In Salt Lake County, the laws regarding pasties and panties are quite specific. Pasties must completely cover the nipple and areola, and cannot be shaped or colored to look like real nipples. As for panties, "at a minimum, the genitals, pubic region and anus shall be fully covered by an opaque covering no narrower than four inches wide in the front and five inches wide in the back which shall not taper to less than one inch wide at the narrowest point."[2] Law enforcement officers have been known to show up with tape measures.

The municipality of South Salt Lake, which—you may have seen this coming—lies south of Salt Lake City, banned totally nude live entertainment in 2001. Before then, South Salt Lake was home to a handful of all-nude, soft drink–serving strip clubs. Some of them are still in business, but today they toe the pasty and panty line.[3]

South Salt Lake was also home to "private modeling" businesses. There, a customer would pay at the front desk and be shown to a small private room where a woman would perform nude for his eyes only. A railing separated model and customer. No touching was allowed. If the customer happened to begin pleasuring himself, which was not at all unusual, the model was required to stop dancing and start dressing. A video camera was mounted in each room for monitoring purposes, a practice that rather undid the "private" in "private modeling."

"Private conversation" was a variation on the private modeling concept in which customers paid by the hour to sit in a small room and chat with a hot woman wearing precious little. In theory, this was mere conversation with no modeling, dancing, or, in theory, touching or nudity, so neither railings nor video cameras were required. In practice, a generous tip could persuade the hot woman to remove some or all of the precious little, and a *very* generous tip could persuade her to engage in a bit more than conversation.

Behind the door separating the hall from the front room, Lexie adjusted her skirt and smoothed the fabric of her top. "We dressed skimpy to greet customers," she said. "It's how they knew they were in the right place. And it made them want to stay, pay, and tip."

Dressing sexy to greet customers was effective. For Lexie on this night, however, it proved a bit embarrassing.

Stepping into the small entry room, she found herself face-to-face with a man she recognized.

It was her uncle.

Well, she thought, *this is creepy*.

I asked Lexie how she handled the situation.

"He pretended he was lost and needed directions," she said. "I acted like I believed him. Then he looked around and said, 'What is this place?' As if he didn't know. He tried to look innocent, but come on."

Did she worry that he might out her to her devout Mormon parents who didn't know what she did for a living?

"No, he's a good Mormon," she said, putting air quotes around "good." She smiled and added, "He couldn't tell anyone about me without giving himself away."

"So," I said, "all ended well? No more awkwardness?"

"There wasn't any awkwardness with family, if that's what you mean. But it was way awkward when he showed up again and pretended to be lost again. He asked what the place was again. I'm pretty sure he visited other times when I wasn't working or when I was there but another girl came to the door." She shook her head and sighed. "I'm just glad he didn't ask to stay and do a session with me."

"Would you have gone along with it?" I asked.

"Oh my god. Hell no."

Lexie eventually left the private conversation business and began providing full service on her own. She saw clients in their homes, offices, and hotel rooms, and sometimes received trusted clients in her apartment.

It wasn't long before the Mormon bishop of the ward within whose boundaries she lived began to suspect what was going on.

He became a regular client.

Afterword

About the Interviews

Thank God we got the criminals, and America got the Puritans.

—Australian folk saying

This book didn't turn out to be as funny as I'd planned. I have no trouble lampooning hypocrisy and other human foibles, of which there are plenty in these pages, but in matters that demand empathy or outrage—like abuse, injustice, self-esteem issues, and other of life's challenges—even I have to wax serious. I hope you laughed where you wanted, wept where you felt so moved, and experienced outrage where humanity demanded.

Every provider, interview, and anecdote in this book is real, though here and there I have fictionalized nonessential details to protect identities. I have reproduced conversations and direct quotes as best as I could from memory and fast-jotted notes.

Some of Salt Lake City's busiest and most popular sex workers were kind enough to sit down with me for 90-minute interviews. They are the ones you heard from most often in these pages. A good deal more didn't care to meet, much less give up 90 minutes, but were more than happy to answer a few quick questions via text or phone. You heard from them here too, albeit less often.

I implore the reader not to generalize the experiences of my interviewees to the broad spectrum of sex workers. This is by no means a statistically valid study. The providers in this book occupy a specific niche.

Some providers spoke with me over lunch or coffee. Others asked me to meet them where they work. Some interviewed on a courtesy basis and some charged me the same rate they charge clients. For some, accepting payment simply to visit was not new. It's not unusual for clients to pay just to talk. An hour in the company of someone attractive and sympathetic is all they want.

Shortly after the first paid interview, I took my CPA to lunch and asked if I could write off fees paid for interviews as a business expense. He said that I could. I reminded him that no provider was going to issue me a receipt, and that in the event of an audit I would not reveal anyone's real name. He said, "Keep a spreadsheet of your expenses and keep it current. If the IRS challenges you, show them the spreadsheet, your notes, your manuscript, and the other books you've published. That should be good enough."

I repeat his tax advice here with some reluctance. I worry that an IRS agent might choose to make this a test case. But I can't resist. How many people get to say they paid sex workers and wrote it off on their taxes?

Lunch wasn't over, so I shared a few anecdotes with him from the interviews. When I mentioned that some massage parlors offer "happy endings," my CPA, who is a model of clean living, blurted, "You mean a hand job?" At that moment, our server was just arriving at our table. She looked a little nonplussed. Looking up at her, I said, "I bet you walk in on some interesting conversations."

"All the time," she said.

Acknowledgments

None of us is as smart as all of us.

—Kenneth H. Blanchard

I owe deep thanks to the sexual service providers, massage therapists, mental health professionals, johns, police officers, and others who, trusting my promise to preserve their anonymity, agreed to speak with me.

Many wonderful people pored over the manuscript of this book, offered great suggestions, challenged my thinking (often persuading me), and helped me avoid looking more foolish than necessary. All remaining vestiges of foolishness are solely my doing. Thanks go to Jeff Bacon (who said, "I just wish you were thanking me for 'field research' instead of proofreading"), Naomi Baker, Ophelia Benson, Jen Blair, Paul and the late Brentz Brandt, John Broadous, Jeff Cuno, Sasha Cuno, Sheryl Ginsberg, Rebecca Cuno Hankey, Josh Hauser, Sue Kim, Susie Lee, Julie Lynn, Lauren and Michael O'Malley, Valerie Merges, Ken Moore, Sandi Olson, Charity Smith, Karen Stollznow, and Cris Echeverria Welmerink.

Finally, mega thanks to my agent, Max Sinsheimer, for his painstaking care in preparing the manuscript and in hunting down a publisher. Speaking of publishers, thanks go to Kurt Volkan of Pitchstone Publishing for taking me on as an author and cooking up a killer concept for the cover.

Glossary

If you have a big enough dictionary,
just about everything is a word.

—Dave Barry

apostasy, apostate, apostatize. *Apostasy* is the abandonment of a cause or organization. One who commits apostasy is an *apostate.* To commit apostasy is *to apostatize.*

AMP. Asian Massage Parlor.

bishop, Mormon. A Mormon bishop presides over a ward, a geographic area roughly equivalent to a parish. Only men can be bishops. The bishop presides over weekly local church services, appoints ward members to serve in various positions such as Sunday school teacher or organist, conducts regular worthiness interviews with ward members from age 12 and up, and counsels members in marriage and personal life. The office of bishop is a temporary, unpaid position taken on over and above regular family and employment duties. It is as time-consuming as a second job and emotionally exhausting.

Unlike Catholic and Protestant ministers, bishops do not attend divinity school, study theology, or receive training in family counseling. The Mormon Church has no shortage of disdain for people who have been "trained for the ministry." Mormon leaders local and general are presumed to rely on inspiration from God.

bishopric. The trio of men in charge of a ward. Comprises the bishop, a first counselor, and a second counselor.

bishop's interview. See *worthiness interview*.

body rub. Offered by people who haven't obtained a license to offer massage per se. A body rub may be massage-like or amount to light touching and caressing.

Book of Mormon. Revered by Mormons as a book of scripture on a par with the Bible. The book tells of a small group of Jews in 600 BCE who crossed the ocean from the Old World to the New World. Not long after their arrival, they separated into two groups, the righteous Nephites and the unrighteous Lamanites. God cursed the latter with "a skin of blackness" to make them sexually unappealing to white people.[1] Until recently, the church claimed that Lamanites were the ancestors of Native Americans, but DNA research necessitated revising the claim. Today it claims that Lamanites were *among* the ancestors of Native Americans. The book also claims that Jesus appeared and ministered to the Nephites shortly after his crucifixion in the Old World.

The wicked Lamanites killed off the righteous Nephites around 400 CE, but not before a Nephite by the name of Mormon wrote down his people's history. It is for him that the book is named. Mormon didn't write on paper, however. To ensure the book would remain intact for over a millennium, he wrote it—that is, engraved it—on book-size plates of gold that he bound on one side with three rings.

Mormon's son, Moroni, added to the book after Mormon's death and then buried it in the woods of what would later be known as New York state. In 1827, Moroni, by this time an angel, appeared to Joseph Smith Jr. and commanded him to dig up the plates and translate them into English. The engravings were in "Reformed Egyptian," a language in which Smith was not fluent and which no one else has encountered before or since. Smith completed the translation by "the gift and power of God," that is, by means of placing a stone in a hat, burying his face in the hat to block out the light, and dictating words to a scribe as they appeared on the stone.

Mark Twain offered a succinct review of the Book of Mormon in *Roughing It*:

> It is chloroform in print. If Joseph Smith composed this book, the act was a miracle—keeping awake while he did it was, at any rate. If he, according to tradition, merely translated it from certain ancient and mysteriously-engraved plates of copper, which he declares he found under a stone, in an out-of-the-way locality, the work of translating was equally a miracle, for the same reason.

Chastity, Law of. Sexual prohibitions incumbent upon Mormons. These include refraining from premarital and extramarital sex, gay sex (married or not), masturbation, porn, groping someone you're not married to ("petting"), viewing pornography, and thinking naughty thoughts.

church membership council. See *disciplinary council.*

cisgender. People who identify with the gender they were assigned at birth.

Conference, General. See General Conference.

counselor, first or second. Assistants whose job is to help a church leader with his or her duties. Bishops, stake presidents, Primary presidents, and even the prophet all have first and second counselors.

cult. A group or organization characterized by behaviors such as: unquestioning loyalty to a leader or council; extreme intrusion into personal life and decision-making; isolationism; a feeling of being among the few with true insight; a tendency toward exclusiveness; strong group loyalty; secrecy; feelings of and taking pride in persecution; active recruitment efforts; showering prospective recruits with attention and favors ("love bombing"); and more.

Not all cults are religions, and not all religions are cults. The greater the number of cultish behaviors a group exhibits and the more it presumes to enforce them, the more you can rightly call it a cult. In the cases of groups exhibiting some cultish traits and not others to greater or lesser extents, it may be useful to think in terms of *degrees of cultishness* rather than *cult/not cult*.

deseret. (dez-uh-ret) According to the Book of Mormon, *deseret* is an ancient American word for *honeybee*.

Disciplinary Council. A formal proceeding wherein a Mormon Church member is tried for having committed a serious sin. The result may be acquittal, admonishment, disfellowshipment, or excommunication. The accused is usually presumed guilty, making acquittals rare. In 2020, the Mormon Church officially changed the term "Disciplinary Council" to "Church membership council."

disfellowshipment. A revocation of certain church privileges such as partaking of the sacrament (communion) or entering a temple. Disfellowshipment is meant to be temporary, a path back to full fellowship. In 2020, the Mormon Church officially replaced the term "disfellowshipment" with "formal membership restrictions." See also *excommunication*.

Doctrine and Covenants. Also referred to as "D&C." A book comprising: 135 revelations given by God to Joseph Smith; a declaration of beliefs about governments; a screed against the State of Illinois and the United States government for Joseph Smith's death; a revelation from God to Smith's successor, Brigham Young; a vision penned by later church president Joseph F. Smith; and one official declaration apiece by church presidents Wilford Woodruff and Spencer W. Kimball. Mormons regard the book as scripture.

escort, escort agency. Escort agencies are legal businesses through which you can hire a date—an "escort"—by the hour. You might hire her or him to accompany you to a restaurant, to the theater, or to a gala as your plus-one, or to keep you company in the privacy of your home or hotel room. Utah law requires escorts to be at least 18 years of age and to pass an initial and thereafter quarterly STI test. The state forbids escorts and clients to touch one another's genitals, and individual municipalities layer on their own additional rules. Keeping up on the rules is no small challenge, since the Salt Lake metropolitan area alone comprises 35 municipalities, townships, enclaves, and other "census-designated places." Salt Lake City proper requires clients to book 24 hours in advance and to sign a statement if they plan to ask an escort to undress—a rule that I bet is often ignored. Midvale, about 12 miles south but well within the contiguous metropolitan area, requires that escort agencies execute a written contract with each client at the outset of a session. Curiously, the Midvale code adds, "The contract need not include the name of the patron." One cannot help but wonder if the city official who inserted that clause was a client looking to ensure his continued anonymity.

excommunication. Revocation of church membership. It is possible to rejoin the church after showing suitable remorse and repentance. In 2020, the Mormon Church officially replaced the term "excommunication" with "withdrawal of membership." See also *disfellowshipment*.

First Presidency. The uppermost echelon and ruling body of the Mormon Church. Comprises the president of the church, esteemed as a "prophet, seer, and revelator," and his counselors. Usually there are two counselors, but on occasion a president of the church has added more.

formal membership restrictions. See *disfellowshipment*.

full service. A euphemism sex workers use to mean "includes sex."

garment(s). In their "Initiatory" temple ceremony, Mormon faithful officially receive special underwear. The church reverently calls it "the garment," whereas members tend to say, simply, "garments." The garment top looks something like a short-sleeved white T-shirt with a scoop neck. The women's version has about a half-inch of embroidery around the scoop neck. The shirt features three sewn-in symbols: an L shape over one breast, a V shape over the other, and a straight line over the navel. The pant resembles a snug, knee-length pair of white boxer briefs. It has one symbol, also a straight line, sewn over the right knee. The symbols, each about a centimeter in length, were taken from Masonry to represent covenants made in the Mormon temple ceremony known as the Endowment.

Mormons are to wear the garment day and night except during sporting activities like swimming or basketball, and, mercifully, except when bathing or having sex.

As the Mormon Church increasingly finds its way into the national and international news, garments inevitably become a topic of discussion. There is even a genre of porn in which actors wear Mormon garments.

Mormons are told the garment will serve them as a "shield and a protection." Exactly what that means is not officially established, leaving ample room for garment lore. Stories abound of people whose garments saved them from bullets and stabbings. Hence, outsiders delight in referring to garments as "magic underwear."

Mormons are touchy about their garments, which they consider sacred. Poke fun at your own risk.

General Authority. A member of the upper echelons of the Mormon Church. There are eight such echelons, but it's the top two that matter most. These are the First Presidency, which comprises the prophet and his two counselors, and the Quorum of the Twelve Apostles, which comprises, as you may have already guessed, twelve apostles. Unlike local leaders, General Authorities receive a salary, usually euphemized as a "living allowance."

General Conference. A semiannual, three-day event held in Salt Lake City in which General Authorities of the church deliver sermons to the general membership. It is broadcast and narrowcast worldwide.

Gentile. To most people, a Gentile is anyone who isn't a Jew. To Mormons, a Gentile is anyone who isn't a Jew or a Mormon.

girlfriend experience (GFE). A romantic, paid encounter that includes kissing, touching, and sex, in contrast to sex or a blowjob without kissing or other foreplay.

hand job. Stimulating the penis by use of the hand, usually leading to ejaculation. Also called a *happy ending*.

happy ending. Another term for *hand job*.

high council. Twelve men who preside over a stake, ranking in authority just under the stake presidency.

hobby. The practice of seeing prostitutes.

hobbyist. One who engages in seeing prostitutes. Another word for *john*.

home teaching. See *ministering*.

interviews. See worthiness interview.

john. A man who patronizes a prostitute. Some johns like to call themselves *hobbyists*.

LDS. Short for Latter-day Saints, from The Church of Jesus Christ of Latter-day Saints. It is generally used as an adjective, e.g., "LDS people" or "the LDS Church."

LE test. Short for "Law Enforcement test," which naïve providers mistakenly believe will root out undercover cops posing as clients. The idea is that undercover cops must answer truthfully when asked if they're cops, aren't allowed to expose themselves, and may not touch a provider in the breast or genital area. As many a provider has learned the hard way, the LE test is bunk. Cops can lie about being cops, and policy as to what they're allowed to expose or touch varies by jurisdiction. Some jurisdictions are quite liberal in that regard.

ministering. Formerly called *home teaching*. Each month, every Mormon in the ward is to receive a visit at home from a pair of local members assigned to see that all is well. The latter are to report needs or problems to the bishop.

morally clean. What you are if you obey the Law of Chastity.

Mormon, Mormon Church. A nickname for The Church of Jesus Christ of Latter-day Saints and its members. "Mormon" comes from the Book of Mormon, which church members esteem as a second bible. Outsiders originally coined "Mormons" and "Mormon Church" as terms of derision, but before long church members embraced the nickname. In 2018, church president and prophet Russell M. Nelson asked the world to stop using the nickname, claiming that its use offended Jesus and handed Satan "a major victory." It was not a new request. Gordon B. Hinckley, Nelson's predecessor, made a similar plea when Utah was gearing up to host the 2002 Winter Olympic Games. The requests have had little effect.

Pearl of Great Price. The briefest of four books regarded by Mormons as scripture, the others being the Bible, Book of Mormon, and Doctrine and Covenants. The title is a reference to the parable of the same name in Matthew 13:45–46. The book contains writings of Moses, Abraham, Matthew as revised by Joseph Smith, Smith's account of his first vision, and the "Articles of Faith," a summation of Mormon beliefs. Smith claimed to have obtained Abraham's writings by translating a set of Egyptian scrolls that found their way into his hands, but later scholarship revealed that the scrolls contain only a common Egyptian funerary text. The church maintains that the alleged writings of Abraham are nonetheless authentic.

polygamy. The practice of having multiple spouses at the same time. As specifically practiced by the Mormons, men were allowed multiple wives, but women were not allowed multiple husbands. Joseph Smith outlined the doctrine of polygamy in Section 132 of the Doctrine and Covenants. Smith tried to keep the doctrine under wraps, but rumors leaked. When the Mormons moved to Utah, Smith's successor, Brigham Young, brought Mormon polygamy into the open.

Primary. What Mormons call their Sunday school for children ages 3 through 12.

priesthood. The authority to act on God's behalf, e.g., to baptize, ordain, bless, etc. Open only to males 12 and older who pass a worthiness interview.

provider. A provider of sexual services. A preferred term in place of *prostitute*.

Relief Society. The Mormon Church's women's organization.

sacrament, the. The Mormon term for what other churches call communion. Mormons substitute water for wine (see *Word of Wisdom*). Mormons do not believe in transubstantiation; they take the sacrament "in remembrance of" Jesus.

sacrament meeting. Regular weekly Mormon Church services during which the sacrament (communion) is served, church announcements are made, and one or two people, usually ward members, are called upon to deliver sermons ("talks").

sex worker. A positive term for people who sell sexual services. Besides prostitutes, it can refer to escorts, strippers, and phone-sex workers.

Smith, Joseph, Jr. Founder of The Church of Jesus Christ of Latter-day Saints, aka the Mormon Church. Mormons regard Smith as a prophet and often refer to him as "the Prophet." He was born in 1805. According to his testimony, Smith at age 14 entered a grove near Palmyra, New York, and prayed to know which church he should join. God and Jesus appeared to him, and Jesus told him to join none of the churches, for "all their creeds were an abomination in his sight; that those professors were all corrupt; that 'they draw near to me with their lips, but their hearts are far from me, they teach for doctrines the commandments of men, having a form of godliness, but they deny the power thereof.'"[2] Smith continued receiving revelations and visions, produced the Book of Mormon, and in 1830 founded the Mormon Church. In 1844, Smith was arrested for ordering the destruction of a newspaper office in the Mormon settlement of Nauvoo, Illinois, where the Mormons had elected Smith as their mayor. He was taken to jail in Carthage, Illinois. Two days later, a mob stormed the jail. A gunfight ensued in which Smith, who was armed with a six-shooter that misfired three times, was shot and killed.

stake. A geographic area comprising five to twelve wards. (See *ward.*)

stake president. A man who presides over a stake. He is higher in authority than a bishop. Like the office of bishop, the office of stake president is unpaid.

stake presidency. Comprises a stake president and his two counselors.

sugar baby, sugar daddy, sugar mama. A *sugar baby* is a provider on retainer with a client. The client, known as a *sugar daddy* or *sugar mama*, pays an agreed-upon monthly fee in exchange for an agreed-upon amount of companionship from the provider. The arrangement may or may not be exclusive on either side, and may or may not include sex.

temple, Mormon. Unlike Mormon meetinghouses, Mormon temples aren't for regular church services, but for specific ceremonies or rituals. These include baptism for the dead, the Initiatory, the Endowment, marriage, and, for the top leaders of the church, the Washing of Feet. To enter a temple and participate in the ceremonies, you must be a Mormon in good standing and pass a biannual worthiness interview with a member of your ward bishopric and a repeat interview with a member of your stake presidency. As of this writing there are over 200 Mormon temples throughout the world in operation, under construction, or announced, whereas Mormon meetinghouses number in the tens of thousands.

temple recommend. A permit about the size of a credit card that is required for entering a Mormon temple and participating in ceremonies within. To obtain a temple recommend, you must pass two identical "worthiness interviews," the first with a member of your bishopric, and the second with a member of your stake presidency. Questions cover obedience to the Word of Wisdom, minding the church's sexual rules, tithe payments, and more. (See *worthiness interview*.)

The Church of Jesus Christ of Latter-day Saints. The formal name of the Mormon Church. "The" with a capital T is part of the official name.

ward. The Mormon term for a geographic area not unlike a parish. Can also refer to a Mormon meetinghouse where regular Sunday services are held.

Word of Wisdom, the. A revelation to church founder and prophet Joseph Smith, recorded as Section 89 in the Book of Doctrine and Covenants, wherein God recommends against consuming coffee, tea, alcohol, or tobacco.

With the Women's Temperance movement well underway, women

throughout the United States were united in the opinion that tobacco and hard liquor were of the devil. Smith's wife, likely a member of the Kirtland, Ohio Temperance Union, suggested to the prophet that he obtain a revelation forbidding alcohol and tobacco. Smith's male buddies countered with the suggestion that he obtain a revelation forbidding coffee and tea, which women in the church happened to enjoy. Smith returned with a revelation advising against, but explicitly not banning, all of the above. Neither the men nor the women were pleased, and both promptly ignored the revelation.

Few Mormons today realize that the Word of Wisdom allows for beer, which in the day was referred to as a "mild drink." The exception is not surprising, for Smith's fondness for beer was no secret. Decades after Smith's death and the church's move to Utah, the church gradually elevated the Word of Wisdom to commandment status, adding beer and drug abuse to the list of no-nos, notwithstanding Smith's introduction to the revelation, which says, "To be sent greeting; not by commandment or constraint."

There was considerable debate among church members as to whether the ban on coffee extended to caffeinated soft drinks. In 2012, the church officially made drinking colas okay.

withdrawal of membership. See *excommunication*.

worthiness interview. A one-on-one meeting with a bishopric or stake presidency member, usually held biannually with adults wishing to obtain a temple recommend and semiannually with youth age 11 and up. The church's *General Handbook* requires leaders to ask all of the following questions:

1. Do you have faith in and a testimony of God, the Eternal Father; His Son, Jesus Christ; and the Holy Ghost?

2. Do you have a testimony of the Atonement of Jesus Christ and of his role as your Savior and Redeemer?

3. Do you have a testimony of the Restoration of the gospel of Jesus Christ?

4. Do you sustain the President of The Church of Jesus Christ of Latter-day Saints as the prophet, seer and revelator and as the only person on the earth authorized to exercise all priesthood keys? Do you sustain the members of the First Presidency and the Quorum of the Twelve Apostles as prophets, seers, and revelators? Do you sustain the other general authorities and local leaders of the church?

5. The Lord has said that all things are to be "done in cleanliness" before Him (Doctrine and Covenants 42:41). Do you strive for moral cleanliness in your thoughts and behavior? Do you obey God's law of chastity?

6. Do you follow the teachings of The Church of Jesus Christ in your private and public behavior with members of your family and others?

7. Do you support or promote any teachings, practices or doctrine contrary to those of The Church of Jesus Christ of Latter-day Saints?

8. Do you strive to keep the Sabbath day holy, both at home and at church; attend your meetings; prepare for and worthily partake of the sacrament; and live your life in harmony with the laws and commandments of the gospel?

9. Do you strive to be honest in all that you do?

10. Are you a full-tithe payer?

11. Do you understand and obey the Word of Wisdom?

12. Do you have any financial or other obligations to a former spouse or to children? If yes, are you current in meeting those obligations?

13. Do you keep the covenants that you made in the temple, including wearing the temple garment as instructed in the endowment?

14. Are there serious sins in your life that need to be resolved with priesthood authorities as part of your repentance?

15. Do you consider yourself worthy to enter the Lord's house and participate in temple ordinances?[3]

Against instructions, some individual leaders have been known to add questions of their own, not all of them appropriate.[4]

Young, Brigham. Second prophet of the Mormon Church and successor to Joseph Smith. Young led the Mormons from Illinois to the Mexican territory of Utah, where they established Great Salt Lake City. "Great" was eventually dropped from the name. Less than a year later, Mexico ceded the territory to the United States, and Young was appointed territorial governor. In his book *Roughing It*, Mark Twain had this to say of his 1861 visit to Salt Lake City: "There is a batch of governors, and judges, and other officials here, shipped from Washington, and they maintain the semblance of a republican form of government—but the petrified truth is that Utah is an absolute monarchy and Brigham Young is king!" Twain was known to sprinkle his nonfiction with a good deal of fiction, but in the case of Young he was not far off.

Notes

Author's Note 1

1. "George Carlin / 7 Words You Can't Say on Television," YouTube, video uploaded by TekClassics, February 18, 2013, youtu.be/8dCIKqkIg1w.

Prelude

1. Dallin H. Oaks, "Pornography," General Conference of The Church of Jesus Christ of Latter-day Saints, April 2005.

2. Gordon B. Hinckley, "The Symbol of Christ" *New Era*, April 1990. See www.churchofjesuschrist.org/study/new-era/1990/04/the-symbol-of-christ?lang=eng.

3. Many in the trade prefer *provider* and *sex worker* to less euphemistic albeit better known terms. Although I tend to use *sex worker* as a synonym for *prostitute* herein, in reality the term also applies to strippers, nude models, escorts, etc.

4. Following the U.S. Congress's passage of the Stop Enabling Sex Traffickers Act and Allow States and Victims to Fight Online Sex Trafficking Act (FOSTA-SESTA) in 2018, TER blocked access to its site from within the U.S. and deleted all U.S. provider and user information.

5. Men who pay for sex are called "johns."

6. No provider I asked had a good answer for why they do that.

7. Johns often refer to seeing providers as *the hobby* and to themselves as *hobbyists*.

8. The most heinous sin a Mormon can commit is to deny a sure witness of the Holy Ghost. No one has ever laid out exactly what a sure witness of the Holy Ghost is, other than to reassure you not to worry because it's so incredibly rare that you will probably never experience it. Why God made it a priority to warn the world about a sin that nearly everyone is incapable of committing is beyond me. The second and third most heinous sins, murder and sexual sin, respectively, are much more attainable.

9. If you're male and an elder in the church's priesthood, which most "worthy" Mormon men are, you'll probably stand before a *Stake* Disciplinary Council, a stake being made up of five to ten wards.

10. On February 19, 2020, the Mormon Church officially changed the terminology. "Disciplinary councils are now called 'Church membership councils.' As before, these councils are an expression of love, hope and concern, designed to help Latter-day Saints through their repentance process. Also, instead of being 'disfellowshipped,' members are given 'formal membership restrictions.' And excommunication is now labeled a 'withdrawal of membership.'" "A Look Inside the New General Handbook for Church Leaders and Members." The Church of Jesus Christ of Latter-day Saints Newsroom, February 19, 2020. See newsroom.churchofjesuschrist.org/article/new-general-handbook.

Chapter 1

1. The church insists on capitalizing "The." It's part of the official name.

2. Every April and October, the church holds a three-day General Conference in Salt Lake City, where top leaders deliver addresses over the course of six two-hour sessions. All sessions are broadcast, but there is cachet to attending in person, which Mormons travel from all over the world to do.

3. Matthew Diebel, "Anthony Weiner, Ex-congressman Jailed for Sexting with 15-Year-Old Girl, to Be Released Early from Prison," *USA Today*, October, 10, 2018, www.usatoday.com/story/news/nation/2018/10/10/anthony-weiner-jailed-sexting-girl-15-get-early-release/1587360002/.

4. Danny Hakim and William K. Rashbaumnov, "No Federal Prostitution

Charges for Spitzer," November 6, 2008, www.nytimes.com/2008/11/07/nyregion/07spitzer.html?mtrref=www.google.com.

5. March 2, 2020, early afternoon.

6. More from Koko in Chapter 4, "Secret Sexual Activities Mormon Men Enjoy."

7. "Cisgender" refers to people who identify with the gender they were assigned at birth.

Chapter 2

1. Overconfidence from not knowing enough not to feel confident is called the Dunning-Kruger Effect.

2. Eros, "Disclaimer," www.eros.com/disclaimer/report.

3. The Tor browser can mask your identity when you surf the web. The U.S. Navy created Tor for undercover agents to infiltrate illicit websites on the Dark Web and, hopefully, shut them down. But to ensure that a masked IP address didn't automatically indicate an undercover cop, the government needed lots of people outside of government using Tor. Therefore, it made Tor freely available to the public. Thanks to the United States government, now everyone can have anonymous access to the very websites it created Tor to infiltrate and shut down.

4. For information on what undercover cops can and cannot do, see Chapter 10, "A Police Officer and a Gentleman."

5. See Glossary, "escort, escort agency."

Chapter 3

1. Pearl of Great Price, Joseph Smith—History 1:19

2. Doctrine and Covenants 107:92. "A prophet is a teacher of known truth; a seer is a perceiver of hidden truth, a revelator is a bearer of new truth. In the widest sense, the one most commonly used, the title, prophet, includes the other titles and makes of the prophet, a teacher, perceiver, and bearer of truth." James A. Widtsoe, *Evidences and Reconciliations* (Salt Lake City:

Bookcraft). See www.cumorah.com/etexts/evidencesreconciliations.txt.

3.   Doctrine and Covenants 1:30.

4.   Doctrine and Covenants 115:4.

5.   The Church of Jesus-Christ of Latter-day Saints Bible Dictionary, "Saint." See www.churchofjesuschrist.org/study/scriptures/bd/saint?lang=eng.

6.   Smith's account claims he translated the Book of Mormon using a Urim and Thummim, first referenced in the Old Testament in Exodus 28:30. That remained the church's official claim, too, until documents describing the hat and seer stone came to the public's attention in 2015. The church then acknowledged the hat and stone and released photos of the stone. See Church History Topics, "Seer Stone." www.churchofjesuschrist.org/study/history/topics/seer-stones?lang=eng.

7.   Linda King Newell and Valeen T. Avery, *Mormon Enigma: Emma Hale Smith, Prophet's Wife, Elect Lady, Polygamy's Foe* (Doubleday Publishing, 1984).

8.   Doctrine and Covenants, Section 132.

9.   King and Avery, op. cit. A popular Mormon version of the angel-and-sword tale goes like this: *When God told Smith to take multiple wives, the prophet, aghast, refused. It took God's sending an armed angel to force his compliance.* There are two problems with this version. The first is that it doesn't match the young women's accounts. The second is that it only removes the blame for polygamy from Smith to God. Either way, there is a word for the act of forcing people to engage in sex under threat of violence. That word is *rape*.

10. King and Avery, op. cit.

11. The entire content of the *Nauvoo Expositor* is available online at archive.org/stream/NauvooExpositor1844Replica/Nauvoo_Expositor_1844_replica_djvu.txt.

12. Alex Beam, *American Crucifixion: The Murder of Joseph Smith and the Fate of the Mormon Church* (New York: Public Affairs, 2014).

13. Ibid.

14. Hinckley was lying. It is not *practiced*, but it remains *doctrinal*. Moreover, Mormons believe polygamy is practiced in heaven. See Doctrine and Covenants, Section 132.

15. "President Gordon B. Hinckley on Larry King Live," YouTube, video uploaded by MovieCraze, June 5, 2014. See www.youtube.com/watch?v=jAsN MWwRXvs&feature=youtu.be&t=676.

16. Joel Campbell, "Larry King's Hard Choice: Provo or 'Eternal Nothingness.'" *Deseret News*, May 30, 2009. See www.deseret.com/2009/5/30/20378998/ larry-king-s-hard-choice-provo-or-eternal-nothingness.

17. You'll hear more from Lilly in Chapter 6, "Mormontown's Asian Massage Parlors."

18. Commercial Street was later renamed Regent Street, the name it bears today. Part of Regent Street runs through downtown Salt Lake City's City Creek Center, an upscale mall built at a cost of about $2 billion and owned by the Mormon Church.

19. No one knows the origin of the term "red light district." Some speculate with little basis that it referred to a red lamp that railroad workers carried with them and placed outside providers' doors during visits.

20. London's real name was Dora B. Topham.

21. Jami Balls, "History of the Stockade and Salt Lake's Red Light District," Utah.gov, historytogo.utah.gov/places/olympic_locations/stockade.html.

22. John S. McCormick, "Red Lights in Zion: Salt Lake City's Stockade, 1908–1911," *Utah Historic Quarterly* 50 (Spring 1982).

23. "This layout is a byproduct of the city's Mormon heritage. In 1833, several years after founding the religion in upstate New York, Joseph Smith outlined how Mormon cities should look and feel. The plan drew from that era's East Coast design principles, as well as the church's desire for order. Smith called for a temple at the center of a grid and for large blocks that enabled family farming." Beyer, Scott. "Why Are Salt Lake City's Blocks SO Long?" Governing States and Localities, November, 2017. www.governing.com/columns/urban-notebook/gov-salt-lake-city-extra-wide-streets.html.

24. Balls, op. cit.

25. McCormick, op. cit.

26. Chris McLaws, "Park City's Red Light District," *Park Record*, March 22, 2016. www.parkrecord.com/entertainment/park-citys-red-light-district/.

27. Jan MacKnell, *Red Light Women of the Rocky Mountains* (Albuquerque,

NM: University of New Mexico Press, 2009).

28. Gary Kimball, *Death and Dying in Old Park City* (Park City, UT: Tramway Books, 2005).

29. McLaws, op. cit.

30. MacKnell, op. cit.

31. See, for instance, Billy Graham, "In the World But Not Of It." billygraham. org/decision-magazine/february-2016/a-classic-billy-graham-message-in-the-world-but-not-of-it/.

32. Tyler Hoffman, "Urban legends of Ogden: Alleged," My Weber Media, October 25, 2015. See signpost.mywebermedia.com/2015/10/25/urban-legends-of-ogden-alleged/.

33. Associated Press, "Notorious Utah Brothel Owner's Interview Eludes Historians," *Salt Lake Tribune*, February 5, 2020, www.sltrib.com/news/2020/02/01/notorious-utah-brothel/.

34. Hoffman, op. cit.

35. Ibid.

36. Admiration began waning when the once-decried generation grew up and became parents. Clean-cut, clean-living Mormon youth began to look not so much admirable as out of touch.

37. Book of Mormon, Alma 39:11.

38. Boyd K. Packer, "To Young Men Only," General Conference, October 1976, www.lds.org/general-conference/1976/10/media/session_5_talk_1?lang=eng.

39. "Hilarious Anti-Masturbation Campaign Waged by BYU," YouTube, video uploaded by Secular Talk, February 5, 2014, youtu.be/Ueuz0-Rnd5c.

40. Bruce R. McKonkie, *Mormon Doctrine*, 2nd ed. (Salt Lake City: Bookcraft, 1966), 708.

41. Lindsay R. Curtis, "What Is Petting? Should It Be Confessed to the Bishop?" *New Era*, November 1985. See www.churchofjesuschrist.org/study/new-era/1985/11/q-and-a-questions-and-answers/what-is-petting?lang=eng.

42. "Morality and Modesty," *Eternal Marriage Student Manual*. See www.churchofjesuschrist.org/study/manual/eternal-marriage-student-manual/

morality-and-modesty?lang=eng.

43. BYU University Policies, "Church Educational System Honor Code," See policy.byu.edu/view/index.php?p=26&s=s1165.

44. Peggy Fletcher Stack, "A Year after Her Mormon Excommunication, Where Do Kate Kelly and the Ordain Women Movement Stand?" *Salt Lake Tribune*, July 3, 2015, archive.sltrib.com/article.php?id=2653329&itype=CMSID.

45. "Intimacy in Marriage," a lesson in the *Eternal Marriage Student Manual*, published by the Mormon Church. See www.lds.org/manual/eternal-mar-riage-student-manual/intimacy-in-marriage?lang=eng.

46. Letter to local church leaders from the First Presidency of The Church of Jesus Christ of Latter-day Saints, dated January 1985, imgur.com/a/ME6ST.

47. From a first presidency letter dated April 14, 1969. See emp.byui.edu/SAT-TERFIELDB/Quotes/Birth%20Control%20Family%20Size.htm.

48. Rulon T. Burton, *Doctrines and Principles of The Church of Jesus Christ of Latter-day Saints* (Draper, UT: Tabernacle Books), 262.

49. Eternal Family Teacher Manual, Lesson 17, "The Commandment to Multi-ply and Replenish the Earth." See www.churchofjesuschrist.org/study/man-ual/the-eternal-family-teacher-manual/lesson-17-the-commandment-to-multiply-and-replenish-the-earth?lang=eng.

50. "Birth Control," an article published by the church on its website. See www.lds.org/topics/birth-control?lang=eng.

51. Ibid.

52. When I served in a local Mormon Church leadership position, a distraught, Mormon woman confessed to me that she had felt lust toward her husband during sex with him. Believing it to have been a sin, she was seeking for-giveness.

53. Burton, op. cit., 261–262.

54. N. Eldon Tanner, "The Blessing of Church Interviews," October 1978, www.lds.org/general-conference/1978/10/the-blessing-of-church-interviews?lang=eng.

55. Bill Hutchinson, "Woman Breaks Her Silence 30 Years after She Says She Was Raped in Secret Room by Mormon Church Official," ABC News, April 8, 2018, abcnews.go.com/US/woman-breaks-silence-30-years-raped-se-

cret-room/story?id=54255419. Some of the plaintiff's later accusations appear to have been discredited, however, her original accusation has legs, thanks to corroborating testimony from another victim and to a recorded admission by the accused. See respectively: Michael Locklear, "Former MTC President Says Church Leaders Knew of Sexual Indiscretions with Missionaries," KUTV, June 17, 2019, kutv.com/news/local/former-mtc-president-says-church-leaders-knew-of-sexual-indiscretions-with-missionaries; and Jana Riess, "Retired Mormon Mission President Admits He Molested a Female Missionary," Religion News Service, March 20, 2018, religionnews.com/2018/03/20/retired-mormon-mission-president-admits-he-molested-a-female-missionary/.

56. Brady McCombs, "Mormon Youth Interviews With Bishops under Scrutiny," NBC Bay Area, March 30, 2018, www.nbcbayarea.com/news/national-international/mormon-youth-interviews-with-bishops-under-scrutiny/2038884/.

57. Peggy Fletcher Stack, "Some Parents and Therapists Say Mormon Bishops' Interviews with Children about Sexual Matters Are 'Intrusive, Inappropriate,'" *Salt Lake Tribune*, December 11, 2017, www.sltrib.com/religion/local/2017/12/12/all-the-buzz-about-sexual-harassment-has-some-mormons-wondering-if-bishops-interviews-go-too-far-and-need-reform/.

58. Hannah Knowles, "LDS Women Say Church Leaders Encouraged Them to Stay with Their Abusers," KUTV, February 13, 2018, kutv.com/news/local/lds-women-say-church-leaders-encouraged-them-to-stay-with-their-abusers.

59. "LDS Utah Child Molestation Cover-Up," YouTube, video uploaded by Ron Karren, February 13, 2016, www.youtube.com/watch?v=0A97odud60o&feature=youtu.be.

60. Ben Winslow, "LDS Church Settles Sex Abuse Lawsuits," Fox 13, Salt Lake City, September 24, 2018, fox13now.com/2018/09/24/lds-church-settles-sex-abuse-lawsuits/.

61. Nate Carlisle, "Latter-day Saint Filmmaker Sterling Van Wagenen Pleads Guilty to Child Sex Abuse in a Second Courtroom," *Salt Lake Tribune*, May 2, 2019, www.sltrib.com/news/2019/05/02/latter-day-saint/.

62. Sarah Jane Weaver, "First Presidency Releases New Guidelines for Interviewing Youth." *Church News*, June 20, 2018, www.churchofjesuschrist.org/

church/news/first-presidency-releases-new-guidelines-for-interviewing-youth?lang=eng.

63. Quentin L. Cook, "Prepare to Meet God," April 2018, www.churchofjesuschrist.org/study/general-conference/2018/04/prepare-to-meet-god?lang=eng&verse=.

64. Richard G. Scott, "Healing the Tragic Scars of Abuse," April 1992, www.churchofjesuschrist.org/study/general-conference/1992/04/healing-the-tragic-scars-of-abuse?lang=eng. Italics added.

65. Barry Meier, "The Mormon Church Has Been Accused of Using a Victims' Hotline to Hide Claims of Sexual Abuse," Vice News, May 3, 2019, www.vice.com/en_us/article/d3n73w/duty-to-report-the-mormon...been-accused-of-using-a-victims-hotline-to-hide-sexual-abuse-claims.

66. Marci A. Hamilton, "A Reply to Von Keetch's Comments on Clergy Child Sex Abuse and the Church of Jesus Christ of Latter-day Saints," FindLaw, supreme.findlaw.com/legal-commentary/a-reply-to-von-keetchs-comments-on-clergy-child-sex-abuse-and-the-church-of-jesus-christ-of-latter-day-saints.html.

67. *General Handbook: Serving in The Church of Jesus Christ of Latter-day Saints* (Salt Lake City: The Church of Jesus Christ of Latter-day Saints, 2021), www.churchofjesuschrist.org/study/manual/general-handbook/38-church-policies-and-guidelines?lang=eng#title_number160.

68. See, for example, "Mormon-LDS Orders for 29 June 2008 on Same-Sex Constitution Ban," WikiLeaks, June 21, 2008, "wikileaks.org/wiki/Mormon-LDS_orders_for_29_June_2008_on_same-sex_constitution_ban.

69. Jesse McKinely and Kirk Johnsonnov, "Mormons Tipped Scale in Ban on Gay Marriage," *New York Times*, November 14, 2008.

70. Gregory A. Prince, *Gay Rights and the Mormon Church* (Salt Lake City: University of Utah Press, 2019). A good many evangelical churches flagrantly ignore the Johnson Amendment. To date the IRS has shown no interest in calling them on it.

71. Peggy Fletcher Stack, "LDS Apostle under Fire for Civil-Rights Analogy," *Salt Lake Tribune*, October 14, 2009, archive.sltrib.com/story.php?ref=/ci_13552589.

72. Prince, op. cit.

73. See Utah's Public Health Indicator Based Information System, ibis.health. utah.gov/ibisph-view/indicator/complete_profile/SuicDth.html.

74. Prince, op. cit.

75. Lee Hale, "Can The LDS Church Be Blamed for Utah's LGBT Suicides?" Kuer. org, www.kuer.org/post/can-lds-church-be-blamed-utah-s-lgbt-suicides# stream/0.

76. Lane Williams, Amy Fife, and Hal Boyd, "No Correlation between Youth Suicide and Church of Jesus Christ of Latter-day Saints," *Idaho Statesman*, September 22, 2019, www.idahostatesman.com/opinion/readers-opinion/ article235270667.html#storylink=cpy.

77. Prince, op. cit.

78. Michelle L. Price, "Utah Officials Unsure Why Youth Suicide Rate Has Nearly Tripled since 2007," Associated Press, July 3, 2016, archive.sltrib. com/article.php?id=4075258&itype=CMSID.

79. Seth Anderson, "Timeline of Mormon Thinking about Homosexuality," Rational Faiths, November 3, 2013, rationalfaiths.com/timeline-of-mormon-thinking-about-homosexuality/.

80. Provided, that is, LGBTQ Mormons remain celibate. It's still unreasonable, but it's progress nonetheless. See "Same-Sex Attraction" under "Gospel Topics" on the official church website: www.churchofjesuschrist.org/study/ manual/gospel-topics/same-sex-attraction?lang=eng.

81. The URL has been updated to mormonandgay.churchofjesuschrist.org.

82. "LGBT people who live God's laws" is code for "LBGT people who don't engage in gay sex or affection, married or not." The church deserves credit in that coming out is no longer cause for excommunication, but the underlying current of disapproval remains. Text and videos avoid terms like "homosexual," "gay," "lesbian," and "transgender" in favor of "same-sex attraction" and "same-gender attraction," usually paired with "struggle," e.g., "members of the church who struggle with same-gender attraction." What seems lost on church leaders is that what LGBTQ Mormons struggle with is not same-gender attraction but *the church's stance* on homosexuality. While the church took a step forward with the website, it could do more.

83. The ordinance carved out an exception for church-owned businesses and housing.

84. "Non-discrimination Ordinances Become Law in Salt Lake City," KSL.com, April 2, 2010, www.ksl.com/article/10247471/non-discrimination-ordinances-become-law-in-salt-lake-city.

85. Laurel Wamsley, "In Major Shift, LDS Church Rolls Back Controversial Policies toward LGBT Members," NPR News, April 4, 2019, www.npr.org/2019/04/04/709988377/in-major-shift-mormon-church-rolls-back-controversial-policies-toward-lgbt-membe.

86. Kathy Stephenson, "'It is Done': LDS Sex Therapist Helfer Is Ousted from the Church," *Salt Lake Tribune*, April 22, 2021.

87. Benjamin Edelman, "Red Light States: Who Buys Online Adult Entertainment?" *Journal of Economic Perspectives* 23, no. 1 (Winter 2009): 209–220, See people.hbs.edu/bedelman/papers/redlightstates.pdf.

88. Alexis C. Madrigal, "The United States of Ashley Madison," *Fusion*, August 20, 2015, fusion.tv/story/185853/the-united-states-of-ashley-.madison/?utm_source=facebook&utm_medium=social&utm_campaign=socialshare&utm_content=desktop+top.

89. Defined as soliciting customers or transporting persons "for prostitution purposes; to own, manage, or operate a dwelling or other establishment for the purpose of providing a place where prostitution is performed; or to otherwise assist or promote prostitution." See "US and State Prostitution Arrests," ProCon.org, prostitution.procon.org/view.resource.php?resourceID=000120.

Chapter 4

1. See Glossary, "sugar daddy, sugar mama."

2. I recommend the walnut shrimp.

3. See Chapter 7, "I Speak with Male, Once-Mormon Sex Workers."

4. Perhaps inevitably, "garment porn" is a thing. See Glossary, "garment(s)."

5. *Seinfeld*, season four, episode 16.

6. "'The 'male G-spot' is the prostate and it's about two inches in the rectum toward the belly,' explains Susan Milstein, PhD, a sex educator and professor in the Department of Health Enhancement, Exercise Science and

Physical Education at the Rockville Campus of Montgomery College in Maryland. That's because the prostate contains a ton of nerve endings (in fact, there are almost as many nerve endings in the prostate as there are in the clitoris). 'It really can open up a whole new avenue of pleasure for men if they are willing to try it,' adds Milstein." Carrie Borzillo, "Yes, There's a Male G-spot—and Here Are 4 Things You Can Do to Find It," *Men's Health*, October 1, 2018, www.health24.com/Sex/Great-sex/yes-theres-a-male-g-spot-and-here-are-4-things-you-can-do-to-find-it-20171219.

7. It wouldn't surprise me if some Mormons would find the smoking more upsetting than the cross-dressing. See Glossary, "Word of Wisdom."

8. In 2019, Utah did away with that danger by passing HB40, which allows sex workers to report a crime without fear of arrest.

9. History has had its share of entertainers known as *flatulists*. Able to break wind at will, they made a living onstage farting in a range of pitches and rhythms.

10. I'm no attorney, so I don't know if Betty's summary is a fair representation of California BDSM laws. Pride Legal warns that it's possible to incur assault charges from practicing BDSM and that consent is not a defense. "Make sure that you 'play' with people that you know and trust," Pride Legal's website advises. "Establish clear boundaries and avoid behavior that can inflict serious injury upon another person. Use 'safe words' that can be enlisted when things are about to cross the line. Avoid the taking of pictures or video or other forms of recording that could be used against you as evidence at a later date." See "BDSM and the Law: Assault or Consent?" Pride Legal, November 16, 2020, pridelegal.com/assault-consent-bdsm-law/.

11. Associated Press, "National News Briefs; Federal Judge Overturns Alabama's Sex Toy Ban," *New York Times*, March 30, 1999, www.nytimes.com/1999/03/30/us/national-news-briefs-federal-judge-overturns-alabama-s-sex-toy-ban.html.

12. The Texas law remains on the books but is no longer enforced. W. Gardner Selby, "Colin Jost, on Weekend Update, Says a Texas Law Bars Ownership of More than 6 Dildos," Politifact Texas, October 13, 2017, www.politifact.com/texas/statements/2017/oct/13/colin-jost/colin-jost-weekend-update-texas-dildos-law-6-own-m/.

13. Lest anyone accuse Springfield of prudery, the same ordinance decriminal-

ized having a boner in public. Grace Sparapani, "The Small Town Banning the Underboob, but Totally Chill With Public Boners," Vice.com, September 23, 2015, www.vice.com/en_us/article/d7aqpw/the-small-town-banning-the-underboob-but-totally-chill-with-public-boners.

Chapter 5

1. "Neurofeedback is a kind of biofeedback, which teaches self-control of brain functions to subjects by measuring brain waves and providing a feedback signal. . . . Although it is a noninvasive procedure, its validity has been questioned in terms of conclusive scientific evidence. . . . Nevertheless, neurofeedback is known as a complementary and alternative treatment of many brain dysfunctions. However, current research does not support conclusive results about its efficacy." Hengameh Marzbani; Hamid Reza Marateb, and Marjan Mansourian, "Neurofeedback: A Comprehensive Review on System Design, Methodology and Clinical Applications," *Basic and Clinical Neuroscience* 7, no. 2 (April 2016): 143–158, www.ncbi.nlm.nih.gov/pmc/articles/PMC4892319/.

2. Utah law requires a massage license to advertise or perform massages. Semi-nude "body rubs" require no license and are not illegal provided there's no touching of body parts normally covered by a bikini. Some practitioners abide by the law, but generally speaking "body rub" is code for a sexy provider who permits groping, performs hand jobs, and possibly offers more.

3. Although the providers I interviewed remain in the trade of their own volition, it's important to note that trafficking is a serious and complex issue. See Chapter 10, "Should It Be Legal?"

4. See Chapter 2, "I Meet Annie (While Avoiding Arrest)."

5. In the same sense, popular Salt Lake City radio announcer Tom Barberi used to refer to the town of Franklin, Idaho, barely north of the Utah-Idaho border, as "the home of the Utah lottery."

6. My father moved our family to Reno, Nevada, in 1966. At the time it was common knowledge that Mustang Ranch and other brothels operated nearby just across the county line. While researching this book I was surprised to learn that Nevada didn't formally legalize brothels until 1971.

7. Joanne Hanks, as told to Steve Cuno, *"It's Not about the Sex" My Ass: Confes-*

sions of an Ex-Mormon, Ex-Polygamist Ex-Wife (Lulu Press, 2016).

8. Try the Mama Burrito. You might want to ask for a side of extra salsa.

9. The concept of sex addiction as a real addiction is contested. See Brian Dunning, "All About Sex Addiction," *Skeptoid Podcast* no. 708, December 31, 2019, skeptoid.com/episodes/4708. Also see Marty Klein, "Why There's No Such Thing as Sexual Addiction—and Why It Really Matters: Part 1," HER, June 8, 2009, www.empowher.com/sex-relationships/content/why-theres-no-such-thing-sexual-addiction-and-why-it-really-matters-part-.

10. National Center for Victims of Crime, https://victimsofcrime.org/.

11. "There is a cult of ignorance in the United States, and there always has been. The strain of anti-intellectualism has been a constant thread winding its way through our political and cultural life, nurtured by the false notion that democracy means that 'my ignorance is just as good as your knowledge.'" Isaac Asimov, "A Cult of Ignorance," *Newsweek*, January 21, 1980, aphelis. net/wp-content/uploads/2012/04/ASIMOV_1980_Cult_of_Ignorance.pdf.

12. "Confirmation bias . . . leads the individual to stop gathering information when the evidence gathered so far confirms the views or prejudices one would like to be true." Shahram Heshmat, "What Is Confirmation Bias?" *Psychology Today*, April 23, 2015, www.psychologytoday.com/us/blog/science-choice/201504/what-is-confirmation-bias.

13. This was the judge to whose courtroom Koko accompanied a friend. See Chapter 1, "Logo for a Call Girl."

14. Brigham Young's folk hero status is largely due to the church's sanitized version of its history. Young was in fact a ruthless despot with no shortage of blood on his hands. I recommend Will Bagley's *Blood of the Prophets* (Norman, Oklahoma: University of Oklahoma Press, 2002); David L. Bigler and Will Bagley's *The Mormon Rebellion* (Norman, Oklahoma: University of Oklahoma Press, 2012); and Jon Krakauer's *Under the Banner of Heaven* (New York: Penguin Random House, 2003).

15. American Civil Liberties Union, "Racial Disparities in Sentencing," October 27, 2014, www.aclu.org/sites/default/files/assets/141027_iachr_racial_ disparities_aclu_submission_0.pdf.

16. According to RAINN (Rape, Abuse & Incest National Network). See RAINN.org/statistics.

17. See Chapter 6, "Mormontown's Asian Massage Parlors."

18. Wendover, Utah, and Wendover, Nevada, are twin cities straddling the Utah-Nevada border. Driving Wendover Boulevard, you will come upon a broad, white line painted across the street with "Utah" and "Nevada" painted in large white letters on their respective sides. Another clue that you have reached the state line is the pair of huge hotel-casinos abutting the Nevada side of the line. Their adjacent parking lots, however, are on the Utah side. Chances are the Utah land, where gambling is illegal, was cheaper than the Nevada land.

19. "What a Sex Worker Can Teach Us about Human Connection, Nicole Emma, TEDxSaltLakeCity," YouTube, video uploaded by TEDx Talks, December 18, 2018, youtu.be/r7xLfeTytns.

20. Jennifer Dobner, "Utah Sex Workers Talk about the Personal, Practical and Political Aspects of Their Jobs," *Salt Lake Tribune*, November 16, 2017, www.sltrib.com/news/2017/11/17/utah-sex-workers-talk-about-the-personal-practical-and-political-aspects-of-their-jobs/.

Chapter 6

1. Not *race* in the socially harmful and biologically meaningless sense, but in the sense of *geographically correlated appearance traits*.

2. If you're a straight American male of Asian extraction, you're likely to have more of a thing for non-Asian women. See Kat Chow, "Odds Favor White Men, Asian Women On Dating App." NPR, November 30, 2013, www.npr.org/sections/codeswitch/2013/11/30/247530095/are-you-interested-dating-odds-favor-white-men-asian-women.

3. "Gravure idols" are youthful-looking, minimally attired Japanese models, many with considerable international followings. Call me cynical, but I doubt AMPs pay to use the photos. I bet they count on the models and photo copyright holders to have better things to do than prosecute individual spas an ocean away.

4. The "arm" was a handle you'd pull after dropping in a coin, setting in motion three or more vertically spinning cylinders that clicked to a stop one at a time. If identical images aligned across the cylinders, you'd win a few coins or, infrequently, a jackpot. Today's version has animated instead of

mechanical cylinders and a "spin reels" button instead of a handle. Though "one-armed" no longer applies, "bandit" still does.

5. "I think I can manage," I said, smiling. She returned the smile, winked, and walked away.

6. "Angels above us are silent notes taking." From "Do What Is Right," a song in the Mormon hymnal.

7. Utah Department of Health, "Asian American," health.utah.gov/disparities/ utah-minority-communities/asian-american.html.

8. Polaris, "Human Trafficking in Illicit Massage Businesses," polarisproject. org/sites/default/files/Full_Report_Human_Trafficking_in_Illicit_Massage_Businesses.pdf.

9. Ibid.

10. Ibid.

11. Ibid.

12. Polaris, op. cit., polarisproject.org/human-trafficking/recognize-signs.

13. Steven Novella, "Trusting Intuition vs Analysis," *NeurologicaBlog*, December 17, 2012, theness.com/neurologicablog/index.php/trusting-intuition-vs-analysis/.

14. No translation app is foolproof. To lessen chances of mistranslation, I used Google to translate my side of the dialog into Chinese, and then to translate the Chinese back into English. When the latter translation was close enough to what I had set out to say, I deemed the Chinese translation good and used it. Many times I had to repeatedly revise an English phrase before attaining a suitable reverse-translation.

15. Alicia and her husband took quite the risk. Penalties for marriage fraud, as ICE calls it, include jail time, up to $250,000 in fines, or both. U.S. Immigration and Customs Enforcement, www.ice.gov/sites/default/files/documents/Document/2016/marriageFraudBrochure.pdf.

16. If workers sleep in the spa, it can be a sign of trafficking. Lilly maintains an apartment for workers, but says that she has "allowed" workers to sleep in the spa to avoid paying rent.

17. IRS.gov, "Understanding Employee vs. Contractor Designation," www.irs. gov/newsroom/understanding-employee-vs-contractor-designation.

18. justworks.com, "Improperly Classifying Employees as Independent Contractors: What are the Penalties?" justworks.com/blog/consequences-misclassifying-workers-independent-contractors.

19. Dan Evon, "Did Mark Twain Say 'It's Easier to Fool People Than to Convince Them That They Have Been Fooled'?" *Snopes*, December 29, 2016, www.snopes.com/fact-check/did-mark-twain-say-its-easier-to-fool-people-than-to-convince-them-that-they-have-been-fooled/.

20. Michelle Jeffs, "Punishing Pimps and Johns: Sex-Trafficking and Utah's Laws," *Brigham Young University Journal of Public Law* 28 (July 1, 2013).

21. United States Code, Chapter 78, "Trafficking Victims Protection," 7102, "Definitions."

22. Victims of Trafficking and Violence Protection Act of 2000, Section 1591, part (a) para. (2).

23. Jennifer Gardiner, "26 Suspects Arrested in 3-day Human Trafficking Sting in Utah County," November 25, 2019, www.abc4.com/news/top-stories/26-suspects-arrested-in-3-day-human-trafficking-sting-in-utah-county/.

24. For an example, see Elizabeth Nolan Brown: "Patriots Owner Robert Kraft's Bust Is Being Billed as a Human Trafficking Bust, but It Looks More Like Ordinary Prostitution," *Reason*, February 2, 2019, reason.com/2019/02/22/robert-krafts-prostitution-arrest-is-par.

25. For my interview with Winder, see Chapter 10, "A Police Officer and a Gentleman."

26. It's also important to remember that, one, my impressions could be wrong and, two, my research was limited to Salt Lake. For all I know, the majority of AMP workers in other cities may be trafficked.

Interlude

1. The names of the people described in this section were widely published in the news media, making their use fair legal game.

2. Lee Davidson, "Rep. John Stanard Resigns Abruptly with Little Explanation," *Salt Lake Tribune*, February 27, 2018, www.sltrib.com/news/politics/2018/02/07/utah-legislator-resigns-abruptly/.

3. "EXCLUSIVE 'Any Toys? Maybe a Corset?' Call Girl Claims Married Republican Lawmaker Secretly Met Her Twice for Sex and Releases Saucy Texts He Sent Her as He Steps Down Citing 'Family Issues,'" *Daily Mail*, February 8, 2018, www.dailymail.co.uk/news/article-5364591/Escort-claims-married-lawmaker-secretly-met-sex.html.

4. Dennis Romboy and Lisa Riley Roche, "News Report Says Resigned Utah Lawmaker Hired Escort," *Deseret News*, February 8, 2018, www.deseret-news.com/article/900009750/resigned-utah-house-member-paid-escort-for-sex-daily-mail-reports.html.

5. *Daily Mail*, op. cit.

6. *Daily Mail*, "Want to Sell a Story to the Daily Mail?" www.talktothepress.co.uk/sell-a-story-to-the-daily-mail/.

7. Nicole Rojas, "LDS Bishop Who Was Formerly on a Police Vice Squad Arrested in Human Trafficking Sting," *Newsweek*, February 2, 2019, www.newsweek.com/lds-bishop-police-vice-squad-arrested-human-trafficking-sting-1338310.

8. Pat Reavy, "Former Utah Vice Squad Lieutenant Arrested in Prostitution Sting," KSL.com, February 20, 2019, www.ksl.com/article/46495111/for-mer-utah-vice-squad-lieutenant-arrested-in-prostitution-sting. KSL Radio, KSL TV, and KSL.com are owned by the Mormon Church.

9. Ibid.

10. Disposable cell phones.

Chapter 7

1. Short for "Latter-day Saint," from The Church of Jesus Christ of Latter-day Saints.

2. The pioneers named Utah's Jordan River after *the* Jordan River, where, as Priest 3 sings in *Jesus Christ Superstar*, "John did his baptism thing." About 51 miles long and varying in width from about 25 to 190 feet, Utah's Jordan River flows north from the freshwater (unless you consider the pollution) Utah Lake and empties into the Great Salt Lake.

3. At 18, Mormon men are expected to put in two years as full-time pros-elytizing missionaries. They are unpaid, covering food, rent, and other liv-

ing expenses on their own or, more often, their parents' dime. Decked out in white shirts, nametags, neckties, and backpacks, they go door-to-door and present memorized lessons in hopes of winning converts. The church decides where they will serve and provides training, including an intensive language course for those headed to non-English speaking areas. The designation "return missionary" means a young man has completed that service. It is a badge of honor, an early indicator of commitment to the faith and suitability as a prospective spouse. Missionary service is not required of Mormon women, and it is less of a badge of honor for them, it being understood that their primary role is not to proselytize but to marry and bear children. Female Mormon missionaries must be 19 or older and serve only for 18 months.

4. The Mormon Church has a lay priesthood. Beginning at age 12, all "worthy" Mormon males are ordained.

5. Short for "pre-exposure prophylaxis."

6. Don't take my word for it. Consult a doctor or pharmacist.

7. She should have kicked Ian Fleming in the nuts, too, for naming her Pussy Galore.

8. "Goldfinger—James Bond & Pussy Galore Barn Scene," YouTube, video uploaded by AvengedS939—The James Bond Network, December 3, 2011, www.youtube.com/watch?v=1pUXH1Bye88.

Chapter 8

1. Just kidding about the humble part.

2. Wards report a variety of statistics up the ladder: monetary receipts and expenditures, of course; also baptisms; attendance; number of people with temple recommends; number of official "ministering" visits members make to one another; number of visits to a temple; and more. The Church Membership Division keeps records on every Mormon, including address, date of baptism, priesthood ordinations (males only), leadership positions, marital status, number of children, and serious transgressions. The church also maintains the Strengthening the Members Committee, whose job is to monitor members' public activities and report anything it finds disturbing to local leaders for possible action.

3. "Investigation on Internet Sex Traffickers," *Congressional Record* 163, no. 8 (January 12, 2017), www.govinfo.gov/content/pkg/CREC-2017-01-12/html/CREC-2017-01-12-pt1-PgS308.htm.

4. U.S. Justice Department, "Justice Department Leads Effort to Seize Backpage.Com," April 9, 2018, www.justice.gov/opa/pr/justice-department-leads-effort-seize-backpagecom-internet-s-leading-forum-prostitution-ads.

5. "While this move is meant to protect people from being sexually exploited," reported *Newsweek*, "some sex workers fear that it will only drive the business into the shadows, or take away a source of income that some desperately need. The organizers of the Women's March on Washington expressed dismay over the shutdown as well, tweeting that 'sex workers rights are women's rights.'" Kristin Hugo, "'People Are Going to Die': Sex Workers Devastated after Backpage Shutdown," *Newsweek*, April 10, 2018, www.newsweek.com/people-are-going-die-sex-workers-devastated-after-backpage-shutdown-876486. On April 6, 2018, Collective Action for Safe Spaces tweeted, "Sex work is consensual. Sex trafficking is coerced. The crackdown on Backpage is not about ending trafficking; it's motivated by the patriarchal notion that women should not be free to do what we want with our bodies." See twitter.com/SafeSpacesDC/status/982429621198249985.

6. Mormons take the whole "Thou shalt not take the name of the Lord thy God in vain" thing seriously. They take greater offense at "Oh my god" than at "shit." And some, apparently, take the not saying "My god!" thing more seriously than the "thou shalt not commit adultery" thing.

7. In 2018, the Utah State Legislature changed sexual solicitation from a Class B to a Class A misdemeanor and increased the fine from $300 to $2,500.

8. Salt Lake City's other daily is the Mormon Church-owned *Deseret News*. Until recently, the *Tribune* and the *News* shared a printing facility, an advertising sales force, and advertising revenues. The *Tribune* no longer carries sexually oriented classified ads, but the *News* has always declined them. In 2019, the *Tribune* became the nation's first not-for-profit daily newspaper.

9. This refers to a longstanding point of bickering between Christians and Mormons. Christians who claim to be "saved" contend that Mormons do not believe in "the Christ the Bible teaches," ergo Mormons are not real Christians, ergo Mormons are not saved. Mormons take umbrage. After all, "Jesus Christ" is kind of right there in the middle of "The Church of Jesus

Christ of Latter-day Saints." But then, fair is fair. Although Mormon Church leaders don't talk about it as bluntly as they once did, Mormon doctrine holds that the Mormon Church is the only true Christian faith and that all others make up the church of the devil. See Book of Mormon, 1 Nephi 14:10.

10. K. J. Petrie, R. J. Booth, and J. W. Pennebaker, "The Immunological Effects of Thought Suppression," *Journal of Personality and Social Psychology* 75, no. 5 (1998): 1264–1272

11. David Eagleman, *Incognito: The Secret Lives of the Brain* (New York: Pantheon, 2011).

12. The Secular Therapy Project (www.seculartherapy.org) provides a directory of nonreligious mental health practitioners.

13. Doctrine and Covenants 1:3

14. Doctrine and Covenants 19:15

15. Doctrine and Covenants 132:39

16. "For whoso eateth and drinketh my flesh and blood unworthily eateth and drinketh damnation to his soul." Book of Mormon, 3 Nephi 18:28–29.

17. *Merriam-Webster*, "Apologetics," www.merriam-webster.com/dictionary/apologetics (accessed January 19, 2020).

18. The Church of Jesus Christ of Latter-day Saints, "Polygamy," newsroom.churchofjesuschrist.org/topic/polygamy.

19. The Church of Jesus Christ of Latter-day Saints, "Race and the Priesthood," www.churchofjesuschrist.org/study/manual/gospel-topics-essays/race-and-the-priesthood?lang=eng.

20. At least, that's what Book of Mormon 2 Nephi 5:21 said until 2010, when the church removed the offending language from the online edition—quite the presumption, given that the Book of Mormon is "the most correct book on earth" and its translation divinely inspired (History of the Church, 4:461). See Joanna A. Brooks, "'Dark Skin' No Longer a Curse in Online Book of Mormon," *Religion Dispatches*, December 17, 2010, religiondispatches.org/dark-skin-no-longer-a-curse-in-online-book-of-mormon/.

21. Richard Lyman Bushman, *Joseph Smith: Rough Stone Rolling* (New York: Alfred A. Knopf, 2005).

22. *Doctrine and Covenants Student Manual,* Section 62 (Salt Lake City: The Church of Jesus Christ of Latter-day Saints), www.lds.org/manual/doctrine-and-covenants-student-manual/section-62-ye-are-blessed-for-the-testimony-ye-have-borne?lang=eng.

23. Really. The Salt Lake area has a number of them. This comes as a surprise to many, given that Utah's predominantly Mormon legislature believes that God forbids alcohol consumption.

24. Mormon afterlife is divided into three kingdoms. These are, from lowest to highest, the Telestial (a term Joseph Smith coined), the Terrestrial, and the Celestial. The Celestial Kingdom is the only place where families can live together for eternity. Doctrine and Covenants 76.

25. Sometimes church leaders remind members to extend love to those who have left the fold. The expressed reason, however, is less that love is the right thing to do for its own sake and more that love might encourage the disaffected to return. See Tad Walch, "Church Leaders Ask Latter-day Saints to Love Those Who Have Left," *Deseret News,* April 6, 2019, www.deseretnews.com/article/900064262/april-2019-general-conference-updates-lds-mormon-saturday-morning-session-president-nelson.html.

26. David A. Bednar, "And Nothing Shall Offend Them," address at the General Conference, October 2006, www.churchofjesuschrist.org/study/general-conference/2006/10/and-nothing-shall-offend-them?lang=eng.

27. "Some [who leave] might say, "I don't think I could live up to your standards." Dieter F. Uchtdorf, "Come, Join with Us," talk at the General Conference, October 2013, www.churchofjesuschrist.org/study/general-conference/2013/10/come-join-with-us?lang=eng.

28. Until recently, the seventh of 15 official worthiness interview questions for admittance to a Mormon temple was, "Do you support, affiliate with, or agree with any group or individual whose teachings or practices are contrary to or oppose those accepted by the Church of Jesus Christ of Latter-day Saints?" In October 2019, the church officially amended the question to, "Do you support or promote any teachings, practices or doctrine contrary to those of The Church of Jesus Christ of Latter-day Saints?" Also, Mormons are counseled not to associate with people who do not share their "standards." See MormonThink, "Temple Recommend Interview and Questions," www.mormonthink.com/glossary/templerecommend.htm and The

Church of Jesus Christ of Latter-day Saints, "Friends," www.lds.org/youth/
for-the-strength-of-youth/friends?lang=eng.

Chapter 9

1. A few months after our interview, Winder accepted a position as chief of
    investigations for the Salt Lake County District Attorney's Office.

2. "Salt Lake County Sheriff Jim Winder Reveals Why He'll Step Down to
    Become Moab Police Chief," *Gephardt Daily*, May 30, 2017, gephardtdaily.
    com/local/salt-lake-county-sheriff-jim-winder-reveals-why-hell-step-
    down-to-become-moab-police-chief/.

3. Brian Donegan, "Winder Owes Moab an Apology," *Times-Independent*, April
    12, 2019, moabtimes.com/2019/04/12/winder-owes-moab-an-apology/.

4. Some jurisdictions call them Community Oriented Patrols or Problem Ori-
    ented Patrols.

5. Who says police work isn't glamorous?

6. Rachel Lovell and Ann Jordan, "Do John Schools Really Decrease Re-
    cidivism?: A Methodological Critique of an Evaluation of the San Fran-
    cisco First Offender Prostitution Program," Erotic Service Provider Legal,
    Educational and Research Project, July 2012, esplerp.org/wp-content/up-
    loads/2012/05/John-Schools.Lovell.Jordan.7.12.pdf.

7. Sirin Kale, "Police Are Allegedly Sleeping with Sex Workers Before Ar-
    resting Them," Broadly.Vice.com, May 7, 2017, broadly.vice.com/en_us/
    article/59mbkx/police-are-allegedly-sleeping-with-sex-workers-before-
    arresting-them.

8. Jessica Miller, "In Busts of Illicit Massage Parlors, Do Some Utah Officers
    Let Touching Go Too Far?" *Salt Lake Tribune*, February 9, 2020, www.sltrib.
    com/news/2020/02/09/busts-illicit-massage/.

9. Ibid.

10. For a more detailed discussion of trafficking, see Chapter 6, "Mormon-
    town's Asian Massage Parlors," and Chapter 10 (which just happens to be
    coming up next), "Should It Be Legal?"

Chapter 10

1. *Ils doivent envisager qu'une grande responsabilité est la suite inséparable d'un grand pouvoir.* ("They must understand that great responsibility follows inseparably from great power.") Convention Nationale, Paris, "Collection générale des décrets rendus par la Convention Nationale" vol. 9, p. 73, books.google.com/books?id=D55aAAAAcAAJ&q=inséparable#v=snippet&q=inséparable&f=false

2. Known variously as *water intoxication*, *water poisoning*, *hyperhydration*, *overhydration*, and *water toxemia*.

3. HMLs also control televised fun. It wasn't until 1987 that bra marketers were allowed to feature blouse-less, bra-wearing women in commercials—until then they used mannequins—even though blouse-less, bra-wearing women had long been allowed in programming as well as in real life. For that matter, next time you see a beer or liquor commercial, watch closely. Everyone is holding a drink, but no one takes a sip. That's thanks to self-imposed network policies that let you advertise alcohol provided you don't show anyone actually consuming it. We wouldn't want commercials to create the impression that people ever do anything with alcoholic beverages beyond holding them inches from their lips while they party and flirt.

4. "After Prohibition's repeal on December 5, 1933, organized crime, with its top unlawful moneymaking racket gone, was forced to regroup and focus on other things." National Museum of Organized Crime & Law Enforcement, "Prohibition Profits Transformed the Mob," prohibition.themobmuseum.org/the-history/the-rise-of-organized-crime/the-mob-during-prohibition/.

5. Janet Burns, "Violent Crime Has Dropped in Border States with Legal Cannabis: Study," *Forbes*, January 16, 2018, www.forbes.com/sites/janetwburns/2018/01/16/violent-crime-has-fallen-in-border-states-with-legal-cannabis-study/#4678c1ac59eb.

6. Ronald Weitzer, *Legalizing Prostitution: From Illicit Vice to Lawful Business* (New York: New York University Press, 2012).

7. Catherine Murphy, "Sex Workers' Rights Are Human Rights," August 14, 2015, www.amnesty.org/en/latest/news/2015/08/sex-workers-rights-are-human-rights/.

8. Weitzer, op. cit., 208.

9. As cited in Devon D. Brewer et al., "Prostitution and the Sex Discrepancy in Reported Number of Sexual Partners," *Proceedings of the National Academy of Science* 97 no. 22 (October 24, 2000), www.pnas.org/content/pnas/97/22/12385.full.pdf; John J. Potterat et al., "Estimating the Prevalence and Career Longevity of Prostitute Women," *Journal of Sex Research* 27 (1990): 233–243.

10. Havocscope, "Number of Prostitutes by Country," www.havocscope.com/number-of-prostitutes/.

11. I don't spy on people in restrooms. Honest. This information comes from easily googled studies and from one personal acquaintance who conducted one.

12. Cited, among many, by the *Washington Post*'s Alexendra Petri in her wonderful takedown of a more recent so-called sexuality study. Alexandra Petri, "Dirty Talk? New Sex Survey's Surprising Stats," *Washington Post*, October 4, 2010, voices.washingtonpost.com/compost/2010/10/dirty_talk_new_sex_surveys_sur.html.

13. Havocscope, op. cit.

14. Potterat et al., op. cit.

15. Their website is www.antlers.com.

16. Potterat et al., op. cit.

17. It may seem odd for a guy whose book is based on interviews to cast doubt on interview-based data. The difference is that I do not represent my findings as statistically significant. They are a glimpse through a window.

18. Maggie McNeill, "Lies, Damned Lies and Sex Work Statistics," *Washington Post*, March 27, 2014, www.washingtonpost.com/news/the-watch/wp/2014/03/27/lies-damned-lies-and-sex-work-statistics/?noredirect=on&utm_term=.26646930ac49.

19. Though some are. Especially those who pursue the crusade by day while patronizing providers by night.

20. Lenora C. Babb, "Utah's Misguided Approach to the Problem of Sex Trafficking: A Call for Reform," *University of Utah Journal of Law and Family Studies* 14 (October 26, 2012).

21. Law.com, "The Prostitution Statistics You Have to Know," sex-crimes.laws. com/prostitution/prostitution-statistics.

22. Someone really should do something about ketchup on scrambled eggs.

23. This may explain why there is no record of anyone in the Victorian Era standing up and saying, "Balderdash! I masturbate all the time, and I'm not blind."

24. I can get away with sticking up for prostitution because I'm single. The publication of this book may guarantee my remaining single.

25. ProCon.org, "Opinion Polls/Surveys 1978–2016," prostitution.procon.org/ view.resource.php?resourceID=000121.

26. World Health Organization, "Sex Work," www.who.int/hiv/topics/sex_ work/about/en/.

27. Murphy, op. cit.

28. Jennifer Wright, "Why Prostitution Should Be Legal," *Harpers Bazaar*, April 26, 2108, www.harpersbazaar.com/culture/politics/a20067359/why-prostitution-should-be-legal/.

29. Elizabeth Nolan Brown, "What the Swedish Model Gets Wrong about Prostitution." *Time*, July 19, 2014, time.com/3005687/what-the-swedish-model-gets-wrong-about-prostitution/.

30. Ahmed Aziza, "Think Again: Prostitution," *Foreign Policy*, January 19, 2014, foreignpolicy.com/author/aziza-ahmed/.

31. Weitzer, op. cit., 89.

32. As cited in Weitzer, op. cit.

33. Marty Klein, "When Prostitution Is a Positive Sign," MartyKlein.com, April 19, 2009.

34. Wright, op. cit.

35. Department of Health and Human Services Nevada, "Regulations—Prostituion," dpbh.nv.gov/uploadedFiles/dpbh.nv.gov/content/Programs/STD/ dta/Providers/Regulations%20-%20Prostitution.pdf.

36. Centers for Disease Control and Prevention, "Condom Effectiveness," www.cdc.gov/condomeffectiveness/latex.html.

37. U.S. Food & Drug Administration, "Condoms and Sexually Transmitted

Diseases," www.fda.gov/patients/hiv-prevention/condoms-and-sexually-transmitted-diseases.

38. Alexa Albert, *Brothel* (New York: Random House, 2001).

39. See, for instance, David H. Rodgers, "The Viability of Nevada's Legal Brothels as Models for Regulation and Harm Reduction in Prostitution," thesis, Florida State University, 2010, diginole.lib.fsu.edu/islandora/object/fsu:176310/datastream/PDF/view.

40. Brown, op. cit.

41. Paul Bisschop, Stephen Kastoryano, and Bas van der Klaauw, "Street Prostitution Zones and Crime," *American Economic Journal: Economic Policy* 9, no. 4 (2017): 28–63, doi.org/10.1257/pol.20150299

42. Ricardo Ciacci and Maria Micaela Sviatschi, "The Effect of Indoor Prostitution on Sex Crimes: Evidence from New York City," Cato Institute, www.cato.org/publications/research-briefs-economic-policy/effect-indoor-prostitution-sex-crimes-evidence-new-york.

43. Cathy Reisenwitz, "Why It's Time to Legalize Prostitution," *Daily Beast*, August 14, 2014, www.thedailybeast.com/why-its-time-to-legalize-prostitution.

44. Eric Sprankle, Twitter, April 18, 2016, twitter.com/drsprankle/status/722307392663199744?lang=en.

45. Stuart Chamber, "Prostitution Is Just the Latest 'Deviance' Targeted by Crusaders," *Montreal Gazette*, July 9, 2014, montrealgazette.com/opinion/prostitution-is-just-the-latest-deviance-targeted-by-crusaders.

46. Reisenwitz, op. cit.

Chapter 11

1. Kaylin Jorge and Kathleen Serie, "Police: Man Who Filmed Woman at Dressing Room Identified as High Member of LDS Church," KUTV News, August 19, 2019, kutv.com/news/nation-world/man-who-filmed-woman-at-opry-mills-dressing-room-identified-as-high-member-of-lds-church?fbclid=IwAR0UwIwpwnJG18OHsCK1JfMozG_9ljtQAaqGjMsoFh1XkLRaHFQHYMLT-N4.

2. "Facts and Statistics," The Church of Jesus Christ of Latter-day Saints Newsroom, newsroom.churchofjesuschrist.org/facts-and-statistics/country/united-states/state/utah.

3. Laurie Goodstein and Sharon Otterman, "Catholic Priests Abused 1,000 Children in Pennsylvania, Report Says," *New York Times*, August 14, 2018, www.nytimes.com/2018/08/14/us/catholic-church-sex-abuse-pennsylvania.html.

4. N. Eldon Tanner, "The Power of Example," *Ensign*, December, 1981, www.churchofjesuschrist.org/study/ensign/1981/12/the-power-of-example?lang=eng.

5. Thomas S. Monson, "Be an Example and a Light," address at the General Conference, October 2015.

6. Russell M. Nelson, "The Love and Laws of God," speech at Brigham Young University, September 17, 2019, speeches.byu.edu/talks/russell-m-nelson/love-laws-god/.

7. Gordon B. Hinckley, "A Chosen Generation," address at the General Conference, April 1992.

8. Thomas S. Monson, "Be a Light Unto the World," devotional at Brigham Young University, November 1, 2011.

9. The Church of Jesus Christ of Latter-day Saints, "Friends," www.lds.org/youth/for-the-strength-of-youth/friends?lang=eng.

10. Doctrine and Covenants 38:42.

11. This doctrine is found in Abraham 3:23 of the Pearl of Great Price, which is the shortest of the Mormon Church's four books of scripture. The others are the Book of Mormon, Doctrine and Covenants, and the Bible. Also see "Foreordination," The Church of Jesus Christ of Latter-day Saints, www.lds.org/topics/foreordination?lang=eng.

12. Apostle Ezra Taft Benson, "In His Steps," devotional at Brigham Young University, March 4, 1979.

13. For over a century, general authorities of the church taught that less valiant pre-mortal spirits were born on Earth as non-Caucasians. Until 1978, Negroes were deemed the seed of Cain and barred from the Mormon priesthood worldwide. The Book of Mormon says that the ancestors of Native

Americans were cursed with "a skin of blackness" so that righteous white people wouldn't find them attractive or, worse, want to make babies with them (2 Nephi 5:21–25). A common Mormon belief held that when Native Americans joined the church, their skin began to lighten. The church used to counsel against interracial marriage of any sort. Today the church tries to distance itself from racist statements in its scriptures and by past leaders. However, the claims are widely found in print, have spread through the Internet, and remain ensconced in the culture, especially among older Mormons.

14. Thomas S. Monson, "Be an Example and a Light," address at the General Conference, October 2015.

15. *Teachings of the Presidents of the Church* (Salt Lake City: The Church of Jesus Christ of Latter-day Saints, 2011), Chapter 41, www.lds.org/manual/teachings-joseph-smith/chapter-41?lang=eng.

16. Dallin H. Oaks, "The Only True and Living Church," at a seminar for new mission presidents, June 25, 2010, www.lds.org/youth/article/only-true-living-church?lang=eng.

17. John 10:27–28. (Mormons accept the Bible alongside its other books of scripture.)

18. Glenn L. Pace, "They're Not Really Happy," address at the General Conference, October 1987.

19. You will find these "reasons" strewn throughout General Conference talks. Self-appointed defender of the faith Greg Trimble dutifully regurgitated them in his blog post, "You Should Not Leave Mormonism for Any of These 5 Reasons." Read it at the risk of insult to your intelligence: www.gregtrimble.com/you-should-not-leave-mormonism-for-any-of-these-5-reasons/.

20. Joseph Smith, Jr., "King Follet Sermon," sermon given at the conference of the Church in Nauvoo, Illinois, April 7, 1844, www.lds.org/study/ensign/1971/04/the-king-follett-sermon?lang=eng.

21. Ezra Taft Benson, "Our Divine Constitution," Saturday Morning Session, October 1987, www.churchofjesuschrist.org/study/general-conference/1987/10/our-divine-constitution?lang=eng.

22. Doctrine and Covenants 18:10–16.

23. I attended a Mormon stake conference in the early 1970s in Reno, Nevada,

during which Mormon apostle Mark E. Peterson asked members not to dine in restaurants attached to casinos. Mormons consider gambling a sin, so I anticipated that his reason would have to do with casinos as unsuitable environments. Nope. His concern was that non-Mormons might assume that Mormons were there to gamble, and that then there'd be no converting them.

24. I ran the "we're better than you" observation by a number of practicing Mormon friends. (Yes, I actually have some.) Every one of them regretfully conceded the point.

25. Vania Grandi, "Utah Non-Mormons Stung by Exclusion," *Los Angeles Times*, September 17, 2000, www.latimes.com/archives/la-xpm-2000-sep-17-me-22382-story.html.

26. Chrisy Ross, "To Mormons, with Love from Your Non-LDS Neighbor," *LDS Living*, December 21, 2017, www.ldsliving.com/To-Mormons-With-Love-from-Your-Non-LDS-Neighbor/s/76513

Postlude

1. See Chapter 5, "The Life of a Mormontown Sex Worker."

2. Sexually Oriented Businesses and Employee Licensing Salt Lake County, Utah, Chapter 5.136, www.naco.org/sites/default/files/documents/ae024.pdf.

3. On September 19, 2019, the 10th Circuit Court of Appeals struck down a Ft. Collins, Colorado, ban on women going topless in public. Besides Colorado, the court has jurisdiction over Wyoming, New Mexico, Kansas, Oklahoma, and Utah. The effect of the 10th Court's ruling on sexually oriented businesses remains to be seen. A complicating factor may be that, two years earlier, the 7th Court of Appeals *upheld* Chicago's topless ban for women. Adam Forgie, "Women Can Now Legally Go Topless in Utah, 5 Other States, after Federal Ruling," KUTV, September 19, 2019, kutv.com/news/local/women-can-now-legally-go-topless-in-utah-5-other-states-after-federal-ruling?fbclid=IwAR0JDpMccCvQjKTGzJNTRThBvT8T41HP3 9zClR2ygcRNXwm8GezEAeqgiR8.

Glossary

1. Book of Mormon, 2 Nephi 5:21

2. Pearl of Great Price, Joseph Smith–History 1:19

3. Taylor Scott, "See the List of Revised Temple Recommend Questions Shared by President Nelson." *Church News*, October 6, 2019, www.thechurchnews. com/members/2019-10-06/general-conference-october-2019-temple-recommend-questions-163456.

4. See Chapter 3, "A Brief History of Mormon Sex," Section 8, "Abuse, Cover-ups, Victim Blaming, and Bishops Who Teach Lasciviousness."

About the Author

We never really grow up; we only learn how to act in public.

—Bryan White

Steve Cuno is an advertising writer, a columnist for *Free Inquiry* magazine, and the as-told-to author of Joanne Hanks's popular memoir, *"It's Not about the Sex" My Ass: Confessions of an Ex-Mormon, Ex-Polygamist, Ex-Wife*. Steve lived in the Salt Lake City area for more than 40 years and now resides in Oregon. His website is stevecuno.com.